Cybersecurity Blue Team Toolkit

Cybersecurity Blue Team
Toolkit

Nadean H. Tanner

Cybersecurity Blue Team Toolkit

Published by
John Wiley & Sons, Inc.
10475 Crosspoint Boulevard
Indianapolis, IN 46256
www.wiley.com

ISBN: 978-1-119-55293-2
ISBN: 978-1-119-55295-6 (ebk)
ISBN: 978-1-119-55294-9 (ebk)

Manufactured in the United States of America

SKY10033279_021022

For general information on our other products and services please contact our Customer Care Department within the United States at (877) 762-2974, outside the United States at (317) 572-3993 or fax (317) 572-4002.

Wiley publishes in a variety of print and electronic formats and by print-on-demand. Some material included with standard print versions of this book may not be included in e-books or in print-on-demand. If this book refers to media such as a CD or DVD that is not included in the version you purchased, you may download this material at http://booksupport.wiley.com. For more information about Wiley products, visit www.wiley.com.

Library of Congress Control Number: 2019933354

*To my wonderful husband Kenneth, who believes I can do anything.
Without your support, this would not have happened.*

To my brown eyes—Shelby, if a film is made, I promise you the lead role.

To my blue eyes—Gavin, thank you for all your electronical advice.

I love you—infinity times googleplex.

About the Author

When my 7-year-old introduced me to his second-grade class, he put it best: "My mom teaches the good guys how to keep the bad guys out of their computers. She has a blue light saber."

I have been in the technology industry for more than 20 years in a variety of positions from marketing to training to web development to hardware. I have worked in academia as an IT director of a private elementary/middle school and as a technology instructor teaching post-graduate classes at Louisiana State University. I have trained and consulted in the corporate world for Fortune 50 companies and have hands-on experience working and training the U.S. Department of Defense, focusing on advanced cybersecurity and certifications. Currently, I am Lead Education Technical Specialist at Rapid7, managing the curriculum and teaching classes in Nexpose, InsightVM, Metasploit, Ruby, SQL, and API.

I love what I do—as an author, a trainer, and an engineer—making the world safer one domain at a time.

Current certifications:

A+	MCITP
Network+	MCTS
Security+	MCP
CASP	AVM
Server+	NCP
CIOS	MPCS
CNIP	IICS
CSIS	IVMCS
CISSP	ITILv3
MCSA	

About the Technical Editor

Emily Adams-Vandewater (SSCP, Security+, Cloud+, CSCP, MCP) is a technical strategies and security manager at Flexible Business Systems, an MSP located on Long Island, New York, where she focuses on network security and vulnerability management, backup and data recovery, endpoint protection, and incident response. She holds certifications and expertise in malware and cyber intrusion analysis, detection, and forensics. Emily is an active and passionate member of a variety of Women in Technology groups and shares her knowledge by volunteering as a cybersecurity subject-matter expert for ICS2 exam development and a variety of cybersecurity conferences. When Emily is not working, she spends her time learning new security tools and technologies to satisfy her drive to learn and unrelenting curiosity of the unknown.

Credits

Associate Publisher
Jim Minatel

Editorial Manager
Pete Gaughan

Production Manager
Katie Wisor

Project Editor
Kathryn Duggan

Production Editor
Barath Kumar Rajasekaran

Technical Editor
Emily Adams-Vandewater

Copy Editor
Kim Wimpsett

Proofreader
Debbye Butler

Indexer
Potomac Indexing, LLC

Cover Designer
Wiley

Cover Image
©igoriss/iStockphoto

Acknowledgments

First of all, I have to thank Jim for seeing my potential and making the ask. Second, thanks to Kathi and Emily for your expertise and patience. I think we made a great team!

To Eric and Spencer, thank you for the green light as well as Josh, the best sounding board.

To my besties Ryan and Tiffany, I love y'all. We are coming down for chicken wings soon!

Shannan, my sister from another mister, you are my original ripple person. Thank you for believing in me and throwing the rock. You didn't know what you started.

Magen, you have no idea just how inspiring you are.

To Nathan and Ajay, we have gone in different directions and yet we're all still teaching. We have been through some stuff and look how strong it has made us.

Rob, aka CrazyTalk, sudo make me a sammich! Thank you for explaining hashes to me.

Nicole, you are the ying to my yang. I'm always pulling up my bootstraps and asking W.W.N.D.

Lisa, you are one of the most patient, loving people I know. Thank you for being patient and loving me. Julie, thank you for being the most amazing mentor and dearest friend.

Contents at a glance

Contents

Foreword

The year was 2012 and I took a big leap in my own career to move across the country. I filled a role to lead a three-person team providing information technology and security training to Department of Defense personnel. This leadership role was new to me having worked for the past eight years in the intelligence and information security world for the most part as a trainer. While building out the team in the fall of 2012, I interviewed a wonderful candidate from Louisiana named Nadean Tanner. She was full of personality, charisma, knowledge, and most importantly, she had the ability to train. She proved this as part of her training demonstration in the interview process. I knew she was the right candidate and hired her almost immediately. Hiring Nadean is still one of the best decisions I made, and she is one of the greatest trainers I know. My philosophy is that a great trainer does not simply regurgitate what they know. Rather, they have the ability to explain a topic in different ways so that each learner can comprehend. Nadean embodies this philosophy.

Nadean has trained thousands of learners on topics from hardware to advanced security. In each class, she takes the time and effort to ensure every learner gets what they need. Whether learning a product for performing their job, building out their professional development, or advancing their career with a certification, Nadean covers it all. If you had the opportunity to attend one of her training classes, consider yourself blessed by a great trainer. If you have not, you picked up this book, which is the next best thing. I am glad to see her move to authorship, allowing everyone to experience her ability to explain complicated topics in simple ways.

In the world of cybersecurity we are constantly bombarded with new products, new tools, and new attack techniques. We are pulled daily in multiple directions on what to secure and how to secure it. In this book, Nadean will break down fundamental tools available to you. This includes general IT tools used for troubleshooting, but ones that can also help the security team understand the environment. She will cover tools attackers use, but also empower you and your team to use them to be proactive in your security. Specifically, you as the reader get to enjoy not only Nadean's ability to impart knowledge but her uncanny ability to explain why. Rather than being technical documentation focusing on the how, Nadean will delve into why use the tools and the specific use cases. For many users fresh to the cybersecurity world, this should be considered a getting started guide. For those in the middle of or more senior in their careers, this book will serve as a reference guide you want to have on your desk. It is not a book that makes it to your shelf and collects dust.

Throughout the years I have been Nadean's manager, colleague, peer, and most importantly dear friend. We have shared stories about how we learned, what we learned, and how we passed the information along to our learners. As the owner of this book, you are well on your way to enjoying Nadean's simple yet thorough explanations of advanced security topics. Rather than spending more of your time on reading this foreword, jump into the book to learn, refresh, or hone your cybersecurity skills.

Ryan Hendricks, CISSP
Training Manager, CarbonBlack

Introduction

> "The more you know, the more you know you don't know."
>
> *—Aristotle*

> "If you can't explain it simply, you don't understand it well enough."
>
> *—Einstein*

If you have ever been a fisherman or been friends with or related to a fisherman, you know one of their favorite things is their tackle box . . . and telling stories. If you ask a question about anything in that tackle box, be prepared to be entertained while you listen to stories of past fishing expeditions, how big was the one that got away, the one that did get caught, and future plans to use certain hooks, feathers, and wiggly things. A great fisherman learns to adapt to the situation they are in, and it takes special knowledge of all the fun things in that tackle box—when and where and how to use them—to be successful in their endeavor.

In cybersecurity, we have our own form of a tackle box. We have our own versions of wiggly things. To be successful, we have to learn when and where and how to use our tools and adapt to the technical situation we find ourselves in. It can take time to develop the expertise to know when to use which tool, and what product to find vulnerabilities, fix them, and, when necessary, catch the bad guys.

There are so many philosophies, frameworks, compliances, and vendors. How do you know when to use which wiggly thing? Once you know which wiggly thing to use, how do you use it? This book will teach you how to apply best-practice cybersecurity strategies and scenarios in a multitude of situations and which open source tools are most beneficial to protect our dynamic and multifaceted environments.

This book will take a simple and strategic look at best practices and readily available tools that are accessible to both cybersecurity management and hands-on professionals—whether they be new to the industry or simply are looking to gain expertise.

Fundamental Networking and Security Tools

WHAT YOU WILL LEARN IN THIS CHAPTER:

- ➤ Ping
- ➤ IPConfig
- ➤ Tracert
- ➤ NSLookup
- ➤ NetStat
- ➤ PuTTY

Before heading off to the cybersecurity conference Black Hat in Las Vegas, a friend of mine, Douglas Brush, posted on his LinkedIn page a warning for other InfoSec professionals. He said, "Don't go to these events to buy curtains for the house when you don't have the concrete for the foundation poured yet."

Too many times in the many years I've been in information technology (IT), I have seen people forget they need the basics in place before they try to use their shiny new tools. Before you can use any new tools, you must have a foundation to build upon. In IT, these tools are fundamental. They are a must for any computer/InfoSec/analyst to know how to use and when to use them. It's also rather impressive when a manager who you assumed was nontechnical asks you to ping that asset, run a tracert, and discover the physical and logical addresses of the web server that is down. Sometimes they *do* speak your language!

Ping

Ping will make you think one of two things. If it makes you think of irons and drivers and 18 holes of beautiful green fairway, then you are definitely CIO/

CEO/CISO material. If it makes you think of submarines or bats, then you're probably geekier like me.

Packet InterNet Groper, or what we affectionately call *ping*, is a networking utility. It is used to test whether a host is "alive" on an Internet Protocol (IP) network. A host is a computer or other device that is connected to a network. It will measure the time it takes for a message sent from one host to reach another and echo back to the original host. Bats are able to use *echo-location*, or bio sonar, to locate and identify objects. We do the same in our networked environments.

Ping will send an Internet Control Message Protocol (ICMP) echo request to the target and wait for a reply. This will report problems, trip time, and packet loss if the asset has a heartbeat. If the asset is not alive, you will get back an ICMP error. The command-line option for ping is easy to use no matter what operating system you are using and comes with multiple options such as the size of the packet, how many requests, and time to live (TTL) in seconds. This field is decremented at each machine where data is processed. The value in this field will be at least as great as the number of gateways it has to hop. Once a connection is made between the two systems, this tool can test the latency or the delay between them.

Figure 1.1 shows a running ping on a Windows operating system sending four echo requests to www.google.com using both IPv4 and IPv6.

```
Administrator: Command Prompt

Microsoft Windows [Version 10.0.16299.611]
(c) 2017 Microsoft Corporation. All rights reserved.

C:\Windows\system32>ping www.google.com

Pinging www.google.com [2607:f8b0:400f:800::2004] with 32 bytes of data:
Reply from 2607:f8b0:400f:800::2004: time=81ms
Reply from 2607:f8b0:400f:800::2004: time=47ms
Reply from 2607:f8b0:400f:800::2004: time=60ms
Reply from 2607:f8b0:400f:800::2004: time=68ms

Ping statistics for 2607:f8b0:400f:800::2004:
    Packets: Sent = 4, Received = 4, Lost = 0 (0% loss),
Approximate round trip times in milli-seconds:
    Minimum = 47ms, Maximum = 81ms, Average = 64ms

C:\Windows\system32>ping 172.217.6.68

Pinging 172.217.6.68 with 32 bytes of data:
Reply from 172.217.6.68: bytes=32 time=108ms TTL=50
Reply from 172.217.6.68: bytes=32 time=82ms TTL=50
Reply from 172.217.6.68: bytes=32 time=96ms TTL=50
Reply from 172.217.6.68: bytes=32 time=78ms TTL=50

Ping statistics for 172.217.6.68:
    Packets: Sent = 4, Received = 4, Lost = 0 (0% loss),
Approximate round trip times in milli-seconds:
    Minimum = 78ms, Maximum = 108ms, Average = 91ms

C:\Windows\system32>
```

Figure 1.1: Running a ping against a URL and IP address

What this figure translates to is that my computer can reach through the network and touch a Google server. The www.google.com part of this request is called a *uniform resource locator* (URL). A URL is the address of a page on the World Wide Web (WWW). The numbers you see next to the URL is called an *IP address*. Every device on a network must have a unique IP network address. If you are attempting to echo-locate another host, you could substitute the URL www.google.com for an IP address. We will do a deeper dive on IPv4 and IPv6 in Chapter 9, Log Management.

There are more granular ping commands. If you type **ping** along with an option or switch, you can troubleshoot issues that might be occurring in your network. Sometimes these issues are naturally occurring problems. Sometimes they could signal some type of attack.

Table 1.1 shows different options you can add to the base command ping.

Table 1.1: ping command syntax

OPTION	MEANING
/?	Lists command syntax options.
-t	Pings the specified host until stopped with Ctrl+C. ping -t is also known as the *ping of death*. It can be used as a denial-of-service (DoS) attack to cause a target machine to crash.
-a	Resolves address to hostname if possible.
-n count	How many echo requests to send from 1 to 4.2 billion. (In Windows operating systems, 4 is the default.)
-r count	Records route for count hops (IPv4 only). The maximum is 9, so if you need more than 9, tracert might work better (covered later in the chapter).
-s count	Timestamp for count hops (IPv4 only).
-i TTL	Time to live; maximum is 255.

Did you know that you could ping yourself? Figure 1.2 shows that 127.0.0.1 is a special reserved IP address. It is traditionally called a *loopback address*. When you ping this IP address, you are testing your own system to make sure it is working properly. If this IP doesn't return an appropriate response, you know the problem is with your system, not the network, the Internet service provider (ISP), or your target URL.

```
C:\Windows\system32>ping -a 127.0.0.1

Pinging DESKTOP-0U8N7VK [127.0.0.1] with 32 bytes of data:
Reply from 127.0.0.1: bytes=32 time<1ms TTL=128
Reply from 127.0.0.1: bytes=32 time<1ms TTL=128
Reply from 127.0.0.1: bytes=32 time<1ms TTL=128
Reply from 127.0.0.1: bytes=32 time<1ms TTL=128

Ping statistics for 127.0.0.1:
    Packets: Sent = 4, Received = 4, Lost = 0 (0% loss),
Approximate round trip times in milli-seconds:
    Minimum = 0ms, Maximum = 0ms, Average = 0ms
```

Figure 1.2: Pinging a lookback address

If you are experiencing network difficulties, this is the first tool to pull out of your toolkit. Go ping yourself and make sure everything is working as it should (see Lab 1.1).

LAB 1.1: PING

1. Open a command prompt or a terminal window.

2. Type `ping -t www.example.com` and then press Enter. (You can use another URL or hostname of your choice.)

3. After a few seconds, hold the Ctrl button and press C (abbreviated as Ctrl+C in subsequent instructions in this book).

4. When the command prompt returns, type `ping -a 127.0.0.1` and press Enter.

What is the name of your host? As you can see in Figure 1.2, mine is DESKTOP-OU8N7VK. A hostname is comprised of alphanumeric characters and possibly a hyphen. There may be times in the future you know an IP address but not the hostname or you know a hostname but not the IP address. For certain troubleshooting steps, you will need to be able to resolve the two on a single machine.

IPConfig

The command `ipconfig` is usually the next tool you will pull out of your toolbox when you're networking a system. A lot of valuable knowledge can be gleaned from this tool.

Internet Protocol is a set of rules that govern how data is sent over the Internet or another network. This routing function essentially creates the Internet we know and love.

IP has the function of taking packets from the source host and delivering them to the proper destination host based solely on the IP addresses in a packet. The datagram that is being sent has two parts: a header and a payload. The header has the information needed to get the information where it should go. The payload is the stuff you want the other host to have.

In Lab 1.2, you'll use the `ipconfig` command.

LAB 1.2: IPCONFIG

1. Open a command prompt or a terminal window.

2. Type `ipconfig` and press Enter if you are on a Windows system. If you are on Linux, try `ifconfig`.

3. Scroll through your adapters and note the ones that are for Ethernet or Wi-Fi or Bluetooth.

> With the preceding steps, you can answer the following questions: Which adapters are connected with an IP address? Which ones are disconnected?
>
> 4. At the command prompt, type `ipconfig /all` and press Enter.

Now you have a wealth of information to begin your troubleshooting hypothesis. In Figure 1.3, you see the IP addresses and default gateways for each network adapter on the machine.

```
Administrator: Command Prompt

C:\Windows\system32>ipconfig

Windows IP Configuration


Ethernet adapter Ethernet:

   Media State . . . . . . . . . . . : Media disconnected
   Connection-specific DNS Suffix  . :

Wireless LAN adapter Local Area Connection* 2:

   Media State . . . . . . . . . . . : Media disconnected
   Connection-specific DNS Suffix  . :

Ethernet adapter Ethernet 2:

   Media State . . . . . . . . . . . : Media disconnected
   Connection-specific DNS Suffix  . :

Ethernet adapter VMware Network Adapter VMnet1:

   Connection-specific DNS Suffix  . :
   Link-local IPv6 Address . . . . . : fe80::cd8d:3b96:32a6:9afa%9
   IPv4 Address. . . . . . . . . . . : 192.168.229.1
   Subnet Mask . . . . . . . . . . . : 255.255.255.0
   Default Gateway . . . . . . . . . :

Ethernet adapter VMware Network Adapter VMnet8:

   Connection-specific DNS Suffix  . :
   Link-local IPv6 Address . . . . . : fe80::d4e9:8916:372a:e132%20
   IPv4 Address. . . . . . . . . . . : 192.168.124.1
   Subnet Mask . . . . . . . . . . . : 255.255.255.0
   Default Gateway . . . . . . . . . :

Wireless LAN adapter Wi-Fi:

   Connection-specific DNS Suffix  . : lan
   IPv6 Address. . . . . . . . . . . : 2600:1:9507:2759:bc87:7fd4:1989:cb35
   Temporary IPv6 Address. . . . . . : 2600:1:9507:2759:88f8:883a:1236:a114
   Link-local IPv6 Address . . . . . : fe80::bc87:7fd4:1989:cb35%5
   IPv4 Address. . . . . . . . . . . : 192.168.128.21
   Subnet Mask . . . . . . . . . . . : 255.255.255.0
   Default Gateway . . . . . . . . . : fe80::895:2734:a5ab:7ea7%5
                                       192.168.128.1

Ethernet adapter Bluetooth Network Connection:

   Media State . . . . . . . . . . . : Media disconnected
   Connection-specific DNS Suffix  . :
```

Figure 1.3: Using `ipconfig /all`

To find your router's private IP address, look for the default gateway. Think of this machine as a literal gateway that you will use to access the Internet or another network. What tool would you use to make sure that the router is alive? Why, ping of course!

THE INTERNET IS DOWN—NOW WHAT?

The Internet is down.

You ping yourself at 127.0.0.1, and everything is fine on your machine. You ping www.google.com, and it times out. You do an ipconfig /all on your host machine. What can you assume if your ipconfig /all command listed the default gateway as being 0.0.0.0? The router!

As an experienced IT person will tell you, the best thing to do is turn any device off and on again—first your host and then the router. Still not working? Expand your hypothesis to another host on your network—can it reach the Internet or the router? Does it pull an IP address from the router? When you are troubleshooting, it is all about the scientific method. Form a hypothesis, test, modify, and form a new hypothesis.

Here are two more acronyms to add to your IT vernacular: DHCP and DNS. DHCP stands for Dynamic Host Configuration Protocol. Let's isolate each word.

Dynamic: Ever-changing, fluid

Host: Asset on a network

Configuration: How the asset is supposed to work

Protocol: Rules that allow two more assets to talk

DHCP is a network management tool. This is the tool that dynamically assigns an IP address to a host on a network that lets it talk to other hosts. Most simply, a router or a gateway can be used to act as a DHCP server. Most residential routers will get their unique public IP address from their ISP. This is who you write the check to each month.

In a large enterprise, DHCP is configured on servers to handle large networks' IP addressing. DHCP decides which machine gets what IP address and for how long. If your machine is using DHCP, did you notice in your ipconfig /all command how long your lease was? If you are not leasing, then you are using a static IP address.

Here are two more commands for you to use if you want a new IP address:

ipconfig /release: This releases all IPv4 addresses.

ipconfig /renew: This retrieves a new IP address, which may take a few moments.

DNS is an acronym for Domain Name System. This is a naming system for all hosts that are connected to the Internet or your private network. As you do what you do on the Internet or in a private network, DNS will remember domain names. It will store this data in something we call a *cache* (pronounced "cash"). This is done to speed up subsequent requests to the same host. Sometimes your DNS cache can get all wonky—sometimes by accident, sometimes by a hacker.

> **NOTE**   Cache poisoning—sometimes called *DNS spoofing*—is an attack where a malicious party corrupts the DNS cache or table, causing the nameserver to return an incorrect IP address and network traffic to be diverted.

Here are two more commands to try:

`ipconfig /displaydns`: This may scroll for a while because this is a record of all the domain names and their IP addresses you have visited on a host.

`ipconfig /flushdns`: If you start encountering HTML 404 error codes, you may need to flush your cache clean. This will force your host to query nameservers for the latest and greatest information.

NSLookup

The main use of `nslookup` is to help with any DNS issues you may have. You can use it to find the IP address of a host, find the domain name of an IP address, or find mail servers on a domain. This tool can be used in an interactive and a noninteractive mode. In Lab 1.3, you'll use `nslookup`.

LAB 1.3: NSLOOKUP

1. Open a command prompt or a terminal window.

2. To work in interactive mode, type `nslookup` at the prompt and press Enter. You will get an `nslookup` prompt, as you see in Figure 1.4. To escape the prompt, press Ctrl+C.

```
C:\Windows\system32>nslookup
Default Server:  myhotspot.lan
Address:  192.168.128.1

>
```

Figure 1.4: Using `nslookup`

3. To work in noninteractive mode, type `nslookup www.example.com` at the prompt to acquire DNS information for the specific site such as Figure 1.5.

Continues

LAB 1.3 (CONTINUED)

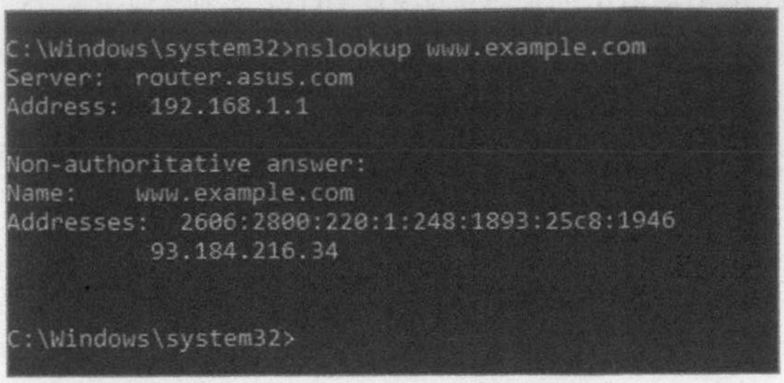

```
C:\Windows\system32>nslookup www.example.com
Server:  router.asus.com
Address:  192.168.1.1

Non-authoritative answer:
Name:    www.example.com
Addresses: 2606:2800:220:1:248:1893:25c8:1946
          93.184.216.34


C:\Windows\system32>
```

Figure 1.5: Using nslookup on a URL

4. Now try nslookup with one of the IP addresses displayed in your terminal window attributed to www.wiley.com. This will do a reverse lookup for the IP address and resolve to a domain name.

5. To find specific type assets, you can use nslookup -querytype=mx www.example.com. In Figure 1.6, you see the result of using qureytype=mx.

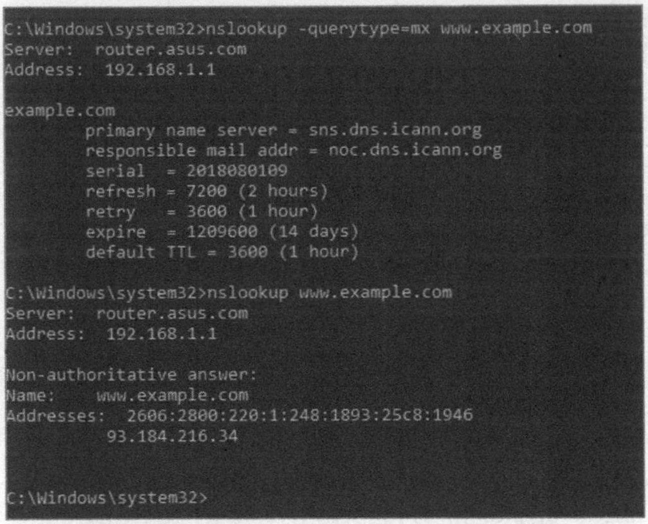

```
C:\Windows\system32>nslookup -querytype=mx www.example.com
Server:  router.asus.com
Address:  192.168.1.1

example.com
        primary name server = sns.dns.icann.org
        responsible mail addr = noc.dns.icann.org
        serial  = 2018080109
        refresh = 7200 (2 hours)
        retry   = 3600 (1 hour)
        expire  = 1209600 (14 days)
        default TTL = 3600 (1 hour)

C:\Windows\system32>nslookup www.example.com
Server:  router.asus.com
Address:  192.168.1.1

Non-authoritative answer:
Name:    www.example.com
Addresses: 2606:2800:220:1:248:1893:25c8:1946
          93.184.216.34


C:\Windows\system32>
```

Figure 1.6: Using nslookup with -querytype=mx

Instead of -querytype=mx, you can use any of the following:

HINFO	Specifies a computer's CPU and type of operating system
UNIFO	Specifies the user information
MB	Specifies a mailbox domain name
MG	Specifies an email group member
MX	Specifies the email server

Tracert

So, now you know that all machines that are on a network need to have an IP address. I live in Denver, Colorado, and one of my best friends, Ryan, lives in Albuquerque, New Mexico. When I send him a message, it does not travel from my house through the wires directly to his house. It goes through "hops" (and not the beer kind, unfortunately for him). These hops are the routers between us.

Tracert is a cool diagnostic utility. It will determine the route the message takes from Denver to Albuquerque by using ICMP echo packets sent to the destination. You've seen ICMP in action before—with the ping command.

ICMP is one of the Internet's original protocols used by network devices to send operational information or error messages. ICMP is not usually used to send data between computers, with the exception of ping and traceroute. It is used to report errors in the processing of datagrams.

Each router along the path subtracts the packets TTL value by 1 and forwards the packet, giving you the time and the intermediate routers between you and the destination. Tracert will print the trace of the packet's travels.

Why is this an important part of your toolkit? This is how you find out where a packet gets stopped or blocked on the enterprise network. There may be a router with a configuration issue. Firewalls can be configured to filter packets. Perhaps your website is responding slowly. If packets are being dropped, this will be displayed in the tracert as an asterisk.

This is a good tool when you have many paths that lead to the same destination but several intermediary routers are involved.

One caveat before Lab 1.4: As I mentioned previously, most of my strengths lie in Windows machines. If you are on a Linux or Mac/Unix-type operating system (OS), then you will want to use the tool traceroute. The commands tracert and traceroute are basically the same thing. The difference lies in which OS you are troubleshooting. If you want to get supremely technical, in Linux the command sends a UDP packet. In Windows, it sends an ICMP echo request.

LAB 1.4: TRACERT

1. Open a command prompt or a terminal window.

2. At the command prompt, type tracert 8.8.8.8 and press Enter.

In Figure 1.7, you can see the hops my machine takes to reach that public Google DNS server. How many hops does yours take?

Continues

LAB 1.4 (CONTINUED)

```
C:\Windows\system32>tracert 8.8.8.8

Tracing route to google-public-dns-a.google.com [8.8.8.8]
over a maximum of 30 hops:

  1     4 ms      2 ms      1 ms   myhotspot.lan [192.168.128.1]
  2    74 ms     76 ms     61 ms   ip-68-29-121-1.pools.spcsdns.net [68.29.121.1]
  3     *          *          *    Request timed out.
  4    90 ms     56 ms     72 ms   66.1.24.242
  5    85 ms     58 ms     61 ms   s1-crs1-che-.sprintlink.net [144.223.173.129]
  6    87 ms     50 ms     50 ms   144.232.12.40
  7    77 ms     55 ms     42 ms   209.85.172.62
  8    80 ms     46 ms     60 ms   108.170.254.81
  9    70 ms     50 ms     59 ms   64.233.175.111
 10    80 ms     54 ms     47 ms   google-public-dns-a.google.com [8.8.8.8]

Trace complete.

C:\Windows\system32>_
```

Figure 1.7: Using `tracert`, counting hops

3. Now try `tracert -d 8.8.4.4`.

This is another public Google DNS server, but now tracert will not try to resolve DNS while counting the hops.

4. For fun, try `tracert 127.0.0.1`. Why is it only one hop?

NetStat

Mathematical statistics is the collection, organization, and presentation of data to be used in solving problems. When you analyze statistics, you are going to use probability to fix issues. For example, in a room of 23 people, there is a 50 percent probability that two of those people share the same birthday. In cybersecurity, a birthday attack is a type of cryptographic attack that exploits the math behind the birthday statistic. This attack can be used to find collisions in a hash function. In our world of networking, learning your network statistics can be quite valuable.

NetStat is a network utility tool that displays networking connections (incoming and outgoing), routing tables, and some other details such as protocol statistics. It will help you gauge the amount of network traffic and diagnose slow network speeds. Sounds simple, yes? From a cybersecurity standpoint, how quickly can you tell which ports are open for incoming connections? What ports are currently in use? What is the current state of connections that already exist?

The output from the netstat command is used to display the current state of all the connections on the device. This is an important part of configuration and troubleshooting. NetStat also has many parameters to choose from to answer the questions presented in the previous paragraph. One thing to remember about the parameters discussed next is that when you type them into your cmd shell, you can literally squish them together. For example, when I am teaching my Metasploit Pro class, we launch a proxy pivot via a Meterpreter shell and scan another network segment. (That might sound like gibberish now, but just finish the book.) How do you know what is actually transpiring on the compromised system? Using the netstat command and the options -a for all and -n for addresses and ports, you will have a list of all active network conversations this machine is having, as shown in Figure 1.8.

```
Administrator: Command Prompt

Microsoft Windows [Version 10.0.16299.547]
(c) 2017 Microsoft Corporation. All rights reserved.

C:\Windows\system32>netstat -an

Active Connections

  Proto  Local Address          Foreign Address        State
  TCP    0.0.0.0:135            0.0.0.0:0              LISTENING
  TCP    0.0.0.0:443            0.0.0.0:0              LISTENING
  TCP    0.0.0.0:445            0.0.0.0:0              LISTENING
  TCP    0.0.0.0:902            0.0.0.0:0              LISTENING
  TCP    0.0.0.0:912            0.0.0.0:0              LISTENING
  TCP    0.0.0.0:3790           0.0.0.0:0              LISTENING
  TCP    0.0.0.0:5357           0.0.0.0:0              LISTENING
  TCP    0.0.0.0:5700           0.0.0.0:0              LISTENING
  TCP    0.0.0.0:7680           0.0.0.0:0              LISTENING
  TCP    0.0.0.0:9012           0.0.0.0:0              LISTENING
  TCP    0.0.0.0:49664          0.0.0.0:0              LISTENING
  TCP    0.0.0.0:49665          0.0.0.0:0              LISTENING
  TCP    0.0.0.0:49666          0.0.0.0:0              LISTENING
  TCP    0.0.0.0:49667          0.0.0.0:0              LISTENING
  TCP    0.0.0.0:49668          0.0.0.0:0              LISTENING
  TCP    0.0.0.0:49669          0.0.0.0:0              LISTENING
  TCP    0.0.0.0:49672          0.0.0.0:0              LISTENING
```

Figure 1.8: NetStat finding active connections

To translate the figure, when running netstat on your host, you may see both 0.0.0.0 and 127.0.0.1 in this list. You already know what a loopback address is. A loopback address is accessible only from the machine you're running netstat on. The 0.0.0.0 is basically a "no particular address" placeholder. What you see after the 0.0.0.0 is called a *port*.

One of my favorite explanations of ports is that you have 65,536 windows and doors in your network ranging from 0 to 65,535. Computers start counting at 0. Network admins are constantly yelling, "Shut the windows and close the doors—you're letting the data out!" Ports can be TCP or UDP. Simply put, TCP means there is a connection made between the host and the destination. UDP doesn't worry about whether there is a connection made. Both TCP and UDP have 65,535 ports available to them. This was the highest number that could be represented by a 16-bit, or 2-byte, number. You may see this represented mathematically as $2^{16} - 1$.

The Internet Assigned Numbers Authority (IANA) maintains an official assignment of port numbers for specific uses. Sometimes this list becomes antiquated at the same time new technologies are becoming available. Some of the most common ones you might see are the "well-known" ports, which are 0–1023. Looking at the list in the previous figure, you see this machine is listening on port 135. Port 135 is traditionally used for a service called epmap/ loc-srv. That should tell you, among other things in Figure 1.8, that this is a

Windows host. When a Windows host wants to connect to an RPC service on a remote machine, it checks for port 135.

The next port that is listening is 443. Most IT professionals memorize this port early in their career. Port 443 is Hypertext Transfer Protocol over TLS/SSL—better known as HTTPS. HTTPS is the authentication of a website that is being accessed and protecting the confidentiality of the data being exchanged. Ports from 1023 all the way up to 49151 are "registered" ports. Above that, you have dynamic or private ports.

NetStat is an abbreviation for "network statistics." If a host is not listening on the correct port for a specific service, then no communication can occur. Take another step in your network path, and these ports may be listening, but this does not mean that a firewall is allowing the traffic to get to the device. To test that hypothesis, you can temporarily disable your host-based firewall causing the networking issue.

Among my favorite `netstat` commands are the statistics options shown in Figure 1.9. In Lab 1.5, you'll use the `netstat` command.

```
Command Prompt

Microsoft Windows [Version 10.0.16299.547]
(c) 2017 Microsoft Corporation. All rights reserved.

C:\Users\Nadean>netstat -sp IP

IPv4 Statistics

  Packets Received                   = 128475
  Received Header Errors             = 0
  Received Address Errors            = 0
  Datagrams Forwarded                = 0
  Unknown Protocols Received         = 0
  Received Packets Discarded         = 1040
  Received Packets Delivered         = 133996
  Output Requests                    = 50228
  Routing Discards                   = 0
  Discarded Output Packets           = 1195
  Output Packet No Route             = 50
  Reassembly Required                = 0
  Reassembly Successful              = 0
  Reassembly Failures                = 0
  Datagrams Successfully Fragmented  = 0
  Datagrams Failing Fragmentation    = 0
  Fragments Created                  = 0

C:\Users\Nadean>netstat -sp UDP

UDP Statistics for IPv4

  Datagrams Received    = 28100
  No Ports              = 1045
  Receive Errors        = 10875
  Datagrams Sent        = 8789

Active Connections

  Proto  Local Address        Foreign Address        State

C:\Users\Nadean>
```

Figure 1.9: NetStat statistics

LAB 1.5: NETSTAT

1. Open a command prompt or a terminal window.

2. At the command prompt, type `netstat -help`.

3. When the prompt is available, use `netstat -an -p TCP`.

4. Next try `netstat -sp TCP`.

INVESTIGATING THE UNEXPECTED

You're sitting in your office, putting the final touches on a presentation that you're giving in an hour on cybersecurity trends that your specific industry is experiencing to the C-level employees at your company. You're feeling confident with your data. You are hitting the Save button after every major change. You're concentrating on the agenda in your presentation when a balloon in your task pane from your anti-virus software pops up and notifies you that an IP address will be blocked for 600 seconds.

As most end users do, you click the X with no hesitation and continue building your presentation. Then you notice you have mail in your inbox from your firewall. It is an alert notification. You start to worry less about your presentation and start thinking a possible breach is being attempted against your host.

You open a command shell and drop a `netstat -nao`. Not only will this give you the protocol, local/foreign address, and state but also the process identifier (PID) associated with that communication. You can easily get overwhelmed by the data displayed, but check your taskbar. Are there any network centric applications running? Close your browsers and try `netstat -nao` again.

Did anything change? Are there any foreign addresses or odd port numbers that you've never seen before?

Two ports to be wary of are 4444 and 31337. Port 4444 is the default port that Metasploit will use as a default listening port. Port 31337 spells *eleet*.

Leet speak originated in the 1980s when message boards discouraged the discussion of hacking. The purposeful misspelling of words and substitution of letters for numbers was a way to indicate you were knowledgeable about hackers and circumvent the message board police. When we substitute letters with numbers to enhance our passwords, we are using leet speak for good.

If either of these two ports shows up in your NetStat statistics, it's time for a procedure that has been previously agreed upon to kick in. Either pull the network cable on this machine or alert your incident response (IR) team so they can triage the situation and make the best decision on how to stop the attack. My own personal recommendation is that if you have an IR team, use it. If you pull the plug on an attacker, you lose valuable forensic information.

PuTTY

Up until now, all the tools discussed are embedded in your operating systems. This tool will require a little more effort on your part. PuTTY is a free, open-source terminal emulation, serial console, and network file transfer program. Originally written for Windows, it has evolved to be used with other operating systems. PuTTY is an amazingly versatile tool that allows you to gain secure remote access to another computer and is most likely the most highly used SSH client for the Microsoft Windows platform.

I believe that many IT professionals who have been in the industry for a while lose track of where we have been. We keep adding knowledge and experience and expertise to our repertoire and think, "Everyone should know that." As an educator, I am not allowed to do that. It's my job to show you how to use all these new shiny things in your toolbox. I can hear some people saying, "You had me until SSH!"

Secure Shell (SSH) is a network protocol for creating an encrypted channel over an unencrypted network. The Internet is *way* unsecured. You don't want your data out there in the World Wide Web dangling freely for all to see! SSH provides a computer administrator with a safe way to reach a system that is remote using strong authentication and secure, encrypted data transmission. There have been times as an administrator when part of my responsibilities were to manage computers I could not reach out and physically touch—execute commands or move files from one computer to another. SSH is the protocol most hosts support. An SSH server, by default, will listen on TCP port 22.

As I mentioned earlier in this chapter, SSH creates an encrypted channel to communicate over. The first version of SSH debuted in 1995. Brad Pitt was the Sexiest Man Alive, Mel Gibson's *Braveheart* won Best Picture, and Match.com was new and the only online dating site. A lot. . .and I mean a lot has changed since then. Over the years, several flaws were found in SSH1, and it is no longer used. The current SSH2 was adopted in 2006 and uses a stronger encryption algorithm to improve security. As of yet, there are no known exploitable vulnerabilities in SSH2, although there have been rumors that the National Security Agency (NSA) may be able to decrypt some SSH2 traffic.

In Lab 1.6, you'll use PuTTY.

LAB 1.6: PuTTY

1. You can download a copy of PuTTY from www.putty.org. There will be a link on the page that takes you to the package file. Make sure you are getting the correct version for the hardware you are running. One size does not fit all.

2. Double-click the file you just downloaded. Follow the instructions until you finish the installation and then open PuTTY by double-clicking the icon that looks like two old computers linked together with a lightning bolt.

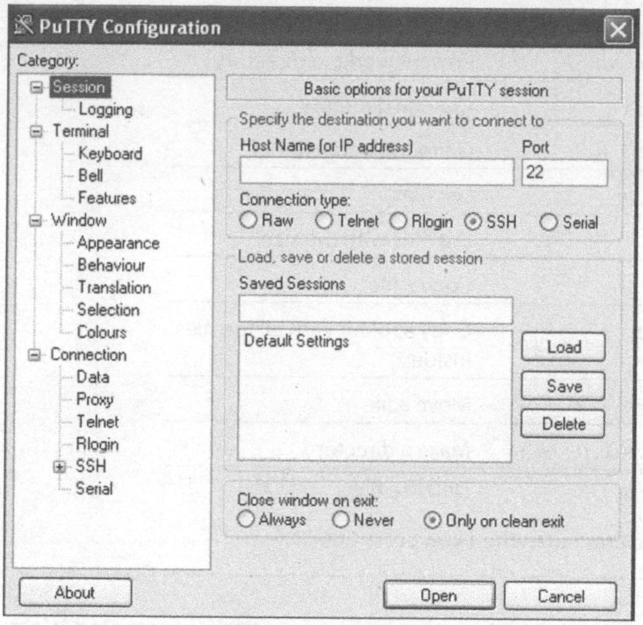

Figure 1.10: PuTTY Configuration window

When the software starts, a PuTTY Configuration window should open, such as what you see in Figure 1.10. The window pane on the left side lists the categories: Session, Terminal, Window, and Connection. The right side of the window will change depending on what category you have selected on the left.

3. In the Session view, enter the domain name or IP address you want to connect to. Port 22 specifies that you will be using SSH. The Connection Type setting lets you choose one of the following options:

   ▪ **Raw:** This is usually used by developers for testing.
   ▪ **Telnet:** Telnet is no longer secure. Passwords are sent in clear text. This is a bad idea.
   ▪ **Rlogin:** This is legacy, which means old (like 1982 old). It uses port 513 and only connects Unix to Unix. Ignore it.
   ▪ **SSH:** This is the protocol most hosts support. An SSH server, by default, will listen on TCP port 22.
   ▪ **Serial:** This is used for controlling some physical machinery or communication devices.

4. After you have supplied the IP or domain address, you should get a terminal window, which will ask for your credentials. If you are able to supply them, you will have a command-line terminal on the machine you just accessed. Some useful commands include the following:

Continues

LAB 1.6 (CONTINUED)

`pwd`	Present working directory
`cd`	Change directory
`cd ~`	Go to the home folder
`ls`	List files
`ls -h`	List files with the size
`cp`	Copy a file
`cp -r`	Copy a folder with all the files inside
`mv`	Move a file
`mkdir`	Make a directory
`rm`	Delete a file

The session will terminate when you press Ctrl+D.

NOTE   The first time you connect another system, you may be prompted to accept the server's SSH key or certificate. It might have some wording like "The server's host key is not cached in the registry." You see an example in Figure 1.11. This is normal. When you click Yes, you are establishing trust between the two hosts.

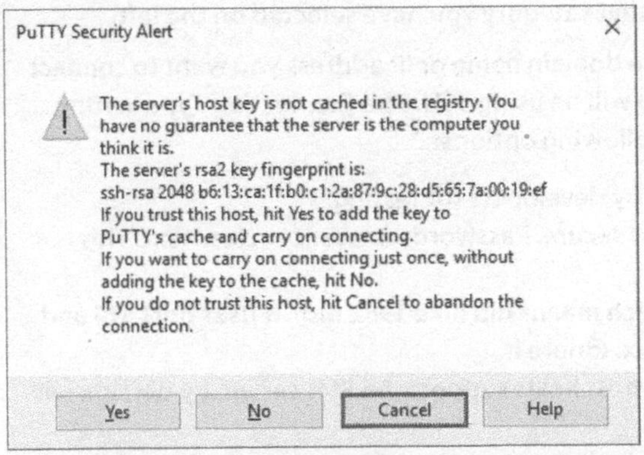

Figure 1.11: PuTTY security alert

I truly hope that I have given you a foundation to start to build on and that you have added these tools to your cybersecurity toolkit. Some of these tools may have just been a review for you, and some of them might have been new. These tools will help you not only with troubleshooting networks but with securing them as well.

CHAPTER

2

Troubleshooting Microsoft Windows

WHAT YOU WILL LEARN IN THIS CHAPTER:

➤   RELI

➤   PSR

➤   PathPing

➤   MTR

➤   Sysinternals

➤   GodMode

In 2012, I left the great state of Louisiana for Colorado to take a position with the Communications-Electronics Command (CECOM) at Fort Carson for the U.S. Army. My job was to train soldiers for information assurance (IA). The Department of Defense has a requirement that any full- or part-time military service member or contractor with privileged access must have certain computer certifications. This was known as DoDD 8570. My role was to teach these certification classes to help soldiers achieve the correct IA level needed so they could perform their job.

My commandant Ryan Hendricks is a networking guru, and he wanted to stay in his Cisco classes. Someone was needed to teach A+, Network+, Security+, Server+, CASP, and CISSP as well as Microsoft Active Directory, SCCM, and SharePoint. We both held the opinion that it wasn't fair for us to teach the class if we didn't hold the certification. He continued down the Cisco path, and I skipped down the CompTIA/Microsoft certification path.

While studying for these certifications, I had many "aha" moments that are still relative today. In fact, when I am teaching my certification classes for Rapid7, I often take a few moments while everyone is getting settled into his or her seat after lunch to show class members some of these cool troubleshooting tricks for Windows. It's a bit of a bonus for coming back to class on time.

Even seasoned professionals who work with massive networks and have years of experience have uttered a few choice words when they see tools that are meant to make their life easier after they've been doing it the hard way for years and years. If nearly 90 percent of your network is Windows, you need these tools to make your administrative life easier.

RELI

I call this tool RELI because when you type these four letters in the Windows search box on the taskbar, there is usually nothing else to choose from besides this one, the Reliability History/Monitor. RELI traces its roots all the way back to Windows Vista. It allows you to see the stability of a machine in a timeline. When you start typing it in the Start menu, you'll notice the name of the tool displays as Reliability History. Once you open the tool, it renames itself to Reliability Monitor. (Thank you, Microsoft.)

Reliability Monitor will build a graph for you of important events, application and Windows failures, and updates and other information that might be important. Figure 2.1 shows the graph that gets generated from application, Windows, and miscellaneous failures. In Lab 2.1, you'll use RELI.

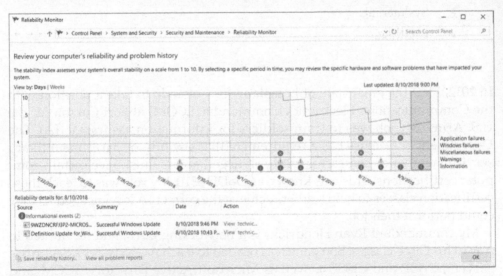

Figure 2.1: Reliability Monitor graph

LAB 2.1: RELI

1. To open this tool, open the Start menu and begin typing **reli.**

2. When you see the blue flag icon next to Reliability History in your Start menu, press the Enter key. Wait while it builds your graphic timeline.

3. Above the graphic in the upper left, notice you can shift your timeline view from Days to Weeks.
   - The first three lines of the graph indicated on the right side are the application, Windows, and miscellaneous failures this system has experienced. These can include when a program stopped working or when Windows did not properly shut down. It is a fantastic indicator of a Blue/Black Screen of Death (BSOD). This will be displayed as a red circle with a white X inside.
   - Under the failures, the yellow triangles with an exclamation point inside indicate a warning. These triangles are called *splats*. They could indicate whether the software did not update properly or errored but did not fail completely.
   - The blue circles across the bottom are informational. They will inform you if software updates were successful or drivers were installed correctly.

4. In the lower-left corner of the Reliability Monitor screen, click the Save Reliability History link to save this timeline as an XML file. This file can be exported and analyzed by other reporting applications.

5. Click the View All Problem Reports link in the lower-right corner next to the Save Reliability History link. This will open a new page that includes all the problems this device has experienced and can be reported directly to Microsoft. When there is a solution, it will appear in Security And Maintenance.

USING RELI

Let's say you are a system administrator. Most system administrators install, upgrade, and monitor software and hardware for their organizations. You have a server in your datacenter that is periodically misbehaving. You attempt to troubleshoot the issue and cannot duplicate the problem that was reported to you. Instead, you get the infamous BSOD.

You will learn that the first thing you ask customers when they report a problem is, "Have you tried turning it off and on again?" If you do unfortunately experience a BSOD, then your only option is to power down and turn the device back on. Check `reli` to determine what caused that crash.

It has been my experience that a BSOD is caused by bad drivers, overheating, or someone installing new software that is incompatible with either the hardware or the operating system. Using `reli` is how you figure out what really happened.

No one ever admits to downloading and playing *Duke Nukem Forever*.

PSR

Are you the one in your organization who is responsible for continuance or documentation? Do you have to train others how to do their job, or have you been asked to train someone to do yours? Do you ever have to troubleshoot an environmental problem on a system or give a presentation at the last minute?

Problem Steps Recorder (PSR) goes back to Windows 7 and Server 2008. PSR is a combination troubleshooting, assistance, screen capture, annotation tool that few IT professionals know about. You can use it to document your steps quickly with annotated screenshots and instructions. You can use it to troubleshoot an issue for a customer who is not as IT-savvy as you. My favorite way to use it is to build documentation.

One of the best questions you can as your IT manager is, "What keeps you up at night?" When I am teaching, I try to learn as much as I can about my students' needs and goals. One of the biggest responses to the question about their security challenges is lack of documentation and continuance. This tool will help solve that problem.

In my experience, I have managed people new to IT who often ask the same questions over and over again. To empower them to find the answers, I created PSRs for repetitive questions like the following and store them on an easily searchable SharePoint site:

"How do I add a static IP?"

"How do I configure a network printer?"

"How do I add a user in Active Directory?"

In Lab 2.2, you'll use PSR.

LAB 2.2: PSR

1. **To open Problem Steps Recorder, go to your Start menu and type in PSR. Press Enter. You will see a menu like Figure 2.2.**

Figure 2.2 : Steps Recorder menu

2. **Click Start Record.**

3. **Open your Calculator application, and on your keyboard, type 9+9 and press Enter. You should get 18 as the answer. As you clicked the screen or typed on the keyboard, a small red bubble indicates that Problem Steps Recorder is taking a picture of the screen.**

4. **Click Stop Record and wait to review your recording.**

To review the Problem Steps Recorder file you just created, in the upper-left corner of the recording, you could click the New Recording button if this did not capture exactly the process you were looking for. If it is a file that you will want to use, click the Save button. When you save this file, it is saved in a `.zip` file by default. If customers/employees are having an IT issue, they can easily email you this file with all the contents for you to examine the issue. When you open the .zip file, you'll notice the file type is MHTML. You can right-click and open this file type with Word and edit it until it reads exactly as you want it to for your continuance or documentation.

Each step recorded has a date and time and is annotated in bright green in the screenshot surrounding what you clicked. Examine your screenshots. In the first frame, your Start button will be highlighted in green with an arrow on it. The explanation at the top of each picture will tell you how the data was entered. When you're troubleshooting, sometimes input makes a difference.

At the bottom of the Recorded Steps page, there will be an Additional Details section. This section contains specific details about software and operating systems that only programmers or advanced IT people will understand. Review this to make sure nothing is in here that you don't want shared.

Have you ever been asked to present in a meeting with 15 minutes prep time? I'm good, but I'm not that good. If you are being asked to present on something that you can show in PSR, scroll up to the top of the page and click the hyperlink "Review the recorded steps as a slide show."

There are a few caveats to PSR. It will look much more professional if you record on just one monitor. This tool will not record text that you type such as passwords; it will record only function and shortcut keys. It also will not capture streaming video or a full-screen game. You may get a static picture, but this tool delivers a flat, one-dimensional file. You are also limited by default to only 25 screenshots. If you need more than 25, you will have to go to the Help menu and adjust the settings. These settings will be temporary and not retained. They go back to the default when you close and reopen the program.

I have had professional IT students tell me this tool alone was worth the price of admission to class.

PathPing

In 2017, Panasonic developed a prototype that not only washes and dries but also folds your clothes. There are some technologies that just belong together.

PathPing is the washer/dryer/folder combination of Windows. If you take a ping and squish it together with a tracert, you have PathPing. Each node is pinged as the result of a single command. Details of the path between two hosts and the echo-location statistics for each node are displayed. The behavior of nodes is studied over an extended time period—25 seconds each, to be exact. This is in comparison to the default ping sample of four messages or default tracert single-route trace.

PathPing will first do a tracert to the destination. Second, it uses ICMP to ping each hop 100 times. This is used to verify latency between the source host and the destination. You cannot completely rely on ICMP when public devices are involved. They are public devices. Occasionally on the Internet, you will run into situations where an ICMP ping destined for one host has 50 percent failure and the next hop has 100 percent success.

Figure 2.3 shows the tracing route to Google's public DNS server 8.8.8.8. From my desktop to the server, it takes 11 hops. Then PathPing will compute the statistics of round-trip time (RTT) as well as the percentage of how many packets were dropped between the two IP addresses. When you see loss rates, it might indicate that these routers are overloaded.

```
Microsoft Windows [Version 10.0.16299.547]
(c) 2017 Microsoft Corporation. All rights reserved.

C:\Users\Nadean>pathping 8.8.8.8

Tracing route to google-public-dns-a.google.com [8.8.8.8]
over a maximum of 30 hops:
  0  DESKTOP-0U8N7VK.HomeRT [192.168.1.18]
  1  router.asus.com [192.168.1.1]
  2  cm-1-acr01.louisville.co.denver.comcast.net [96.120.13.37]
  3  ae-101-rur02.louisville.co.denver.comcast.net [162.151.15.41]
  4  ae-2-rur01.louisville.co.denver.comcast.net [162.151.51.173]
  5  ae-15-ar01.denver.co.denver.comcast.net [162.151.51.201]
  6  be-33652-cr02.1601milehigh.co.ibone.comcast.net [68.86.92.121]
  7  be-12176-pe02.910fifteenth.co.ibone.comcast.net [68.86.83.94]
  8  as1239-pe01.ashburn.va.ibone.comcast.net [75.149.228.174]
  9  108.170.254.81
 10  64.233.175.43
 11  google-public-dns-a.google.com [8.8.8.8]

Computing statistics for 275 seconds...
              Source to Here   This Node/Link
Hop  RTT      Lost/Sent = Pct  Lost/Sent = Pct  Address
  0                                             DESKTOP-0U8N7VK.HomeRT [192.168.1.18]
                                0/ 100 =  0%    |
  1   1ms     0/ 100 =  0%      0/ 100 =  0%    router.asus.com [192.168.1.1]
                                0/ 100 =  0%    |
  2   11ms    0/ 100 =  0%      0/ 100 =  0%    cm-1-acr01.louisville.co.denver.comcast.net [96.120.13.37]
                                0/ 100 =  0%    |
  3   15ms    0/ 100 =  0%      0/ 100 =  0%    ae-101-rur02.louisville.co.denver.comcast.net [162.151.15.41]
                                0/ 100 =  0%    |
  4   13ms    0/ 100 =  0%      0/ 100 =  0%    ae-2-rur01.louisville.co.denver.comcast.net [162.151.51.173]
                                0/ 100 =  0%    |
  5   14ms    0/ 100 =  0%      0/ 100 =  0%    ae-15-ar01.denver.co.denver.comcast.net [162.151.51.201]
                                0/ 100 =  0%    |
  6   14ms    0/ 100 =  0%      0/ 100 =  0%    be-33652-cr02.1601milehigh.co.ibone.comcast.net [68.86.92.121]
                                0/ 100 =  0%    |
  7   12ms    0/ 100 =  0%      0/ 100 =  0%    be-12176-pe02.910fifteenth.co.ibone.comcast.net [68.86.83.94]
                                0/ 100 =  0%    |
  8   13ms    0/ 100 =  0%      0/ 100 =  0%    as1239-pe01.ashburn.va.ibone.comcast.net [75.149.228.174]
                                0/ 100 =  0%    |
  9   13ms    0/ 100 =  0%      0/ 100 =  0%    108.170.254.81
                                0/ 100 =  0%    |
 10   ---     100/ 100 =100%    100/ 100 =100%  64.233.175.43
                                0/ 100 =  0%    |
 11   13ms    0/ 100 =  0%      0/ 100 =  0%    google-public-dns-a.google.com [8.8.8.8]

Trace complete.
```

Figure 2.3: PathPing combining both traceroute and statistics of each hop

PathPing is a better diagnostic tool to use if latency in your network is a concern. The interpretation of the data from a PathPing will give you a more robust hypothesis. If you see anomalies or peaks and valleys in the data on hop 6, it doesn't necessarily mean that hop 6 is the problem. It could be that hop 6 just happens to be under immense pressure or the processor has priorities other than your PathPing at the moment. A tool that ISPs use to prevent overwhelming floods of ICMP is called *control-plane policing* (CoPP). This type of flood prevention can also alter the results you see from PathPing. In Lab 2.3, you'll use PathPing.

LAB 2.3: PATHPING

1. Open a command prompt, PowerShell, or a terminal window.

2. Type the following command to display options that you can use with the PathPing tool:

   `pathping /?`

3. At the next command prompt, type the following:

   `pathping -q 50 8.8.8.8`

   By using `-q 50` as an option, you cut your time in half, although it will still be a very long 137 seconds.

MTR

My TraceRoute (MTR) is another tool that combines multiple tools into one. MTR was originally named for Matt Kimball in 1997 and was called Matt's TraceRoute.

WinMTR is a Windows application that combines the `tracert` and `ping` commands. At the time of publication, it can be downloaded from www.winmtr.net. The tool is often used for network troubleshooting. By showing a list of routers traveled and average time and packet loss, it allows administrators to identify issues between two routers responsible for overall latency. This can help identify network overuse problems. In Lab 2.4, you'll use MTR.

LAB 2.4: MTR

1. Open a command prompt or a terminal window.

2. Download the WinMTR file from www.winmtr.net, and choose the appropriate file for your hardware (e.g., x86 x64).

3. Extract the `.zip` file, making note of the location.

4. Open the WinMTR folder and double-click the application. PathPing along with other information will be displayed in a graphical user interface (GUI), making the data much easier to document.

5. Next to Host, type **8.8.8.8** and click Start. In Figure 2.4, you see the results.

Continues

LAB 2.4 (CONTINUED)

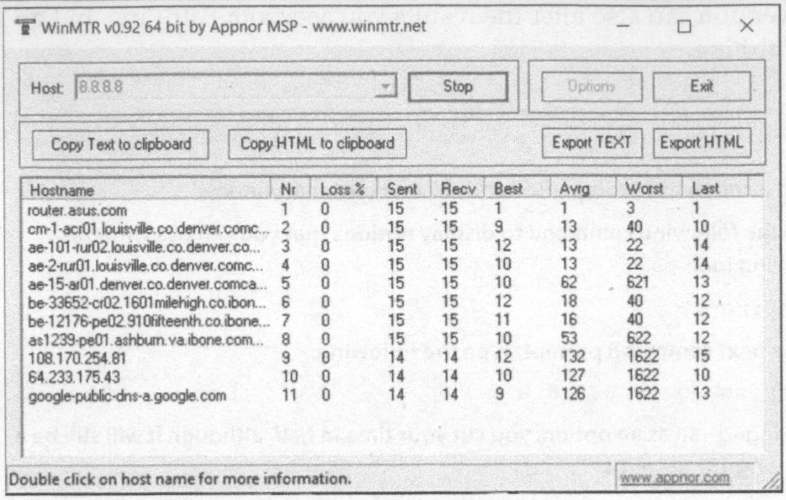

Figure 2.4: WinMTR combining ping with traceroute

6. Copy or export your results by clicking either the Export TEXT or Export HTML button.

7. Double-click a hostname for more information. Select the down arrow at the end of the host field and clear your history.

Sysinternals

Microsoft TechNet is a treasure-trove of all things Microsoft, including troubleshooting, downloads, and training. From the website https://technet .microsoft.com, you can find free training, libraries, wikis, forums, and blogs. When your Microsoft workstation fails hard with a BSOD, where do you go to look up the error codes and event IDs? TechNet! Where do you go to find utilities to help you manage, troubleshoot, and diagnose your Windows machines *and* applications? TechNet!

When you visit the TechNet website, the fastest way to find the Sysinternals suite is to just search for it in the upper-right corner. The Sysinternals suite bundles many smaller utilities into one big beautiful tool. One of the best things about the Sysinternals suite is that it is portable. Figure 2.5 shows the download link. You do not have to install each tool. You can put the entire suite of tools on a USB drive and use them from any PC.

The tools include utilities such as Process Explorer, which is a lot like Task Manager with a ton of extra features, or Autoruns, which helps you deal with startup processes. Another tool inside the suite is PsExec, which is a lightweight

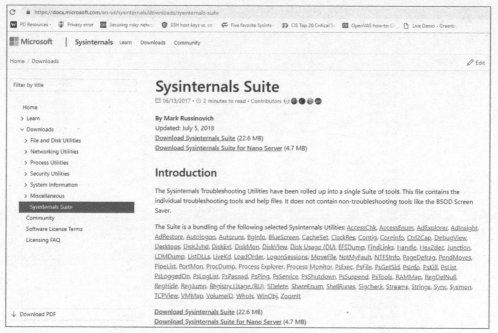

Figure 2.5: Microsoft Sysinternals suite download

replacement for Telnet. One of my favorite tools is Notmyfault. Seriously, that's the name of the tool. You can use it to crash or handle kernel memory leaks—helpful when troubleshooting device driver issues, which has been the cause of at least half of my BSODs. In Lab 2.5, you'll use Sysinternals.

LAB 2.5: SYSINTERNALS

1. Open a browser and navigate to `https://technet.microsoft.com`.

2. In the Search field, look for *Sysinternals*. The first link you should see is "Download Sysinternals Suite."

    The zipped file will be about 24MB. Unzipped, it will be approximately 60MB. It will easily fit on a USB drive.

3. Save the file to your hard drive and extract all files. Make a conscious note of the location. (I say this because I have been known to misplace my tools.)

4. Once the tools are unzipped, open the folder and change the view to List, as you see in Figure 2.6. This will allow you to see everything at one time.

Continues

LAB 2.5 (CONTINUED)

Figure 2.6: List of all Sysinternals tools

There are so many wonderful tools in this file that it can be difficult to know where to start. The following list includes the tools that I have used quite regularly as well as some that I may not use as much but have been helpful in certain situations:

Process Explorer   This tool is one of the most used utilities in Sysinternals. It is a simple tool, but it can clue you in on every process, every DLL, and every activity occurring on your PC. In Figure 2.7, you see processes, CPU usage, PID, and other information. One of my favorite features of Process Explorer is the ability to check processes with VirusTotal if you suspect your machine is compromised.

PsList   One way to see processes on a machine is to press Ctrl+Alt+Delete on your keyboard and navigate to your Task Manager. The Task Manager is a great tool but works only on the local machine. You can run PsList remotely to get a list of processes running on someone else's machine.

PsKill   This tool can be used to kill or terminate processes running on either your machine or someone else's machine. Find the process ID with PsList and terminate it with PsKill.

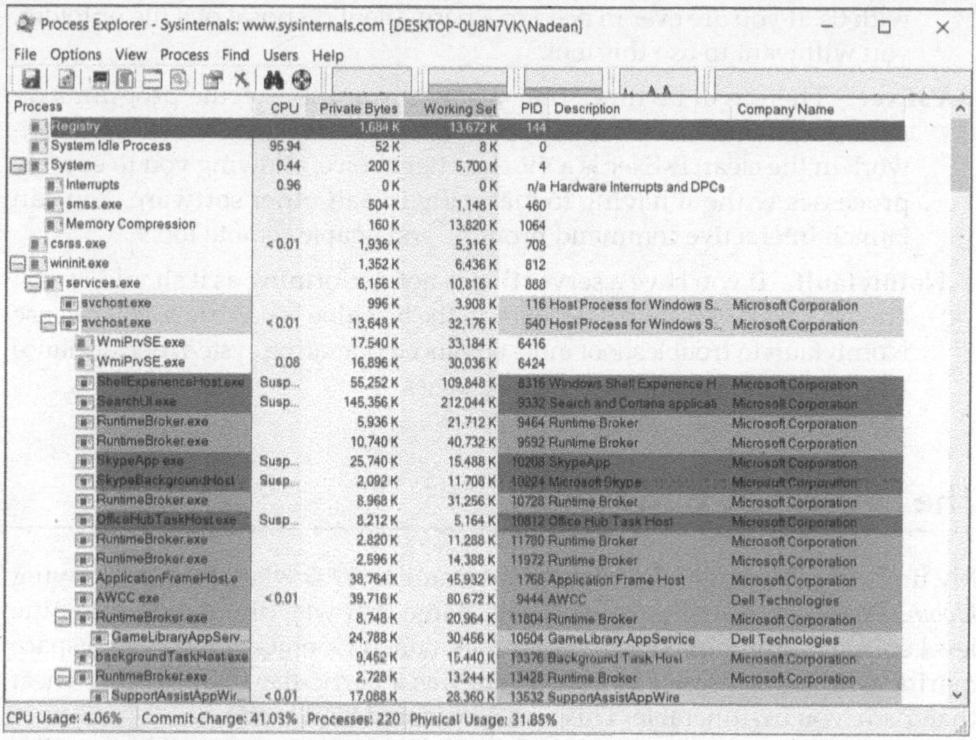

Figure 2.7: Sysinternals Process Explorer

Autoruns   Malware is the bane of our IT existence. It can be insidious and invade the startup folder. It will be one the hardest things you will ever try to clean. Autoruns can help by looking through all possible locations where applications are listed to autostart. You can filter Autoruns so that the good things you need to start are not listed, and you can concentrate on the number of things that invade a system.

ZoomIt   This utility can be used to magnify a certain area of the screen. It can integrate with PowerPoint so that during a presentation you can trigger certain functions with macro keys. You can live zoom, draw, type, and even configure a break timer if your audience requires one during a class.

PsLoggedOn   This tool can find users who are logged on to a system. PsLoggedOn uses a scan of the registry to look through the HKEY_USERS key to see what profiles are loaded. This can be extremely helpful when you need to know who has a session established on a PC.

SDelete   This is a tool that you should not need often but could definitely come in handy. If you ever need to delete something permanently so that even the best of the best file recovery tools cannot retrieve the data, SDelete will take the sectors where the file is stored and write over them with 0s. If you are ever in need of a permanent disposal of a file or folder, you will want to use this tool.

PsExec   There will be times that you will want to execute programs on remote systems. Telnet runs on port 23 and sends credentials over a network in the clear. PsExec is a much better choice, allowing you to execute processes without having to manually install other software. You can launch interactive command prompts and enable remote tools.

Notmyfault   If you have a server that is not performing as it should or you are seeing out-of-resources errors and the machine is very slow, you can use Notmyfault to troubleshoot more advanced operating system performance issues and application or process crashes.

The Legendary God Mode

My first experience with invulnerability came in 1993 when I started playing *Doom. Doom* was a first-person shooter game that was divided up into nine level episodes. You played a character nicknamed DoomGuy who was a space marine who finds himself in Hell. There was a particular IDBEHOLDV cheat that made you invulnerable. This was considered God mode.

In 2007, with the debut of Windows 7 came a tool that was nicknamed *God mode*. Its real name is Windows Master Control Panel, although I personally think God mode sounds more epic.

Windows Master Control Panel gives you access to all the operating systems control panels within one folder. You can enable God mode in Windows 8.1 and Windows 10 as well. The feature is useful for those in IT, those who manage a computer, and advanced Windows experts. Enabling God mode creates a folder that gives you access to every single Windows OS setting. The icon you see in Figure 2.8 is for the folder that gets created.

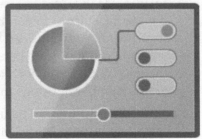

Figure 2.8: God mode folder

In Lab 2.6, you'll enable Windows Master Control Panel.

LAB 2.6: ENABLING WINDOWS MASTER CONTROL PANEL

1. Make sure you are using an account with administrative privileges.
2. Right-click your Windows 7, 8.1, or 10 desktop and choose New ⇨ Folder.
3. Name the folder **GodMode.{ED7BA470-8E54-465E-825C-99712043E01C}**.
4. Press Enter and double-click the Windows Master Control Panel icon to open the file.

It's not quite as exciting as being completely invulnerable in *Doom*, but as far as being in IT, having all these tools in one spot is pretty awesome. Before you start experimenting with the wide assortment of tools, you may want to consider taking a backup of your machine. As shown in Figure 2.9, when you open the GodMode folder, creating a backup and restore file will be one of the first options you see.

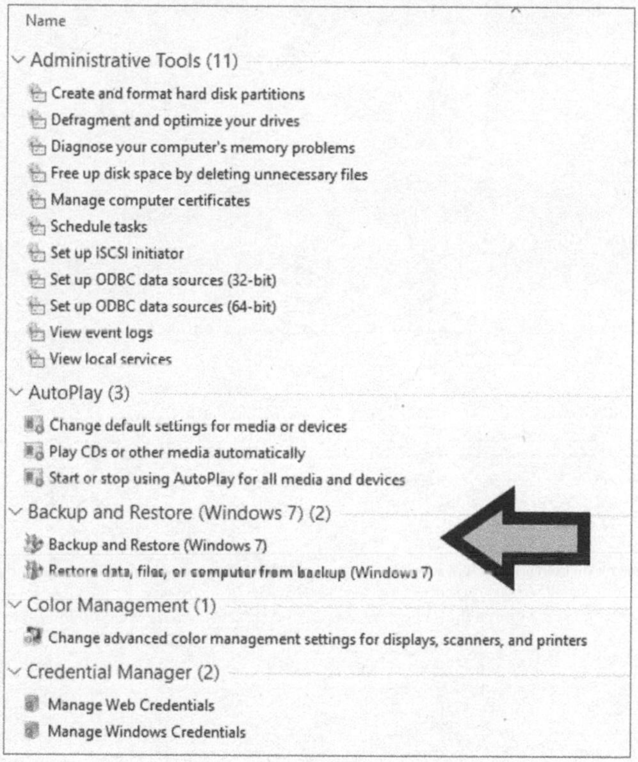

Figure 2.9: Just a few of the 260+ tools in God mode

Nmap—The Network Mapper

WHAT YOU WILL LEARN IN THIS CHAPTER:

➤ Ports

➤ Protocols

➤ Services

➤ OS

➤ ZenMap

One of my favorite nonprofit organizations is the Center for Internet Security (CIS). The mission of CIS is to "identify, develop, validate, promote, and sustain best-practice solutions for cyber defense and build and lead communities to enable an environment of trust in cyberspace." CIS is a collection of subject-matter experts (SMEs) who are able to work together to identify effective security measures for the good of everyone. CIS has an important role in cybersecurity. One of its many contributions is maintaining the most powerful and current cybersecurity best-practices documentation called the "CIS Controls Version 7."

The controls are divided into basic, foundational, and organizational actions so that you can protect your organization and safeguard your data from cyber-attacks. Attackers all over the world are scanning public-facing IP addresses, attempting to find weaknesses in a network.

This chapter will focus on the top CIS-recommended set of actions that all organizations should take. The first is the inventory and control of hardware assets, and the second is the inventory and control of software on those assets. When you are able to track and manage devices and software on your network, you ultimately prevent unauthorized devices and software. You have increased your security posture.

One of the first things you will do to build a security program is implement inventory control. The tool we will start this process with is Nmap, an open source network mapper. Many system administrators find Nmap to be useful when they need to build their documentation around network inventory and topology. In the background, Nmap manipulates IP packets in several ways, attempting to determine what assets are on the network. It will also attempt to find what services, applications, and operating systems are on those assets.

Nmap was originally built as a command-line tool you could execute through a shell or terminal window. The goal was to build a flexible and extremely powerful free open source tool. Originally built on Linux for pure-hearted system administrators, it evolved and is available for Windows as well as in a graphical user interface (GUI) format, Zenmap. There are more than 100 command-line options in Nmap, and some of these were never fully documented by the author, Gordon Lyon.

In any size network but especially large, dynamic networks, it is vitally important to break down these complex networks and analyze traffic, facilitate issues, and fix connection problems. Network scanning is a process of finding assets that are alive or have a heartbeat, communicating and then gathering as much vital information about those assets as possible. Network scanning can be divided into four stages:

- Network mapping
- Open ports
- Services running
- Operating systems

Network Mapping

Network mapping uses a process to discover and visualize assets by actively probing them. Nmap sends both TCP and UDP packets to a targeted machine. These are called *probe packets*. A probe packet is a packet used in an active tool to collect information on a network segment of interest. Data is collected after sending those probe packets that hop from node to node and asset to asset, which returns that information to Nmap.

If you were to scan 65,536 ports on every single machine in your ecosystem, this scan could take an astronomically long time and is really unnecessary. Occasionally, you may hear someone refer to a host discovery scan as a ping scan. In Nmap, you could choose to skip the ping itself and use other targeted methods to find the active hosts on your network.

Network environments are all different; therefore, host discovery needs are going to be very different. The hosts on your network serve multiple purposes, and from a priority standpoint, not all assets are created equal. Some assets are mission critical, while some are used only occasionally and are not as important.

By default, Nmap starts its process by launching host discovery. By default, Nmap will send an ICMP echo request, ICMP timestamp request, and a TCP packet to port 80 (HTTP) and a TCP packet to port 443 (HTTPS). There are several options you can add to a basic Nmap scan to tailor it to your environment. You will definitely want to be using administrator credentials to execute these commands to achieve the best results. For example, Address Resolution Protocol (ARP) is enabled when scanning networks when you are using administrator credentials. ARP is a protocol for mapping an IP address to a physical address on a host called a *Media Access Control (MAC) address*. The table that gets created during an ARP request is called the ARP cache and matches a host's network address with its physical address.

To launch a scan on a network segment, use the following command:

```
>nmap -sn <target addresses>
```

The results will include all active hosts that respond to the probes sent by Nmap. The option `-sn` disables port scanning while leaving the discovery phase untouched. Figure 3.1 shows how Nmap does a ping sweep of assets, meaning you will see only the available hosts that responded to the probes sent out. Most system administrators find this option to be extremely useful and quick to verify which assets are active on the network.

```
Administrator: Command Prompt
Microsoft Windows [Version 10.0.17134.228]
(c) 2018 Microsoft Corporation. All rights reserved.

C:\WINDOWS\system32>nmap -sn 192.168.1.0/24
Starting Nmap 7.70 ( https://nmap.org ) at 2018-09-12 20:49 Mountain Daylight Time
Nmap scan report for 192.168.1.1
Host is up (0.010s latency).
MAC Address: 60:45:CB:B2:08:40 (Asustek Computer)
Nmap scan report for 192.168.1.9
Host is up (0.46s latency).
MAC Address: 10:7B:44:55:48:1B (Asustek Computer)
Nmap scan report for DESKTOP-A07RRLO.HomeRT (192.168.1.74)
Host is up (0.019s latency).
MAC Address: E0:D5:5E:69:1B:14 (Giga-byte Technology)
Nmap scan report for 192.168.1.93
Host is up (0.0080s latency).
MAC Address: AC:16:2D:CE:59:05 (Hewlett Packard)
Nmap scan report for 192.168.1.97
Host is up (0.0056s latency).
MAC Address: 84:1B:5E:26:FC:54 (Netgear)
Nmap scan report for 192.168.1.18
Host is up.
Nmap done: 256 IP addresses (6 hosts up) scanned in 110.46 seconds
```

Figure 3.1: `nmap` command

It is important to scan periodically for new assets that have been added to your network without notification. Change management procedures are not followed or, in a new business, not even written. New machines can be added to networks without being scanned for vulnerabilities.

I had a situation once where the system administrator would scan systems for vulnerabilities in the evenings and on weekends to avoid production hours. Over the weekend, he would see a server pop up in his scans. When this admin would come back in on Monday, he couldn't ping this server. It had disappeared. This happened for a couple weeks until he finally found the problem. One of the networking support people who were supposed to be working over the weekend had a gaming server under his desk. They were having LAN wars instead of patching systems. When they were done "working," the server was unplugged from the network.

Port Scanning

A port scan is a way to figure out which ports on a network are open and which are listening and possibly show whether there are any security devices such as firewalls between the sender and receiver. This process is called *fingerprinting*.

Ports are numbered from 0 to 65,535, but the lower range of 0 to 1,023 consists of the "well-known" ones. A port scan will carefully craft a packet to each destination port. There are some basic techniques to choose from, depending on the network topology and scanning goals.

- **Vanilla scan:** This is the most basic scan, fully connecting to 65,536 ports. It's accurate but easily detectable.

- **SYN scan:** This scan sends a SYN but does not wait for a response. It's faster, but you still learn if the port is open.

- **Strobe scan:** This selectively attempts to connect to only a few ports, typically fewer than 20.

There are some other techniques that penetration testers use, such as Stealth, FTP Bounce, and XMAS, which are scans that were developed so the sender could scan undetected. The sender's location can be obfuscated so that an attacker can get the information while not being tracked.

Now that you know a machine is alive on the network, it's time to determine which ports are open on that host. From a security viewpoint, it is vital to the health and well-being of your network to know exactly which of the 65,536 ports might be exposed. There are six port states that are currently recognized by Nmap.

- **Open:** An application is actively listening for a connection.

- **Closed:** A probe has been received, but no application is listening.

- **Filtered:** It's unknown if port is open; packet filtering typically from a firewall has prevented a probe from reaching the port. Sometimes you get an error response, and sometimes filters will just drop the probe.

- **Unfiltered:** A port is accessible, but Nmap hasn't a clue if the port is open or closed.

- **Open/filtered:** The port is filtered or open, but no state is established.

- **Closed/filtered:** Nmap is unable to determine whether the port is closed or filtered.

The most popular port scan to use by default is the -sS, or SYN, scan you see in Figure 3.2. It is a fast scan, scanning thousands of ports per second relatively stealthily since it's not waiting around for an acknowledgment.

To launch a port scan on a network segment, use the following command:

```
>nmap -sS <target addresses>
```

```
C:\WINDOWS\system32>nmap -sS 192.168.1.0/24
Starting Nmap 7.70 ( https://nmap.org ) at 2018-09-12 22:16 Mountain Daylight Time
Nmap scan report for 192.168.1.1
Host is up (0.0045s latency).
Not shown: 993 closed ports
PORT     STATE SERVICE
53/tcp   open  domain
80/tcp   open  http
139/tcp  open  netbios-ssn
445/tcp  open  microsoft-ds
515/tcp  open  printer
8200/tcp open  trivnet1
9100/tcp open  jetdirect
MAC Address: 60:45:CB:B2:08:40 (Asustek Computer)

Nmap scan report for 192.168.1.74
Host is up (0.0035s latency).
Not shown: 992 filtered ports
PORT     STATE SERVICE
135/tcp  open  msrpc
139/tcp  open  netbios-ssn
443/tcp  open  https
445/tcp  open  microsoft-ds
902/tcp  open  iss-realsecure
912/tcp  open  apex-mesh
2968/tcp open  enpp
6646/tcp open  unknown
MAC Address: E0:D5:5E:69:1B:14 (Giga-byte Technology)

Nmap scan report for 192.168.1.93
Host is up (0.0020s latency).
All 1000 scanned ports on 192.168.1.93 are filtered
MAC Address: AC:16:2D:CE:59:05 (Hewlett Packard)

Nmap scan report for 192.168.1.97
Host is up (0.0042s latency).
Not shown: 991 closed ports
PORT      STATE SERVICE
80/tcp    open  http
111/tcp   open  rpcbind
139/tcp   open  netbios-ssn
443/tcp   open  https
445/tcp   open  microsoft-ds
548/tcp   open  afp
631/tcp   open  ipp
8200/tcp  open  trivnet1
50000/tcp open  ibm-db2
MAC Address: 84:1B:5E:26:FC:54 (Netgear)
```

Figure 3.2: Nmap SYN scan

Services Running

Many moons ago, I taught the CompTIA classes for Iron Horse University at Fort Carson in Colorado Springs. My soldiers would sit in my classroom for two weeks of instruction and hands-on learning. So, if someone wanted to talk to one of my soldiers, they would come down the hall and into classroom 4. They needed a specific person, so they would go to that person's seat so they could talk to him or her.

As an example, let's say the soldier's name was Carla, who was seated in seat 23. So, Carla's socket was classroom.4:23. A socket is a point of ingress or egress. The combination of an IP address and a port is called an *endpoint*. A socket is one of the endpoints in a two-way conversation between two programs communicating over a network. A socket is bound to a port number so we know which application that data is destined for.

The person sitting in seat 23 is like the program that is registered with the operating system to listen at that port. What if Carla was absent? What if someone else was sitting in seat 23? Programs listening on a certain port may or may not be the usual listener. You need to know whether Carla and Robert swapped seats. Table 3.1 describes the most common ports and the services that should be running on them.

Table 3.1: Top Ports Defined

PORT NUMBER	NAME	DEFINED	USED FOR
20	FTP-data	File Transfer Protocol	Moving files between client and server
21	FTP-control	File Transfer Protocol	Control information for moving files
22	SSH	Secure Shell	Security for logging in and file transfer
23	Telnet	Telnet Protocol	Obsolete unencrypted communication
25	SMTP	Simple Mail Transfer Protocol	Sending/routing email
53	DNS	Domain Name System	Phonebook of the Internet; translates names of websites to IP addresses
80	HTTP	Hypertext Transfer Protocol	Foundation of the World Wide Web
110	POP3	Post Office Protocol	Receiving email by downloading to your host

PORT NUMBER	NAME	DEFINED	USED FOR
123	NTP	Network Time Protocol	Synchronizes the clocks on computers on your network
143	IMAP	Internet Message Access Protocol	View email messages from any device; does not download to a host
161	SNMP	Simple Network Management Protocol	Collects information and configures different network devices
443	HTTPS	Hypertext Transfer Protocol Secure	The secure version of HTTP; information between a browser and website is encrypted
445	Microsoft DS	Microsoft-Directory Services	SMB over IP; preferred port for Windows file sharing
465	SMTPS	Secure SMTP	Authenticated SMTP over SSL
1433	MSSQL	Microsoft SQL	Microsoft SQL database management system
3389	RDP	Remote Desktop Protocol	Application sharing protocol

If you want to run a services scan against the machines in your ecosystem, Nmap will tell you which of the hundreds of thousands of ports might be open on a host. If a port is open, communication can occur. Sometimes that communication is unwanted and is what you are trying to protect against. For example, in Figure 3.3 you see the Nmap scan report showing the ports that are open, the service, the state, and the version.

```
Nmap scan report for 192.168.1.18
Host is up (0.00015s latency).
Not shown: 994 closed ports
PORT     STATE SERVICE         VERSION
135/tcp  open  msrpc           Microsoft Windows RPC
139/tcp  open  netbios-ssn     Microsoft Windows netbios-ssn
443/tcp  open  ssl/http        VMware VirtualCenter Web service
445/tcp  open  microsoft-ds?
902/tcp  open  ssl/vmware-auth VMware Authentication Daemon 1.10 (Uses VNC, SOAP)
912/tcp  open  vmware-auth     VMware Authentication Daemon 1.0 (Uses VNC, SOAP)
Service Info: OS: Windows; CPE: cpe:/o:microsoft:windows
```

Figure 3.3: Nmap scan report

To launch a services scan on a network segment, use the following command:

```
>nmap -sV <target addresses>
```

When you do a service scan with Nmap, it will tell you which ports are open and will use a database that lists more than 2,000 well-known services that are typically running on those ports. It has been my experience that network administrators are opinionated and will have their own ideas of how services in their enterprise environment should be configured, so sometimes that database and reality do not match up. If you are doing inventory or vulnerability management, you want to be as accurate as possible and know the version and patch level of systems whenever available.

Version detection investigates those ports to figure out what is actually running. The nmap-services-probes database contains certain probe packets for discovering services and matching them to responses. Nmap will attempt to determine the service, application, version number, hostname, device type, and operating system.

Operating Systems

Nmap is often used to detect the operating system of a machine. Being able to correctly identify the operating system is key for many reasons, including doing inventory and finding vulnerabilities and specific exploits. Nmap is known for having the most robust and comprehensive OS fingerprint database.

When you are identifying specific operating systems, the key is how the operating system responds to Nmap probe packets. Windows XP and Windows Server 2003 are nearly identical, while Windows Vista and Ubuntu Linux 16 are completely different in the way they respond. In Figure 3.4, you see the response of an nmap -O command. To enable operating system detection, use the following command:

```
>nmap -O <target addresses>
```

```
C:\Users\Nadean>nmap -O 192.168.1.97
Starting Nmap 7.70 ( https://nmap.org ) at 2018-09-16 22:08 Mountain Daylight Time
Nmap scan report for 192.168.1.97
Host is up (0.00052s latency).
Not shown: 991 closed ports
PORT      STATE SERVICE
80/tcp    open  http
111/tcp   open  rpcbind
139/tcp   open  netbios-ssn
443/tcp   open  https
445/tcp   open  microsoft-ds
548/tcp   open  afp
631/tcp   open  ipp
8200/tcp  open  trivnet1
50000/tcp open  ibm-db2
MAC Address: 84:1B:5E:26:FC:54 (Netgear)
Device type: storage-misc
Running: Netgear RAIDiator 4.X
OS CPE: cpe:/o:netgear:raidiator:4.2
OS details: Netgear ReadyNAS device (RAIDiator 4.2.21 - 4.2.27)
Network Distance: 1 hop

OS detection performed. Please report any incorrect results at https://nmap.org/submit/ .
Nmap done: 1 IP address (1 host up) scanned in 7.68 seconds
```

Figure 3.4: nmap -O

Zenmap

Everything in this chapter thus far has been done through the command line or terminal interface. As Nmap has matured, so has the interface. Zenmap is the GUI of Nmap. It is a multiplatform, free, and open source application. There are some benefits to Zenmap that the good old command-line Nmap cannot do, such as building topology, creating interactive maps, showing comparisons between two scans, keeping and tracking the results of a scan, and making the scan duplicable. Zenmap's goal is to make scanning easy and free for beginners and experts alike. You only have to identify your target and hit the Scan button, as you see in Figure 3.5.

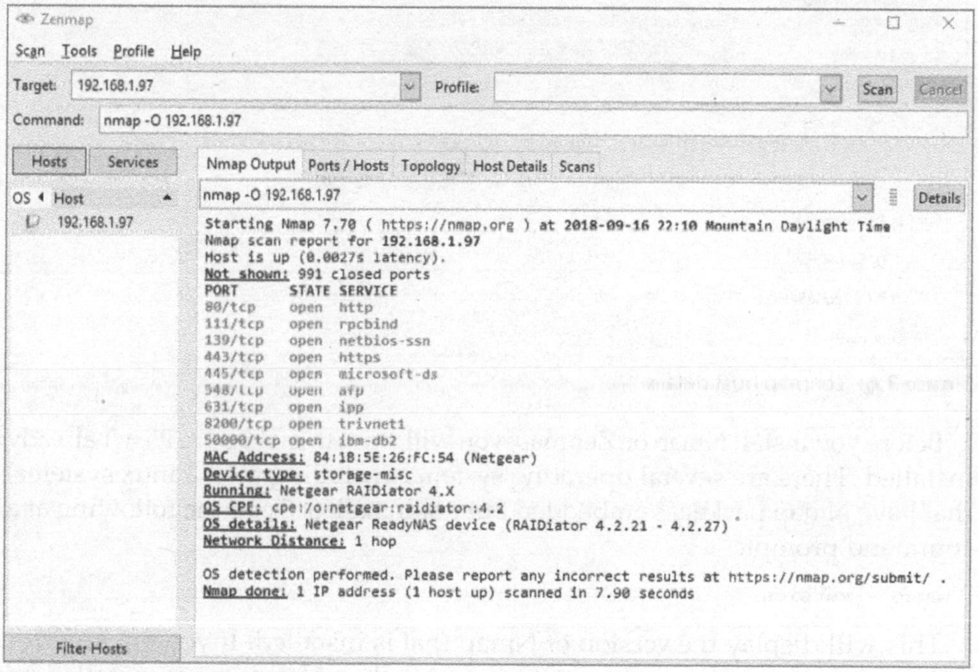

Figure 3.5: Zenmap GUI scan

As you can see, this scan is the exact previous scan, just done in a GUI. If you clicked the tabs across the middle, you would see a list of all ports open, the network topology, the host details, and the history of scans of this asset, as you see in Figure 3.6.

To save an individual scan to a file, choose the Scan menu and select Save Scan from the drop-down. If there is more than one scan, you will be asked which one to save. You have a choice of saving in .xml or .txt format. The .xml format can only be opened and used again by Zenmap. By default, all scans are saved automatically, but only for 60 days.

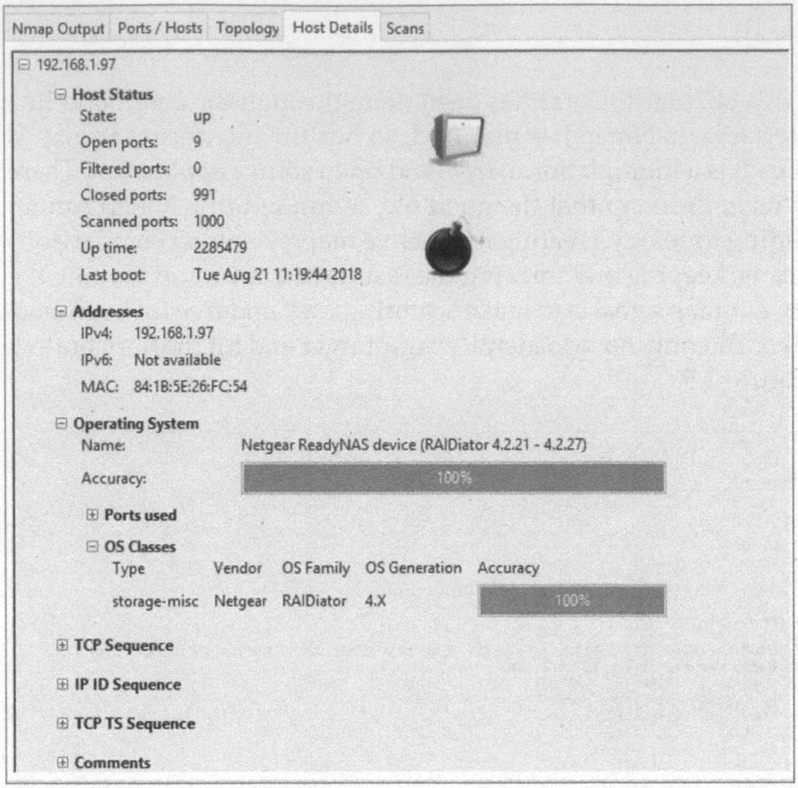

Figure 3.6: Zenmap host details

Before you install Nmap or Zenmap, you will want to make sure it isn't already installed. There are several operating systems (including most Linux systems) that have Nmap packages embedded but not installed. Type the following at a command prompt:

```
nmap --version
```

This will display the version of Nmap that is installed. If you get an error message such as `nmap: command not found`, then Nmap is not installed on your system.

Zenmap is found in the executable Windows installer. The latest stable release will be on the `www.nmap.org/download` page. To download the executable file, click the link shown in Figure 3.7.

Latest **stable** release self-installer: nmap-7.70-setup.exe

Figure 3.7: Downloading `nmap-7.70-setup.exe`

As with most executable files for Windows, the file is saved by default in the Downloads folder. Double-click the executable to start the install process. Click

Next through the windows, keeping all the defaults, until you get to Finish. Once the install has completed, open the Start menu on your taskbar and begin typing **Nmap**. At the top of your menu, you should see Nmap-Zenmap GUI. Click the application, define the target assets, and click Scan to launch.

The white paper "CIS Controls Implementation Guide for Small- and Medium-Sized Enterprises (SMEs)" published at www.cisecurity.org breaks down into these three phases:

1. Know your environment.

2. Protect your assets.

3. Prepare your organization.

In phase 1, Nmap is described as a famous multipurpose network scanner, and Zenmap is described as an easy-to-use graphic user interface for Nmap. You must know your environment better than an attacker and use that attacker's mind-set in key controls to develop your security program.

Vulnerability Management

WHAT YOU WILL LEARN IN THIS CHAPTER:

➤ Managing vulnerabilities

➤ OpenVAS

➤ Continuous assessment

➤ Remediation

➤ Nexpose Community

I have years of vulnerability management experience. At first, it was theoretical when I was teaching at Louisiana State University. It became a more hands-on role when I worked as an IT director for a small private school and then again when I worked for the U.S. Department of Defense (DoD) as a contractor. If you are planning to take any security certification exams—whether it's ISACA, ISC2, or CompTIA—you need to be aware that the management of the vulnerability lifecycle and risk is a key component on those exams.

Some ships are titanic, and some boats are small. Some boats, like a kayak, could represent your home network, while a Fortune 50 company would be more like the *Queen Elizabeth II*. The goal of both vessels is the same: Don't sink. If you have been tasked with vulnerability management, your task is the same: Don't sink.

Managing Vulnerabilities

As I mentioned earlier, you must know your environment better than an attacker and use that attacker's mind-set in key controls to develop your security program. Now that you have all the open-source tools to troubleshoot your network and you know what assets you have to protect, you have to be able to assess those assets for vulnerabilities. It is a cyclic endeavor, as shown in Figure 4.1.

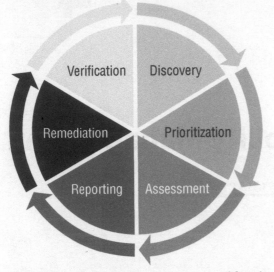

Figure 4.1: The vulnerability management lifecycle

In the discovery phase, you have to figure out what is on your network communicating to other devices. You cannot protect what you don't know you have. Once you're able to map out the assets, hosts, nodes, and intermediary devices on your network, then you're able to move to the next step.

Not all devices are created equal. A domain is a group of computers and other devices on a network that are accessed and administered with a common set of rules. A Windows domain controller (DC) is a Microsoft server that responds to login authentication requests within a network. In an enterprise environment, if a DC fails, your help desk will explode with calls because of the inability for users to log in to the domain. However, if you have a marketing department with a small file server that it backs up to once a month, if this machine fails, then it might warrant a phone call or two. After you know what machines exist on your network, you must prioritize which assets are mission critical.

Once you have identified which assets have a heartbeat and you know which assets would cause chaos through failure or compromise, the next step is to determine the assets' vulnerabilities. This is usually accomplished by analyzing the operating system, ports that are open, services running on those ports, and applications you have installed on those assets.

Now you're ready to build a report. Some reports will bubble up to upper management and require information such as trending analysis and vulnerability remediation plans. The decisions that upper management will make based on these reports could be budgetary or based on head count. The more technical reports will usually trickle down to the asset owner and contain what needs to be fixed on that device.

With the report in hand, you now have a list of vulnerabilities in your environment and on what device they reside. Some software with advanced capabilities will generate instructions on how to remediate those vulnerabilities. Most of these technical reports will give you a severity rating typically based on the Common Vulnerability Scoring System (CVSS), as listed in Table 4.1. The National Institute of Standards and Technology (NIST) maintains the National Vulnerability Database (NVD). In this database, you can see a quantitative analysis of every vulnerability based on access vector, complexity, and authentication as well as the impact to confidentiality, integrity, and availability. Basically, this means every vulnerability will have a score of 0 to 10, with 0 being good and 10 being horrendously awful.

Table 4.1: CVSS v3.0 Ratings

SEVERITY	BASE SCORE RANGE
None	0
Low	0.1–3.9
Medium	4.0–6.9
High	7.0–8.9
Critical	9.0–10.0

Source: National Institute of Standards and Technology

In the vulnerability management lifecycle, building your remediation attack plan is a critical step. After completing the asset classification and vulnerability assessment, you correlate the findings to compile your plan of action. There are some organizations I have worked with that have the goal of becoming 100 percent free of vulnerabilities, and that just isn't a realistic goal to have in our modern digital infrastructure. If you have devices connected and communicating to the world, there is a way into your network and a way out. On mission-critical devices, prioritize the repair of critical and high-severity vulnerabilities. Save the less critical devices to be remediated later.

There is nothing more frustrating than taking apart a PC, fixing what you think is the problem, putting that PC completely back together, and then realizing you didn't fix it and having to start over. Verification is vital to this process. If you do not rescan assets looking for the same vulnerability and you assume that your fix worked but it didn't, you will have a false sense of confidence in that item and leave yourself open to attack.

It has been my experience that the IT industry is one of the most dynamic, with constant change and evolution. There will be times in an enterprise environment that risky behavior will happen when change management processes and procedures are not followed. Our networks are constantly changing and evolving. The networking infrastructure staff throws a new server with no patches on the domain because the people who requested it have the authority to bypass security controls. There are people in the DoD with enough brass on their shoulders to ask for something like this without understanding the repercussions. Those assets still need to be scanned, and if they're not scanned before being added to your network, you get to scan them after.

Some organizations I have worked with have compliance needs that require they scan monthly. Some organizations have a robust security policy where they require assets to be scanned at least once a week. Either way, you vulnerability scanning is not just a one-time action. It is something that needs to be maintained to ensure your network/infrastructure is secure.

OpenVAS

The Open Vulnerability Assessment System (OpenVAS) is an open-source framework of several tools and services that offers powerful vulnerability scanning and management systems. It was designed to search for networked devices, accessible ports, and services and then test for vulnerabilities. It is a competitor to the well-known Nexpose or Nessus vulnerability scanning tool. Analyzing the results from tools like these is an excellent first step for an IT security team working to create a robust, fully developed picture of their network. These tools can also be used as part of a more mature IT platform that regularly assesses a corporate network for vulnerabilities and alerts IT professionals when a major change or new vulnerability has been introduced.

At the center of this modular service-oriented product is the OpenVAS scanner, sometimes called an *engine*. The scanner uses the Network Vulnerability Tests (NVT) maintained by Greenbone Networks based in Germany. Greenbone Networks was founded by experts for network security and free software in 2008 and provides an open-source solution for analyzing and managing vulnerabilities, assessing risk, and recommending an action plan. According to the OpenVAS website, there are more than 50,000 NVTs, and this number is growing weekly.

The OpenVAS Manager is the actual manager of the processes, controlling the scanner using OpenVAS Transfer Protocol (OTP) and OpenVAS Management Protocols (OMP). The Manager component schedules scans and manages the generation of reports. The Manager runs on a SQL database where all the scan results are stored. The Greenbone Security Manager (GSM) web application interface is the easiest alternative to the command-line client to control the scanner, schedule scans, and view reports. Once you have OpenVAS installed, you will log in through the Greenbone Security Assistant, as shown in Figure 4.2.

Figure 4.2: The Greenbone Security Assistant login for OpenVAS

An ISO file is a replication of an entire CD or DVD that you use to install operating systems or software. Sometimes called an *ISO image*, you will need this file to deploy the OpenVAS image. Once you have the OpenVAS .iso file from the website, you can install on bare metal or in a virtual environment. If you want to install this on a Linux system, I suggest 16.04. You will need a newly deployed Ubuntu server, a nonroot user with sudo privileges, and a static IP address. You also need to know how to use the following commands:

```
sudo apt-get update -y
sudo apt-get upgrade -y
sudo reboot
```

The sudo command is used on Linux systems and means "superuser do." If you are more familiar with the Windows environment, sudo is similar to right-clicking a program and choosing Run As Administrator. When you add the -y option, it will bypass any yes/no prompt with an affirmative answer.

The apt-get update command will update the list of available packages and versions. The apt-get upgrade command will install the newer versions.

A little like plug-and-play in the old days, you need to install the required dependencies using the following commands:

```
sudo apt-get install python-software-properties
sudo apt-get install sqlite3
```

OpenVAS is not a default in the Ubuntu repository, so to use the personal package archive (PPA), you must add it, update it, and install it using the following commands:

```
sudo add-apt-repository ppa: mrazavi/openvas
sudo apt-get update
sudo apt-get install openvas
```

By default, OpenVAS runs on port 443, so you need to allow this through your firewalls to enable the update of the vulnerability database. The NVT database contains more than 50,000 NVTs, and this is always growing. For online synchronization, use the following command:

```
sudo openvas-nvt-sync
```

If you skip this step, you will most likely have critical errors later. If you prefer, you can wait until you launch the program and go to the Administration feature inside the software to update the vulnerability database feed. Either way, it must be done.

Once the database is synced, use your browser (preferably Mozilla Firefox) to log into `https://your static IP address` with the default credentials *admin/admin*. You should then see the OpenVAS Security Assistant welcome page displayed on your screen, as shown in Figure 4.3.

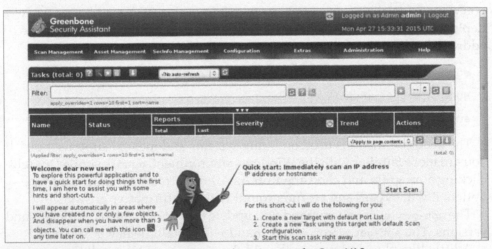

Figure 4.3: Greenbone Security Assistant welcome screen for OpenVAS

The blue star icon is one of the most important buttons on the home page. It will allow you to add a new object such as the configuration of a scan or host list. If you are looking to scan just one IP address, you can use the super-quick Scan Now button on the home page. To get familiar with the software, start with one such as in Figure 4.4 and then branch out to many.

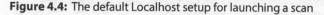

Name	Hosts	IPs	Port List	SSH Credential	SMB Credential	Actions
Localhost	localhost	1	OpenVAS Default			

Figure 4.4: The default Localhost setup for launching a scan

As you may have noticed, there are multiple star icons. If you use the star icon on the right side of the program, you will create a new filter. To add a list of subnets, use the star icon in the top header of the Targets page. The process from start to finish will look like what's shown in Figure 4.5.

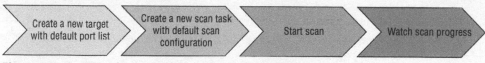

Figure 4.5: Workflow for a scan of assets for vulnerabilities

1. To configure a list of hosts after you're done with the one, navigate to the Configuration tab. Look for Targets in the header portion of the page. This is where you can add a new list of subnets of IP address ranges. Please be aware that, depending on the size of your subnets of IP address ranges, CIDR notation can occasionally error out. You may just need to itemize the list of individual IP addresses. Your local host will be listed on the home page by default.

2. Name the scan appropriately. I usually try to name the scan in a way that allows me to refer to the name and know what I scanned rather than some type of numerical name where I have to actually open the scan to know what I was thinking at the time. The scanning configuration can be left at the default of Full And Fast Ultimate. Select your targets and click Create Task. The new task will show up with a green bar next to the status of New.

3. When you're ready, click the green arrow under Actions to run this new task and start your scan.

4. This is the part I love—watching in the task details page. To watch the scan live, set the No AutoRefresh option to Refresh Every 30 Sec. It's better than television. Depending on how many targets you listed, the scan should be done within a few minutes.

Reporting is vital to your vulnerability management lifecycle. After the scan has completed, check the summary of scan results. They will be classified into High, Medium, and Low and will also contain logs. Each issue that has been discovered will be detailed into vulnerabilities, impact, affected software, and (my favorite if it's available) how to fix what is broken. You can download and export this file as a .pdf, .txt, .xml, or .html file.

Figure 4.6 is an example of filtered results to include in a report. You have the IP address of the host, what operating system is on the host, and the security issues and threat level below.

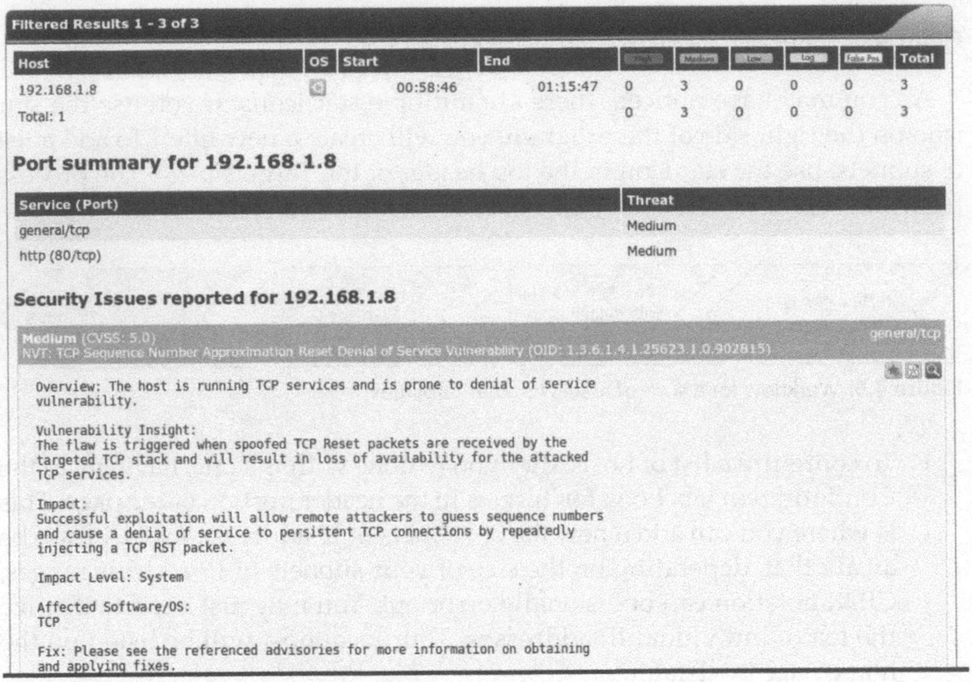

Figure 4.6: Summary results of an asset

Nexpose Community

A lot of organizations offer free or community editions of their software. These editions are usually a lighter version of the paid copy with limited features. Once such community vulnerability management software is Nexpose by Rapid7. There are several versions of Nexpose but the community version is an excellent place to start learning because it's free. If you search in a browser for "Nexpose Community," one of the first options should be the community software directly from Rapid7. You could download from other third parties but I find it safer to download and verify software directly from the vendor whenever possible.

After you complete the form to receive your community license, you will end up on a page to download either the Windows or Linux version with its MD5 sum hash. The hash will verify that your download is not corrupt. Once the download is finished, run the installer. You will notice the community version of Nexpose will only work on 64-bit architecture. To scan an enterprise for vulnerabilities takes a lot of resources including CPU and RAM. Historically, 32-bit architecture can only recognize 4GB of RAM. Nexpose Community cannot do a proper scan with only 4GB of RAM.

LAB 4.1: INSTALLING NEXPOSE COMMUNITY

1. Download and open the executable file. Click Next as you see in Figure 4.7.

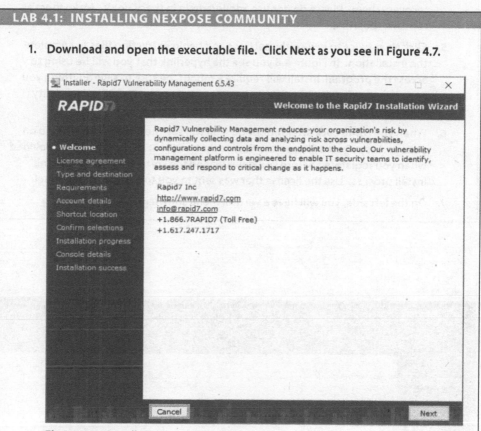

Figure 4.7: Installing Nexpose Community GUI

2. You will choose Security Console with local Scan Engine. You will see the option for Scan Engine only which gives you the ability to deploy scanning engines close to the assets to do the scanning work and then bubble that information up to the scan console without compromising bandwidth. Nexpose runs on a PostgreSQL 9.4.1 database which comes included in the console. Because of the size of most environments, the recommended storage for the database is 80GB. The console will naturally bind to port 3780, which is important when we access the software through the browser through https://yourIpaddress:3780. The PostgreSQL database will communicate over 5432 unless you change it at this stage of installation.

Continues

3. You will add user details including First Name, Last Name, and Company. This is done to create the SSL certificate should you ever need to request help or send data to tech support.

4. Create secure credentials and remember them. You will not be able to easily recovery them. Please do not use admin/admin in these fields. Make them as robust as possible.

5. Click Next twice to review the settings and begin extracting files to complete the installation. In Figure 4.8 you see the hyperlink that you will be using to access the program. Install will require a reboot, be sure to save anything you have open and grab a bite to eat. Nexpose loads over 130,000 vulnerability definitions at startup and can take up to 30 minutes.

6. When you come back after rebooting, you will see the orange Rapid7 logo on your desktop. You will need the license that was sent to the email you provided when you registered before you downloaded the software to complete the install process. Use the license that was sent to you to activate the product.

7. On the left side, you will have a vertical menu shown in Figure 4.8.

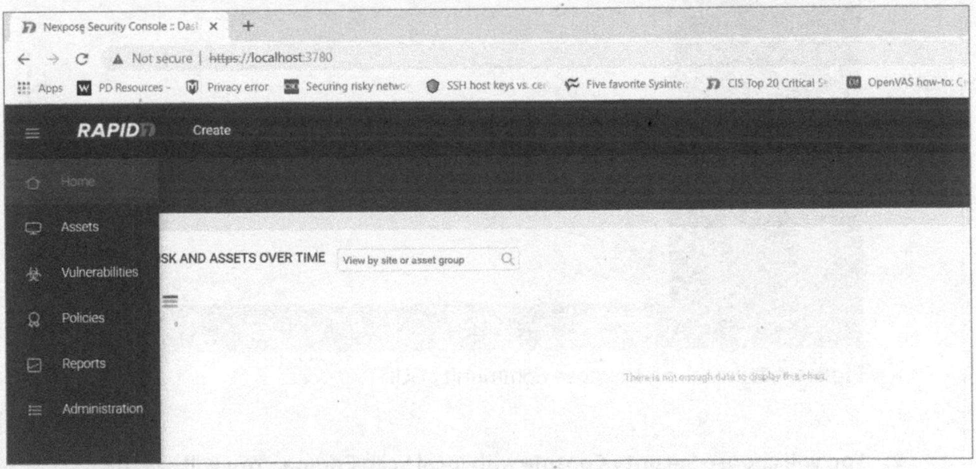

Figure 4.8: Nexpose Community Menu

The home menu gives you a summary of assets, risk scores, and asset groups. The asset page will break down individual items you have scanned and the vulnerability page will give you information on those assets from a different vantage point, where and what makes you vulnerable. The policy tab will be empty since this is the community version but in a paid-for version, you can scan an asset to CIS or a federal guideline of configuration. Reports will be below policies.

LAB 4.2: CREATE A SITE AND SCAN

1. Click on the Create button at the very top of the page. Slide down to Site. You have seven sections to consider for optimal scanning and performance.

2. The General Tab is where you can name the site for future reference and reporting. Add the name TEST.

3. The Assets Tab will allow you to enter a single name, address, or CIDR range of IP addresses you would like to scan. In the community version, it may be wise to do an nmap scan first to build an inventory and then bring in those assets individually since you're limited to 32 assets. For this TEST site, add your IP address. If you are unsure of your IP address, open up a command prompt and do an ipconfig /all.

4. The Authentication tab gives you the ability to be authorized to scan those assets listed on the Assets tab. If you would like a deeper scan, use administrator credentials on this page. Skip this the first time and you will have the ability to create a baseline comparison report in the future.

5. There are several scan templates on the next tab to choose from. The default scan template is a full audit without web spidering. This Is an ideal template to use first.

6. You only have one engine available to you in the community version. This is the local scan engine you installed in Lab 4.1.

7. Alerts are configured to notify an administrator that a scan has failed.

8. The schedule tab will allow you to stay on top of your assets vulnerabilities as Nexpose is updated and new assets are added to your environment.

9. Click Save And Scan in the upper right. This test scan on a single asset will start and you can watch the progress.

10. When the scan completes, review the vulnerabilities on your host. On the asset page, they will look like Figure 4.9.

VULNERABILITIES		
Vulnerability	Severity ⌄	Instances
X.509 Certificate Subject CN Does Not Match the Entity Name	Severe	1
SMBv2 signing not required	Severe	1
Untrusted TLS/SSL server X.509 certificate	Severe	1
TLS/SSL Server is enabling the BEAST attack	Severe	1
TLS Server Supports TLS version 1.0	Severe	1
Self-signed TLS/SSL certificate	Severe	1
TLS Server Supports TLS version 1.1	Moderate	1
TLS/SSL Server Supports The Use of Static Key Ciphers	Moderate	1
TLS/SSL Server Does Not Support Any Strong Cipher Algorithms	Moderate	1

Figure 4.9: List of Vulnerabilities found in Nexpose Community sorted by severity

LAB 4.3: REPORTING

1. Click on the reports menu on the left.

2. Using the carousel under the reports, navigate to the circle that displays the last four default document reports as you see in Figure 4.10.

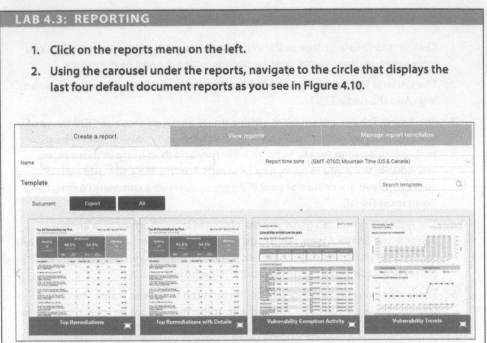

Figure 4.10: Document report menu in Nexpose Community

3. At the top of the page, name this report "Best VM Report EVER."

4. You will see the Top Remediations with Details. Single-click on the report to select.

5. Leave the file format as PDF.

6. Under Scope, choose the big plus in the center and select your test site made in Lab 4.2.

7. Choose Save And Run The Report. The report will generate and when done, you will be able to click on the report name to open.

8. Scroll down through the preview of the report to see the impact of remediated vulnerabilities, the list of vulnerabilities, and the host the vulnerability is on, as displayed in Figure 4.11. Navigate to page two to view the instructions on how to fix the vulnerabilities listed above.

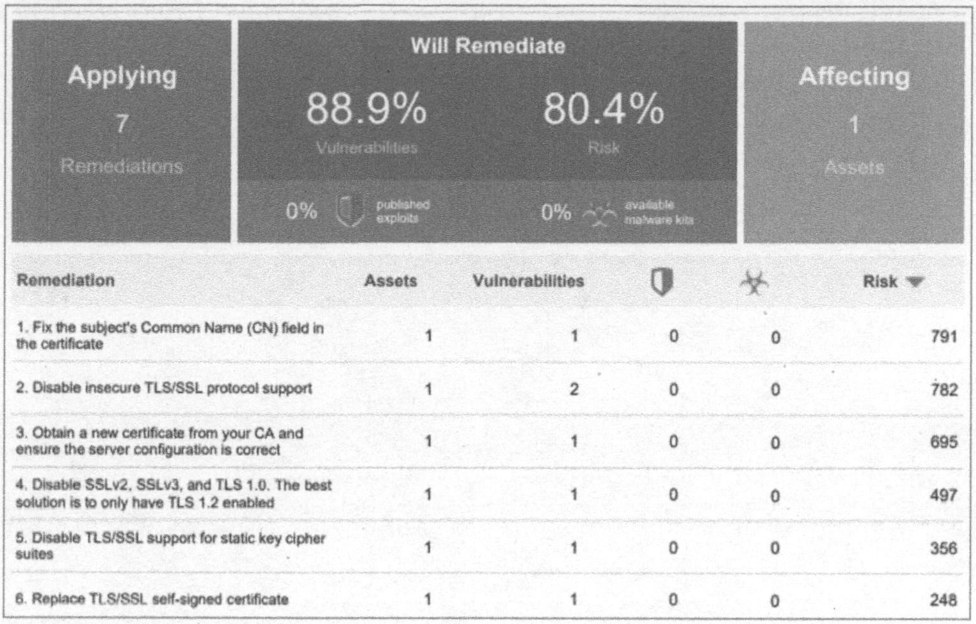

Remediation	Assets	Vulnerabilities	🛡	☣	Risk ▼
1. Fix the subject's Common Name (CN) field in the certificate	1	1	0	0	791
2. Disable insecure TLS/SSL protocol support	1	2	0	0	782
3. Obtain a new certificate from your CA and ensure the server configuration is correct	1	1	0	0	695
4. Disable SSLv2, SSLv3, and TLS 1.0. The best solution is to only have TLS 1.2 enabled	1	1	0	0	497
5. Disable TLS/SSL support for static key cipher suites	1	1	0	0	356
6. Replace TLS/SSL self-signed certificate	1	1	0	0	248

Figure 4.11: Top Remediations

You now have a picture of how an attacker might see you and your network. This is exactly the methodology attackers would use to find the landscape of your environment and attempt to exploit what they find. If you can thwart their efforts by closing up the vulnerabilities that are exposed to the world, you will have a much safer ecosystem.

# CHAPTER 5

Monitoring with OSSEC

WHAT YOU WILL LEARN IN THIS CHAPTER:

➤ Log-Based Intrusion Detection Systems

➤ Agents

➤ Log Analysis

Open Source Security (OSSEC) is a free, open-source, host-based intrusion detection system (HIDS). Daniel Cid, the author of OSSEC, often refers to it in the log analysis portion of OSSEC as a *log-based intrusion detection system* (LIDS). Log analysis for intrusion detection is the process of using the recorded events to detect attacks on a specific environment.

With the proper agents installed on your assets and logs being processed by OSSEC, you meet the criteria for another CIS control. CIS Control 6 is the maintenance, monitoring, and analysis of logs. You must ensure that logging is enabled locally on your systems and it is actively being monitored. Sometimes logging is the only record or evidence of a successful attack. Without solid logs, an attack may go undetected, and damage can be ongoing for months, if not years. Not only can a LIDS protect against an external threat, it also can protect against an internal threat such as detecting a user who is violating an acceptable use policy (AUP).

Log-Based Intrusion Detection Systems

On your hosts across your network, it is vital to monitor the current state of a machine, check the files that are stored on that machine (the log files), and check to make sure that these files have not been changed. OSSEC operates on the principle that attackers who are successful at exploiting a vulnerability and have gained access to a machine will leave evidence of their activities. Once attackers gain access to a system, they of course will not want to lose access. Some attackers will establish some type of backdoor that allows them to return, bypassing all security you may have in place. A computer system should be able to detect these modifications and find persistent threats that penetrate firewalls and other network intrusion systems.

OSSEC is a security log analysis tool and is not known to be useful for log management. It will store the alerts but not every single log. You should have another mechanism for log storage if you need to store logs for your internal security policies or compliance. If you choose to use OSSEC as a HIDS, you will be using a database to monitor file system objects. OSSEC can remember size, attributes, and dates as well as a hash of contents on a machine. For example, if integrity is the most important aspect of file monitoring, an MD5sum hash will use an algorithm to create a digital fingerprint of the file.

With any new project/program implementation, there comes a need for current evaluation. Your team needs to define what success will look like, analyze your current situation, start with a few key components, and take a look at your incident response (IR) plan. An IR plan will contain policies, procedures, and guidelines surrounding processes to complete if an unplanned event occurs.

The benefits to using OSSEC is that it is an open-source free tool that doesn't require a lot of hardware. This HIDS tool will give you visibility into logs generated by firewalls, applications, servers, and routers. You also gain visibility to encrypted protocols such as SSH and SSL logs.

A challenge with OSSEC is it focuses on reactive remediation, reacting to an event that already occurred rather than proactive remediation, where you mitigate and remediate the issue before it occurs. Another challenge you may face is "alert fatigue." This happens when a system floods you with alerts hundreds of times to an event or incident. These can be managed with log correlation and fine-tuning.

OSSEC can be used to monitor thousands of servers with OSSEC agents. These will be monitored by the OSSEC manager.

OSSEC is fairly easy to install, is easy to customize, is extremely scalable, and can use many different platforms, including Windows, Solaris, Mac, and Linux. Secure by default, there are hundreds of rules that can be used straight out of the box. One of the key benefits to OSSEC is how it helps customers meet specific compliance requirements such as those in the Payment Card Industry (PCI) and the Health Insurance Portability and Accountability Act (HIPAA). It lets users detect and alert on a file system modification that was unauthorized or if there is any malicious behavior in any log files. If your organization does have to subscribe to a compliance like PCI, you have to implement only one primary function per server to prevent functions that require different security levels from co-existing on the same server. Web servers, database servers, and

DNS should be implemented on separate servers. A database, which needs to have strong security measures in place, would be at risk sharing a server with a web application, which needs to be open and directly face the Internet. Each server may generate its own unique type of logs, and that may require some configuration of OSSEC. In Figure 5.1, you see the process that OSSEC will use to gather, analyze, and possibly alert you to activity.

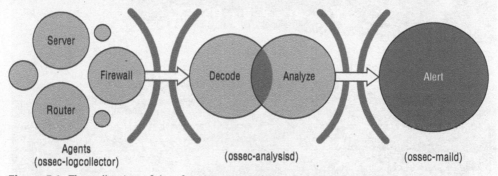

Figure 5.1: The collection of data from agents analyzed and possibly generating alerts

The log analysis flow for the client/server/agent architecture begins with the collection of logs from the assets that need monitoring. After the logs are collected, generic information is extracted such as hostname, program name, and time from the syslog header.

The OSSEC is a virtual appliance based on CentOS and includes Elastic search-Logstash-Kibana (ELK). It comes with its own library of log decoders that will be used by default. These decoders can parse or analyze the logs from Windows, SSH, or Apache using default tags within the logs that help identify what they are and where they came from. The decoders in OSSEC are written in XML and organized into libraries to make them easy to open, decode, define, and close. As you see in Figure 5.2, the virtual appliance spins up ready for you to begin interacting with the dashboard, libraries, and parsing data.

OSSEC must first understand what is in a log before it can tell you if something is wrong or alert you to an event. After parsing the log and normalizing the data, it will match fingerprint with fingerprint and syntax with syntax, forwarding the log file to be evaluated by the rules for processing. If OSSEC receives a log that it doesn't understand, it will generate an event 1002, "Unknown problem somewhere on the system," as you see in Figure 5.3. One of the best solutions is to configure some type of trigger that lists a unique field in the log so it's no longer unknown.

Straight out of the box, there is an extensive set of rules embedded in OSSEC. The rules themselves can be correlated and grouped. After decoding the log, the next step is to check the rules. The rules are internally stored in a tree-type structure and allow you to match on user-defined expressions based on the decoded information. There are more than 400 rules available by default. Please do not modify the default rules inside OSSEC as they will be written over when you upgrade.

Figure 5.2: The OSSEC appliance

Time ▾	Agent	Rule	Alert_Level	Description	Details	File	Syslog_Host	Syslog_Program
▸ October 20th 2018, 19:18:01.207	ossec-server	1002	2	Unknown problem somewhere in the system.	Oct 20 19:17: 55 ossec-ser ver dbus[655]: [system] Fa iled to activat e service 'org bluez': timed	/var/log/ message s	ossec-server	ossec

Figure 5.3: An OSSEC 1002 alert

There are two basic types of rules: atomic and composite. Atomic rules are based on a single event occurring, while a composite rule is based on patterns across multiple logs. When you're learning to write rules, it requires a rule ID, a level that is a number between 0 and 15, and a pattern. For example, if a log is decoded as SSH, generate rule 123. If you want to add a secondary rule, it will be dependent on the first. You can add more rules to be called if the second one matches; for example, you can specify whether the IP address comes from inside or outside the network. Be careful—don't write new rules dependent on composite rules. You should look at the original atomic rule that the composite rule is based on.

OSSEC can generate thousands of alerts a day and, if misconfigured, in a much shorter period of time. You must tune your instance or else you will start to ignore these alerts. Make sure your alerts are relatively rare and relevant to your environment.

Agents

To get started with these processes, OSSEC has many different options for installation. From the www.ossec.net website, you can choose from a server/agent tar.gz file, a virtual appliance, a Docker container, and an .exe file for the Windows agents.

The easiest install for a new user is the virtual appliance. Inside the virtual appliance, which is based on a CentOS Linux 7 distribution, you have the files needed, so getting the .ova file set up is fairly easy. Do not forget: When you download an .ova file, there is usually a .readme file. Be sure to open and read the file for any helpful hints such as default passwords, ports to open or connect on, or ways to bridge with your host network. Two CentOS users are predefined in the virtual appliance: ossec and root. The root password is _0ssec_. The ossec user does not have a password, so you can just press Enter to log on.

If you are working with the OSSEC Virtual Appliance 2.9.3 and downloaded it from OSSEC's GitHub, it already contains the following:

- OSSEC 2.9.3
- Elasticsearch-Logstash-Kibana (ELK) 6.1.1
- Cerebro 0.7.2
- CentOS 7.4

You can import this virtual appliance into most virtual systems. OSSEC recommends VirtualBox for creating and running the appliance, but VMware works as well. The appliance network interface is configured to NAT mode. To use this as a server, you must configure the network to use bridged mode and set a static IP. In Figure 5.4, you see the Kibana OSSEC dashboard is built to visualize alerts, including how many over time, top alerts per agent deployed, and alert data.

Two types of agents will feed data into OSSEC: installable and agentless. Installable agents are installed on hosts, and they report to the server; agentless agents require no installation on a remote host. Both of these processes are started and maintained from the OSSEC manager. After information is gathered, it uses SSH, RDP, SNMP, or WMI to send the data to the manager for processing and decoding.

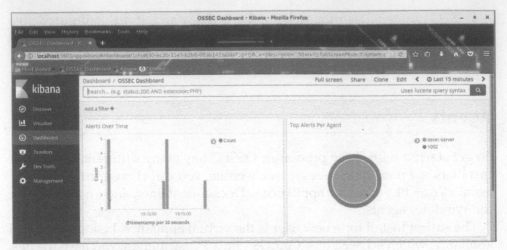

Figure 5.4: The OSSEC dashboard

To add an agent, you will need to do the following:

1. Run manage_agents.

2. Add an agent.

3. Extract and copy the key for the agent.

4. Run manage_agents on the agent.

5. Import the key.

6. Restart the OSSEC server.

7. Start the agent.

In Figure 5.5, you can see the OSSEC agent manager. To run manage_agents from the terminal, ensure that you have root privileges and type in the following:

```
# /var/ossec/bin/manage_agents
```

```
****************************************
* OSSEC HIDS v2.8 Agent manager.       *
* The following options are available: *
****************************************
   (A)dd an agent (A).
   (E)xtract key for an agent (E).
   (L)ist already added agents (L).
   (R)emove an agent (R).
   (Q)uit.
Choose your action: A,E,L,R or Q: A

- Adding a new agent (use '\q' to return to the main menu).
  Please provide the following:
   * A name for the new agent: client_ossec
   * The IP Address of the new agent: 192.168.100.1
   * An ID for the new agent[004]: 004
Agent information:
   ID:004
   Name:client_ossec
   IP Address:192.168.100.1

Confirm adding it?(y/n): Y
Agent added.
```

Figure 5.5: OSSEC agent manager

Several options are available in the agent manager. You can choose to add an agent, extract a key for an agent, list existing agents, remove an agent, and quit. Each of these has a corresponding letter to those actions.

Adding an Agent

To perform this action, type **a** at the Choose Your Action prompt on the manage_agents screen and press Enter.

You are then prompted to provide a name for the new agent. This can be the hostname or another string to identify the system. Figure 5.6 shows an example of how to create a name for an agent. For best practice, create a constant naming convention using some type of spreadsheet that allows you to track your agents.

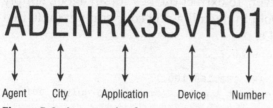

ADENRK3SVR01

| Agent | City | Application | Device | Number |

Figure 5.6: An example of a representative agent name

From this agent name, I know that it is an agent in Denver in rack 3. It's a server, and the agent sequence number is 01. Too many times organizations will name their machines what they are and give a road map to exploitation to the hacker on a silver platter. Security through obfuscation is a pillar of our industry. You wouldn't name a machine WIN2K8SQL, would you?

After you have named the agent, you have to specify the IP address for the agent. This can be either a single IP address or an entire range of IPs. If you use a specific IP address, it should be unique. If you duplicate any IP addresses, it will most definitely cause issues in the future.

Using a network range is preferable when the IP of an agent changes frequently because of DHCP or if different systems appear to come from the same IP address (NAT). For ease of use, you can use CIDR notation when specifying ranges.

After you specify the ID you want to assign to the agent, manage_agents will suggest a value for the ID. This value will be the lowest number that is not already assigned to another agent. The ID 000 is assigned to the OSSEC server. To accept the suggestion, simply press Enter. To choose another value, type it in and then press Enter.

As the final step in creating an agent, you have to confirm adding the agent. For example, you would enter the values shown in bold here:

```
ID: 001
Name: ADENRK3SVR01
IP Address: 192.168.100.1
```

```
Confirm adding it?(y/n): y
Agent added.
```

After that, `manage_agents` appends the agent information to `/var/ossec/etc/client.keys` and goes back to the start screen. If this is the first agent added to this server, the server's OSSEC processes should be restarted by running the command `/var/ossec/bin/ossec-control restart`.

Extracting the Key for an Agent

Each agent shares a key pair with the manager. If you have 100 agents, you need 100 keys. After you add an agent, a key is created. To extract the key, type **e** at the Choose Your Action prompt on the `manage_agents` screen. You will be given a list of all agents on the server. To extract the key for an agent, simply type in the agent ID as shown in bold in the following code snippet (note that you have to enter all digits of the ID):

```
Available agents:
    ID: 001, Name: ADENRK3SVR01, IP: 192.168.100.1
Provide the ID of the agent to extract the key (or '\q' to quit): 001

Agent key information for '001' is:
WERifgh50weCbNwiohg'oixjHOIIWIsdv1437i82370skdfosdFrghhbdfQWE332dJ234
```

The key is encoded in the string and includes information about the agent. This string can be added to the agent through the agent version of `manage_agents`, and the best approach is to cut and paste it.

Removing an Agent

If you want to remove an OSSEC agent from the server, type **r** at the Choose Your Action prompt on the `manage_agents` screen. You will be given a list of all agents already added to the server. Type in the ID of the agent, press Enter, and then confirm the deletion when prompted to do so. It is important to note that you have to enter all digits of the ID. Here's an example:

```
Choose your action: A,E,L,R or Q: r
Available agents:
    ID: 001, Name: ADENRK3SVR01, IP: 192.168.100.1
Provide the ID of the agent to be removed (or '\q' to quit): 001
Confirm deleting it?(y/n): y
```

There is no secondary confirmation. Please double-check that you are removing the proper agent because once `manage_agents` invalidates the agent information in `/var/ossec/etc/client.keys`, you will have to start all over again if you have made a mistake. Yes, I have done it. Learn from my mistakes. Only the values for ID and the key are kept to avoid conflicts when adding agents. The deleted agent can no longer communicate with the OSSEC server.

When you have installed your agents on Windows and Linux machines, they should automatically start checking in with the manager. When you open up the Kibana OSSEC dashboard, you will see there are three major panels.

- OSSEC Alerts Over Time—There is a bar graph that displays the number of events by a unit of time.

- Top Alerts Per Agent—This pie chart shows the top alerts for each active agent.

- OSSEC Alert Data—This table displays the individual alerts and the fields being alerted on, as you see in Figure 5.7.

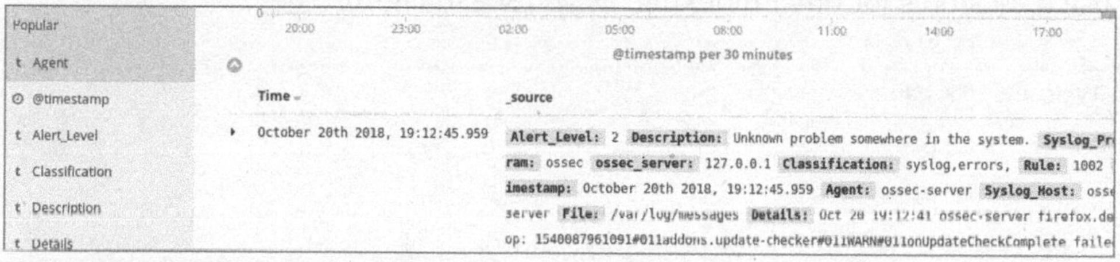

Figure 5.7: OSSEC individual agent alert

Log Analysis

Now that you have your agents gathering logs and bringing them into your OSSEC server, it is time for decoding, inspecting, filtering, classifying, and analyzing. The goal of LIDS is to find any attacks, misuse, or errors that systems are generating using the logs.

Logs are monitored in real time by the manager. By default, log messages from host agents are not retained. Once analyzed, OSSEC deletes these logs unless the <logall> option is included in the OSSEC manager's ossec.conf file. If this option is enabled, OSSEC stores the incoming logs from agents in a text file that is rotated daily. The resources used by the agent are minimal, but the resources used by the manager can fluctuate depending on the events per second (EPS). There are two major ways you can analyze your logs: either by the processes that are running or by the files you are monitoring.

When you are monitoring processes on an asset with OSSEC, the logs that are generated are parsed with the rules contained within the database. Even if some information is not readily available in the logs, OSSEC can still monitor it by examining the output of commands and treating the output as if it was a log file. File log monitoring will monitor log files for new events. When a new log arrives, it forwards the log for processing and decoding.

Configuring a log to be monitored can be pretty easy if you are familiar with Extensible Markup Language (XML). XML is a programming markup language that defines a set of rules used to make a document that is both human readable and machine readable. The design of XML makes it simple and applicable in many scenarios. All you have to do is provide the name of the file to be monitored and the format of the log. For example, the XML may look like this:

```
<localfile>
        <location>/var/log/messages</location>
        <log_format>syslog</log_format>
</localfile>
```

On a virtual machine, you will have the ability to display the dashboard, visualizations, and searches; query the logs; and filter the raw data as well as use data stores for other indexing, as you see in Figure 5.8.

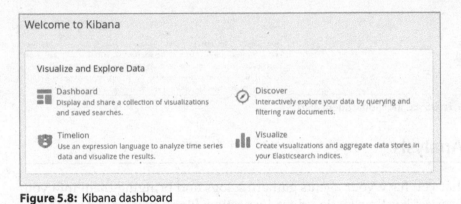

Figure 5.8: Kibana dashboard

Protecting Wireless Communication

WHAT YOU WILL LEARN IN THIS CHAPTER:

➤ 802.11

➤ inSSIDer

➤ Wireless Network Watcher

➤ Hamachi

➤ TOR

The wireless technology that we use today can trace its origin to radiotelegraphy, which transmitted information using electromagnetic waves. Wireless communication today travel over the same electromagnetic waves including radio frequencies, infrared, cellular, and satellite. The Federal Communications Commission (FCC) regulates how the wireless spectrum is used in the United States to ensure stability and reliability. It is up to the users to protect their data at rest as well as their data in transit.

802.11

The Institute of Electrical and Electronics Engineers Standards Association (IEEE) is an organization that develops standards for wireless communication gathering information from subject-matter experts (SME). IEEE is not an institution formed by a specific government but is a community of recognized leaders who follow the principle of "one country, one vote."

The IEEE 802.11 is a set of specifications on implementing wireless over several frequencies. As technology has evolved, so has the need for more revisions. If you were to go shopping for wireless equipment, you would see the array of choices you have based on those revisions of 802.11. Most consumer and enterprise wireless devices conform to 802.11a, 802.11b/g/n, and 802.11ac standards. These standards are better known as Wi-Fi. Bluetooth and wireless personal area networks (WPANs) are specialized wireless technologies, and they are defined by IEEE 802.15.

In Figure 6.1, you see a simple wireless topology; you have a laptop, a printer, and a mobile device all connecting through one wireless access point (WAP) via a router that connects directly to the Internet service provider (ISP), giving the end devices access to the Internet all at the same time.

Figure 6.1: Simple star wireless topology

To best utilize and protect this wireless environment, you need to understand how it works. If you can control electromagnetic waves, you can use them to communicate. Information is sent from one component called a *transmitter* and picked up by another called a *receiver*. The transmitter sends electrical signals through an antenna to create waves that spread outward. The receiver with another antenna in the path of those waves picks up the signal and amplifies it so it can be processed. A wireless router is simply a router that uses radio waves instead of cables. It contains a low-power radio transmitter and receiver, with a range of about 90 meters or 300 feet, depending on what your walls are made of. The router can send and receive Internet data to any computer in your environment that is also equipped with wireless access. Each computer on the wireless network has to have a transmitter and receiver in it as well. A router becomes an access point for the Internet, creating an invisible "cloud" of wireless connectivity called as a *hotspot*.

There are advantages and disadvantages to communicating wirelessly. Networks are pretty easy to set up and rather inexpensive, with several choices of frequencies to communicate over. Disadvantages can include keeping this communication secure, the range of the wireless devices, reliability, and, of course, speed. The transmitter and the receiver need to be on the same frequency, and each 802.11 standard has its own set of pros and cons. Table 6.1 describes the IEEE 802.11 standards for wireless devices. As with any technology, wireless devices have evolved to become faster with more range depending on the standard. 802.11ac is sometimes referred to as Wi-Fi 5 and is what most current wireless routers are compliant with. These devices will have multiple antennas to send and receive data reducing errors and boosting speed. There is a new Wi-Fi technology coming in the near future called 802.11ax or Wi-Fi 6. 802.11ax will be anywhere from four to ten times faster than existing Wi-Fi with wider channels available and promises to be less congested and improve battery life on mobile devices since data is transmitted faster.

Table 6.1: IEEE 802.11 standards

FEATURE	802.11A	802.11B	802.11G	802.11N	802.11AC
Frequency	5 GHz	2.4 GHz	5 GHz	2.4/5 GHz	5 GHz
Maximum data rate	54 Mbps	11 Mbps	54 Mbps	600 Mbps	1 Mbps
Range indoors	100 feet	100 feet	125 feet	225 feet	90 feet
Range outdoors	400 feet	450 feet	450 feet	825 feet	1,000 feet

As with any technology, as it evolves, you will start making decisions on what scenario is best for you and your organization. There may be trade-offs on frequency used, speed, or the range of a device from a Wi-Fi hotspot. A hotspot is merely an area with an accessible network.

When building a typical wireless small office or home office (SOHO) environment, after you identify what technology and design is best for your situation, you configure the settings of your router using a web interface. You can select the name of the network you want to use, known as the *service set identifier* (SSID). You can choose the channel. By default, most routers use channel 6 or 11. You will also choose security options, such as setting up your own username and password as well as encryption.

As a best practice, when you configure security settings on your router, choose Wi-Fi Protected Access version 2 (WPA2). WPA2 is the recommended security standard for Wi-Fi networks. It can use either TKIP or AES encryption, depending on the choices you make during setup. AES is considered more secure.

Another best practice is configuring MAC filtering on your router. This doesn't use a password to authenticate. It uses the MAC address of the device itself. Each device that connects to a router has its own MAC address. You can specify which MAC addresses are allowed on your network as well as set limitations to how many devices can join your network. If you set up your router to use MAC filtering, one drawback is every time you need to add a device, you have to grant network permission. You sacrifice convenience for better protection. After reading this book, the more advanced user will know how to capture packets, examine the data, and possibly identify the MAC address of a device in the list of permitted devices. MAC filtering with WPA2 encryption will be the best way to protect your data.

inSSIDer

One of my favorite tools is called inSSIDer by MetaGeek. inSSIDer is a wireless network scanner. It was meant to replace NetStumbler, which was a Microsoft Windows Wi-Fi scanner. There is a free version with limited features called inS-SIDer Lite, and you can download it from https://www.metageek.com/products/inssider/free/.

inSSIDer intercepts information from wireless devices and will report all of the wireless networks that are nearby. It will report details such as the SSID of the WAP and what channels the device is using, as well as signal strength, the physical type of the WAP, if it's secured, and the minimum/maximum data rate. You also get a graph of the WAPs divided up by channels 2.4 and 5 GHz. In Figure 6.2, you see that inSSIDer Lite captures the SSID of the broadcasting router, channel, signal, 802.11 type, and kind of security that is being used as well as minimum and maximum data rates.

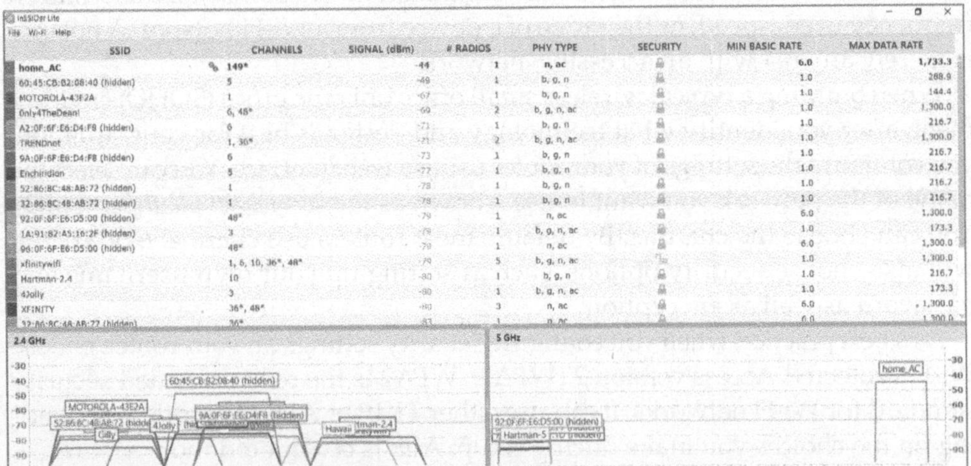

Figure 6.2: inSSIDer capture of Wi-Fi

If you know what is happening around you, you can use this data to fix problems you might be having or improve your network performance. Most people will use inSSIDer to pick the best channel that no one else is using for the best reception and no interference. You can check to see whether your network is secure and what other networks have been discovered.

If there is a lot of traffic on wireless devices around you, you will see this displayed in the visualizations of what channel each access point is on. They can overlap and basically compete for airspace. Using inSSIDer, you can make sure your router is using the best channel. Looking at Figure 6.2, notice that there is a router in the 5 GHz channel all the way over to the right that is not sharing airspace with anyone. Yes, that's me.

One issue everyone experiences from time to time are dead spots. They are one of the most common pain points of Wi-Fi technology. Depending on which version of inSSIDer you use, there is an option to change from Physical to Logical mode. If you change to Physical mode, you can walk around your work or home environment to evaluate whether your router is in the correct spot. If signal strength dips below -70 dBm, you have a weak area. If it falls below -80 dBm, you have a dead spot.

Wireless Network Watcher

inSSIDer will help you manage the wireless connections around you for a stable, reliable connection. Now that you have that stable connection, you may want to monitor who else is attached to the network you are connected to. Wireless Network Watcher by NirSoft is a small program that scans the wireless network you are attached to and displays the list of all computers and devices that are connected to the same network. You can download the latest version from https://www.nirsoft.net/utils/wireless_network_watcher.html.

For every computer or network device attached, you will see the IP address, the MAC address, the company that manufactured the network interface card, and the computer name. You can take that list and export the connected devices into an HTML, XML, CSV, or TXT file. You can even copy the list and paste it into Excel or another spreadsheet application where you can use tools to list, sort, and pivot the information depending on the volume of data.

This program works well when hosted on a Windows machine but can find other platforms such as Linux or Cisco. Wireless Network Watcher will only find assets connected to the network you are currently connected to, not other wireless networks. In some cases, if your network adapter is not found, you can go to Advanced Options and choose the correct network adapter. Under the View tab, you can add gridlines or shaded odd/even rows. If you're actively monitoring the status of your wireless networks, you can even have the program beep when a new device is found. Figure 6.3 shows a list of IP addresses, the device name, MAC address, and other information including whether the device is active on the current network.

IP Address	Device Name	MAC Address	Network Adapter Comp	Device Information	User Text	First Detected On	Last Detected On	Detection Count	Active
192.168.1.1	router.asus.com	60-45-CB-B2-08-40	ASUSTek COMPUTER INC.	Your Router	router.asus.com	11/9/2018 5:00:39	11/9/2018 5:01:58	1	Yes
192.168.1.18	DESKTOP-0UBN7VK.Ho...	00-E1-8C-E7-0C-48	Intel Corporate	Your Computer	DESKTOP-0UBN7VK.HomeRT	11/9/2018 5:00:39	11/9/2018 5:01:43	1	Yes
192.168.1.74	DESKTOP-A07RRLO.Ho...	80-D5-5E-69-18-14	GIGA-BYTE TECHNOLO...		DESKTOP-A07RRLO.HomeRT	11/9/2018 5:00:43	11/9/2018 5:01:36	1	No
192.168.1.93	LaserJet.HomeRT	AC-16-2D-CE-59-05	Hewlett Packard		LaserJet.HomeRT	11/9/2018 5:00:43	11/9/2018 5:01:55	1	Yes
192.168.1.97	NAS-UNIT	84-1B-5E-26-FC-54	NETGEAR		NAS-UNIT	11/9/2018 5:00:44	11/9/2018 5:01:55	1	Yes
192.168.1.61	BOS-T450-3398.HomeRT	4C-34-88-9F-64-24	Intel Corporate		BOS-T450-3398.HomeRT	11/9/2018 5:00:55	11/9/2018 5:01:00	1	No
192.168.1.109		10-78-44-55-48-1B	ASUSTek COMPUTER INC.			11/9/2018 5:01:02	11/9/2018 5:01:02	1	No

Figure 6.3: Wireless Network Watcher capture

In Table 6.2, there are command-line options for scanning and saving in specific file types while using Wireless Network Watcher.

Table 6.2: Wireless Network Watcher command-line options

OPTION	RESULT
/stext *<filename>*	Scan the network; save in TXT file
/stab *<filename>*	Scan the network; save in tab-delimited file
/scomma *<filename>*	Scan the network; save in CSV file

Hamachi

Hamachi by LogMeIn is a cloud-based, professional-level application that allows you to easily create a virtual private network (VPN) in minutes. A VPN seems complicated, but Hamachi is not. Unlike traditional software-based VPNs, Hamachi is on-demand, giving you secure access remotely to your business anywhere you have an Internet connection. Without protection, the information you send will be out in the open, and anyone interested in intercepting your data can capture it. Figure 6.4 shows an example of a laptop sending an email using VPN to secure transmission over the Internet.

Figure 6.4: Securing the transmission of data using a VPN

Based on the fact that you are reading this book, I would probably bet you are the tech support for your friends and family. I've used Hamachi to help friends who are not technically savvy to install printers, troubleshoot issues, and share files and games with other friends around the globe. If you have remote computers that you would like to access, this software gives you access to that remote machine, imitating a local area network.

Using Hamachi, you can add friends, family, and mobile employees to a virtual network where you share resources. Your foundational network configuration does not change. With the VPN connection, information you send to your bank, business email, or other sensitive data is protected. When you use a VPN service, the data is encrypted when it gets to the Internet. The destination site sees the VPN server as the origin of the data. It is extremely difficult to identify the source of the data, what websites you visit, or money you are transferring. The data is encrypted, so even if it is intercepted, no one gets the raw data.

To use Hamachi to create a VPN, you must first download the executable file that will allow you to be a client. The term *client* refers to both the software and any device you've installed the software on. With the correct permission, your client can become a member of any network. The client can be used only with a LogMeIn ID that you create as part of your LogMeIn account when you open and power up the client for the first time. There is no obligation and no credit card required. This ID provides a single sign-on login experience. Once you're logged in to Hamachi, as you see in Figure 6.5, you have your IPv4 and IPv6 address.

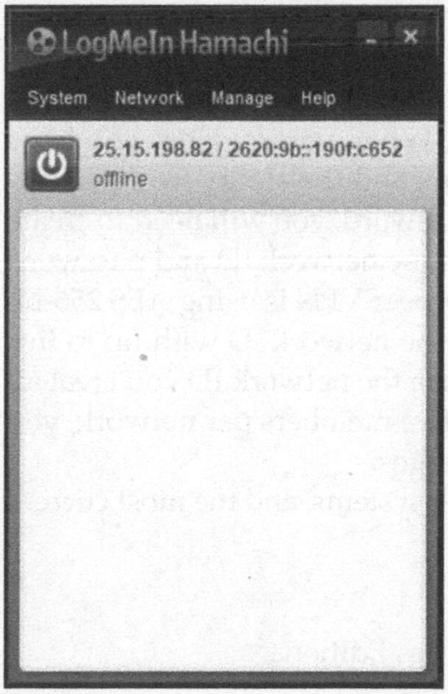

Figure 6.5: Hamachi VPN management console

Every client will have one IPv4 address in the 25.X.X.X range and one IPv6 address. This virtual IP address is globally unique and is used to access any other Hamachi network. As shown in Figure 6.6, when you set up your network, you will have an option to choose Mesh, Hub-And-Spoke, or Gateway.

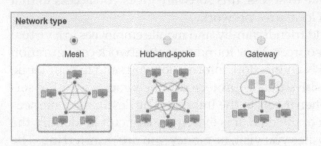

Figure 6.6: Hamachi network type options

In a meshed network, every single member of the network is connected to every other member, which makes it easier to relay data. A mesh topology can handle high amounts of network traffic since every device is considered a node. Interconnected devices can transfer data at the same time, and data moves smoothly, which makes this an ideal choice for gaming. The hub-and-spoke topology provides more control than the meshed network topology. Hubs are connected to everyone, and you have spokes connected to hubs but not to each other. This is a typical choice for a corporate environment where you have workstations connecting to a server. A gateway network will integrate well with a physical network, giving members access to the physical network. There will be only one gateway, and there can many members.

You must sign up for a free account with LogMeIn to complete the install process, and you will need an email address. When you register, you have improved network management, administration, and the ability to create networks. When you have entered an email and password, you will need to create a client-owned network. This will include a unique network ID and password so you can manage your new VPN. This peer-to-peer VPN is using AES 256-bit encryption to secure your data. You can share the network ID with up to five people for free, and they can install the client, use the network ID you created, and join your network. If you need more than five members per network, you may want to look at standard or premium packages.

LogMeIn has been tested with many operating systems, and the most current version supports the following:

- Windows Vista (all versions)
- Windows Server 2008 R2 Standard, Business Editions
- Windows 7, 8.1, and 10

- Windows Server 2012
- Mac OS 10.6 (Snow Leopard) and above
- Ubuntu 16.04 and above
- CentOS 7.2 and above

Depending on the topology you have chosen, keep in mind that you cannot assign the Gateway Node functionality to a Mac or Small Business Server.

LAB 6.1: INSTALLING AND USING HAMACHI

1. On the LogMeIn website, you will you see the download link that attaches your networks to your login *only after you have created a user account and logged in*. If you attempt to download the client without being signed in, any network you create will be unable to be joined by anyone else but you.

2. In the menu on the left in Figure 6.7, there's a Networks menu item. Click Add Clients, and your options will be to install the software on your current machine or a remote machine or add this client to a mobile device. Leave the default of adding LogMeIn Hamachi on this computer and click Continue.

3. Click the Download Now button to allow the installer to download, and follow all the setup wizard's on-screen instructions. You're now ready to configure your first network.

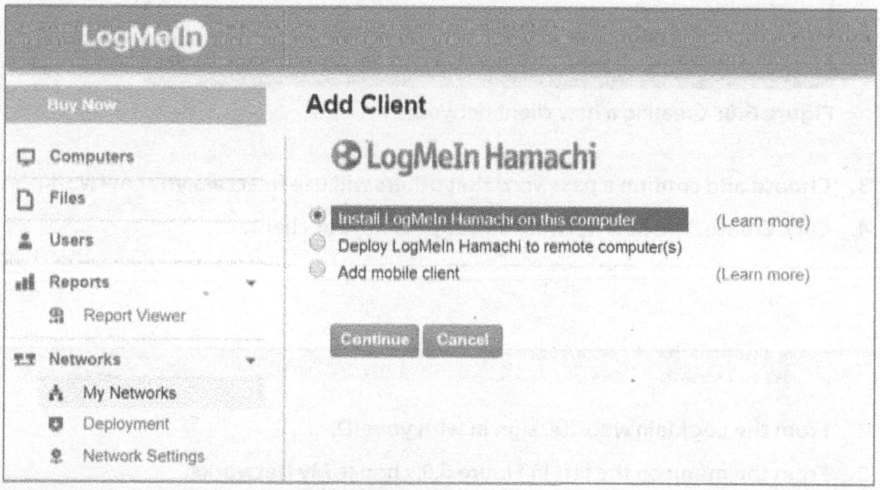

Figure 6.7: LogMeIn Hamachi client menu

NOTE The welcome screen will show you which LogMeIn Account this client will be attached to.

LAB 6.2: CREATING A CLIENT-OWNED NETWORK

1. From the LogMeIn Hamachi menu in Figure 6.5, click Network and then Create Network.

2. As you see in Figure 6.8, create a unique network ID. This is the ID that others will use to join your network. An error message will be displayed if the network ID you've entered is already taken.

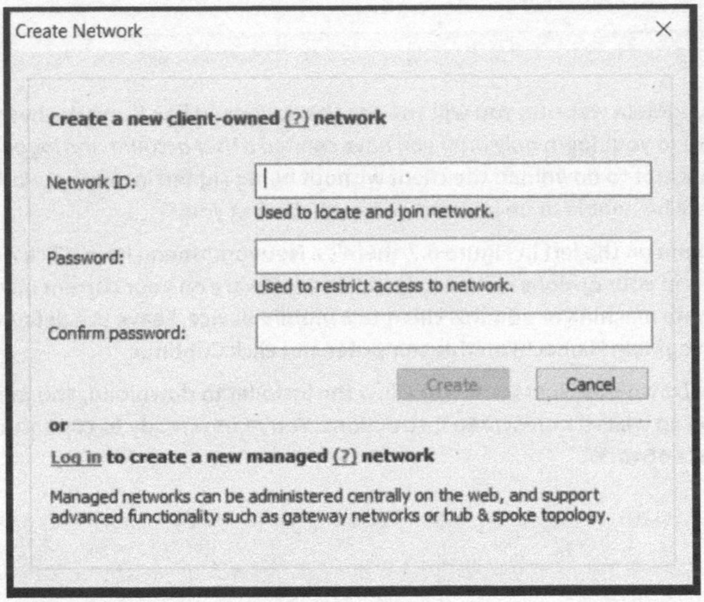

Create Network   ×

Create a new client-owned (?) network

Network ID: |

Used to locate and join network.

Password:

Used to restrict access to network.

Confirm password:

Create   Cancel

or

Log in to create a new managed (?) network

Managed networks can be administered centrally on the web, and support advanced functionality such as gateway networks or hub & spoke topology.

Figure 6.8: Creating a new client network

3. Choose and confirm a password that others will use to access your network.

4. Click Create. The new network will appear in your client.

LAB 6.3: CREATING A MANAGED NETWORK

1. From the LogMeIn website, sign in with your ID.

2. From the menu on the left in Figure 6.9, choose My Networks.

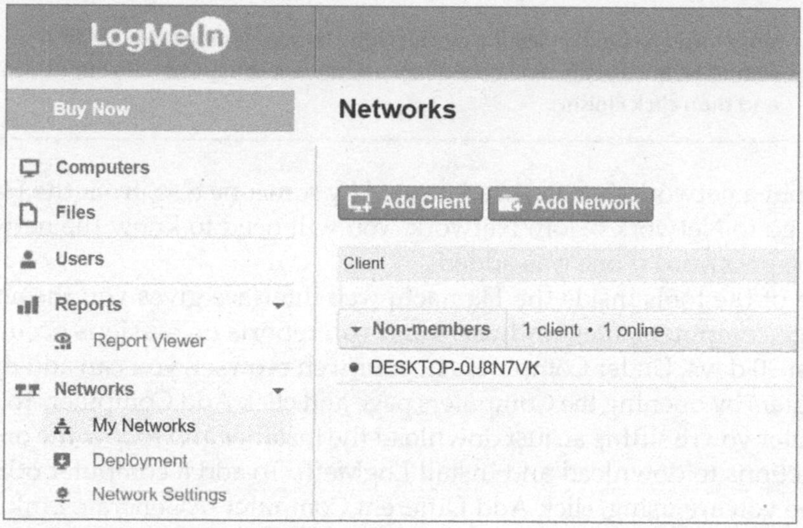

Figure 6.9: Creating a managed network

3. Click **Add Network**. Choose a network name, description, and type, and then click **Continue**. After you click Continue, you cannot change the network type—you will have to delete it.

4. You have an option to accept or approve join requests as well as give the network a password.

5. Click **Continue**.

6. If you chose the hub-and-spoke topology, you will now choose the computer that will act as the hub, as shown in Figure 6.10. If you chose a gateway topology, choose the computer that will act as the gateway computer. The gateway computer cannot be a member of any other VPN. It is typically a server on the physical network. You can change the gateway at any time.

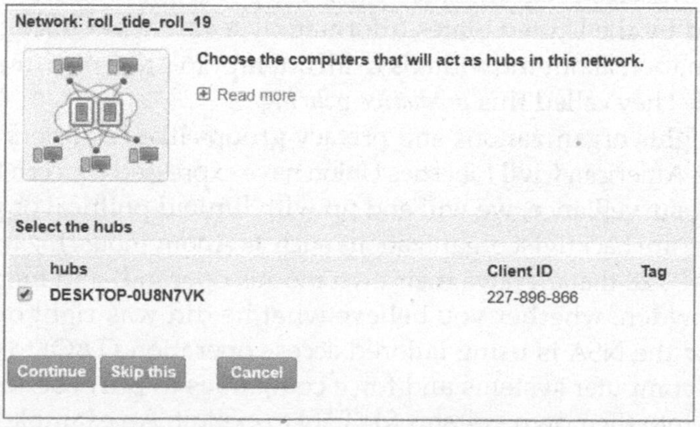

Figure 6.10: Selecting the hub for your network

Continues

LAB 6.3 (CONTINUED)

7. Under Add Network, step 3, you select the hub for your network. Click Continue, and on the next screen, step 4, choose the spokes of your network and then click Finish.

To join a network that has been created by someone else, from the Hamachi client, go to Network ⇨ Join Network. You will need to know the network ID and the password if one was added.

One of the tools inside the Hamachi web interface gives you the ability to manage computers, files, and users and run reports on sessions occurring in the last 30 days. Under Computers in your web browser, you can add different computers by opening the Computers page and click Add Computer. To add the computer you're sitting at, just download the installer and follow the on-screen instructions to download and install LogMeIn. To add a computer other than the one you are using, click Add Different Computer ⇨ Generate Link. Follow the on-screen instructions, but be aware this link does expire after 24 hours. This is where others can download and install the software for the client. With the Files menu, you can upload files, share links, and connect storage space for easy access. Figure 6.11 shows the Users section where you can choose to add users to an account and select which computers you want them to have access to.

Tor

The more you learn about cybersecurity, the more paranoid you may seem to those who do not understand the interworking of the Internet. Monitoring of traffic on the Internet is widespread, and there are many organizations, including governments, corporations, and criminals, that can monitor your traffic covertly. In 2003, a program called Total/Terrorism Information Awareness was established by the United States Information Awareness Office to gather detailed information about individuals in an attempt to prevent crimes before they happened. They called this *predictive policing*.

Many civil rights organizations and privacy groups like Reporters Without Borders and the American Civil Liberties Union have expressed concern that with ever-increasing surveillance, we will end up with limited political or personal freedoms. There are hacktivist organizations such as Anonymous, Lizard Squad, Morpho, and APT28 that all have their own modus operandi and moral code.

Edward Snowden, whether you believe what he did was right or wrong, showed us how the NSA is using tailored access operation (TAO) to compromise common computer systems and force companies to purposefully insert vulnerabilities into their own systems for TAO to exploit. An example of this is

WARRIOR PRIDE, which is iPhone and Android software that can turn on a phone remotely, turn on the microphone, and activate geolocation. The modules of this kit have cartoon names, including Dreamy Smurf, which handles power management; Nosey Smurf, which can turn on the microphone; and Tracker Smurf, which turns on high-precision geolocation.

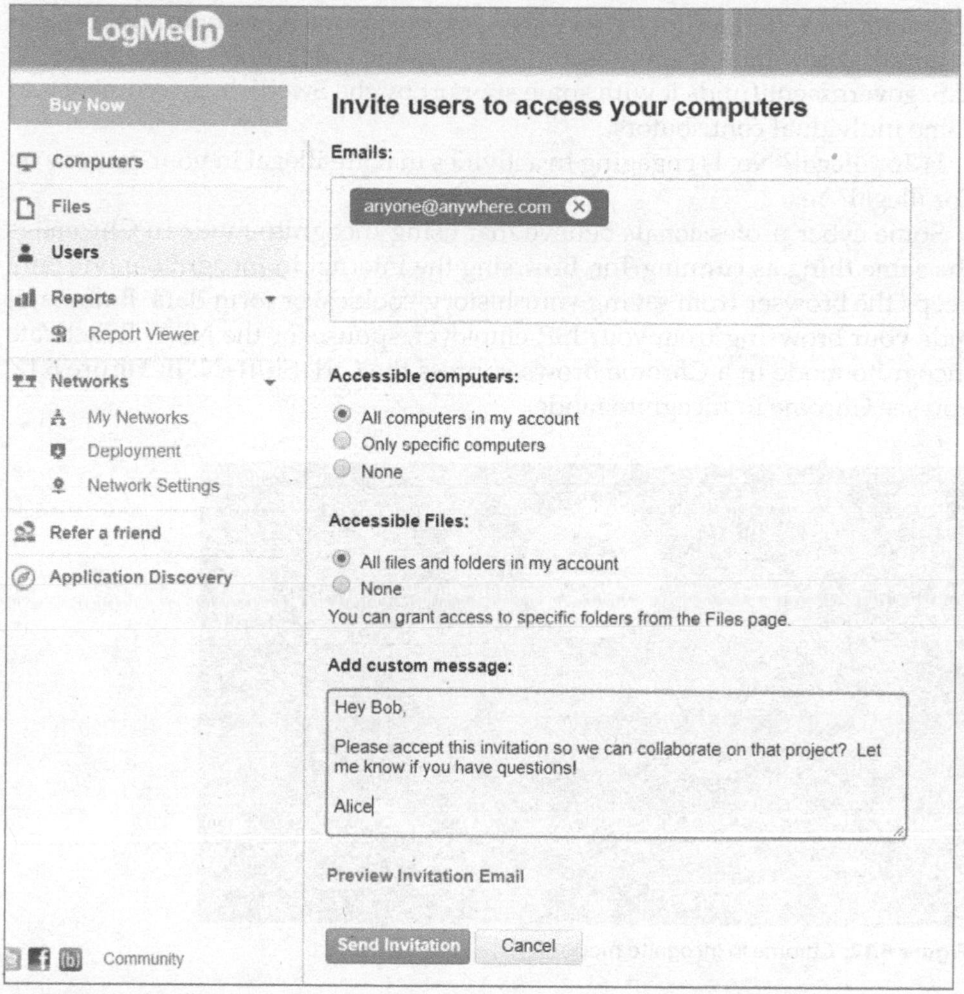

Figure 6.11: Adding users to your computer, granting access to files and folders

According to www.statistica.com, Google had more than 2 billion users in 2017. There are a little more than 7 billion people on the planet. One of the first things I do when teaching a Metasploit class or an open-source intelligence (OSINT) class is to have my students Google themselves. When you get to the My Activity page in Google, depending on your privacy settings, you'll see a timeline of activity, websites you've visited, and images you've viewed. Have you ever had a conversation with a friend and the very next ad you see on your PC or your phone is in direct correlation to the conversation you had?

Tor (also called The Onion Router) is the answer to much of this. Tor is a network that enables you to stay anonymous on the Internet. Tor is based on "onion routing" developed at the U.S. Naval Research Laboratory and was launched in 2002. The Tor Project (www.torproject.org) is a nonprofit organization that currently maintains and develops the free Tor Browser client. The U.S. government funds it with some support by the Swedish government and some individual contributors.

Is Tor illegal? No. Is engaging in activities that are illegal in your country on Tor illegal? Yes.

Some cyber professionals believe that using Incognito mode in Chrome is the same thing as running Tor. Browsing the Internet in Incognito mode only keeps the browser from saving your history, cookies, or form data. It does not hide your browsing from your ISP, employer, spouse, or the NSA. To activate Incognito mode in a Chrome browser, press the Ctrl+Shift+N. In Figure 6.12, you see Chrome in Incognito mode.

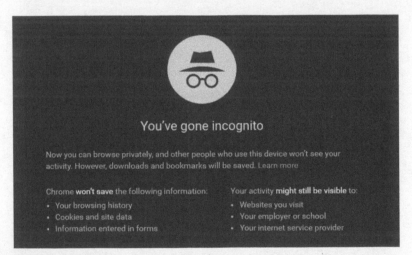

Figure 6.12: Chrome in Incognito mode

By contrast, Tor reduces the risk of traffic analysis by distributing it so that no single point can link you to your destination. To create a private network path, the users of the Tor Browser client will incrementally build a circuit of encrypted connections through different relays on the network. In Figure 6.13, you see the route that data takes from your Tor Browser client to the destination. The circuit is built one hop at a time so that each relay only knows to whom it's giving data and where it is sending that data. No individual relay knows the entire path. For security, after 10 minutes, a new circuit is created to keep anyone from attempting to figure out the path through the nodes.

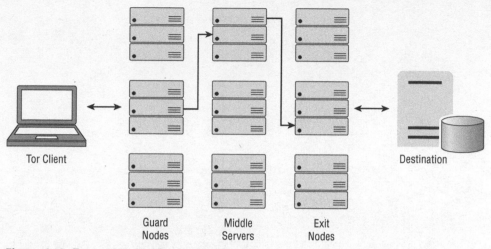

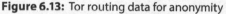

Figure 6.13: Tor routing data for anonymity

To use the Tor Browser client, download the install file from www.torproject.org, run the setup program, choose your desired language, choose a destination folder (I usually choose the Desktop), and click Install.

Open your Tor folder and double-click the Tor Browser client. You will have an option to configure the tool to work with a proxy. Click the Connect button to create the first encrypted relay and open the tool. If you are used to a quick response, you may need to take a deep breath. Because of the architecture of Tor, be prepared for slight delays. It's the exchange you make for privacy. In Figure 6.14, you see the default search engine that Tor uses is DuckDuckGo, layering even more protection of your privacy.

Figure 6.14: DuckDuckGo browser

Now you have end-to-end protection for your wireless communications. You know which networks around you are encrypted; what assets are on your network; which users, devices, and data you're sharing on your virtual private network; and that your browser cannot be traced.

Wireshark

WHAT YOU WILL LEARN IN THIS CHAPTER:

➤ Wireshark

➤ OSI Model

➤ Capture

➤ Filters and Colors

➤ Inspection

Wireshark

My first real experience using Wireshark was in a forensics class with Sherri Davidoff, CEO of LMG Security. Sherri walked us through many tools to investigate a case study where money had been stolen. Wireshark was the tool we kept returning to time and time again to prove what had been planned and executed, and eventually we were able to prove who the threat actors were.

Wireshark is a tool that every network or security administrator should know. It is an open-source tool used for capturing network traffic and analyzing packets at an extremely granular level. Sometimes Wireshark is called a *network analyzer* or a *sniffer*. Packet capturing can tell you about transmit time, source, destination, and protocol type. This can be critical information for evaluating events that are happening or troubleshooting devices across your network. It can also help a security analyst determine whether network traffic is a malicious attack, what type of attack, the IP addresses that were targeted, and where the attack originated from. As a result, you will be able to create rules on a firewall to block the IP addresses where the malicious traffic originated.

Wireshark shows packet details captured from different network media, breaking down the Open Systems Interconnection (OSI) model into the data link, network, transport, and application layers. At the bottom of the workspace, you have an option to open the hexadecimal with corresponding ASCII values on the right.

Wireshark is a powerful tool and technically can be used for eavesdropping. When you plan to use this in a business environment, you will want to get written permission to use it and make sure your organization has a clearly defined security privacy policy that specifies the rights of individuals using the network. Stories abound of network administrators capturing usernames, passwords, email addresses, and other sensitive user data. Wireshark is legal to use, but it can become illegal if you attempt to monitor a network that you do not have explicit authorization to monitor.

Determining the resources that Wireshark needs depends on the size of the .pcap file you are examining. If you have a busy network, then the files will be large. Wireshark can run on Windows and Linux machines. You will need a supported network card for capturing data, such as an Ethernet card or a wireless adapter. To get the latest copy of Wireshark, visit www.wireshark.org. The download page will have the proper version for your computers architecture and version operating system. A new version typically comes out every other month.

To install Wireshark, double-check the name of the file you have downloaded. If you have downloaded Wireshark-win64-2.6.4.exe, you will be installing Wireshark 2.6.4 for Windows 64-bit architecture. The download will include WinPcap, which allows you to capture live network traffic, not just examine saved packet captures (.pcap files).

Once you have installed the Wireshark executable, you will see the list of the different network interfaces that are functioning on the device as well as a graph to the right of current network activity on each interface. It reminds me of an electrocardiogram (EKG) that measures heart rhythms. As you see in Figure 7.1, if you have peaks and valleys, then you have traffic on that interface. If the line is flat, then that interface is not active.

When you double-click a network interface that is displaying activity, the main window will open to display all the traffic on that network. The major components of this page include the menu; the packet list, details, and bytes panes; and the status bar at the bottom, which can give you a great deal of detail regarding your capture.

The packet list pane is located in the top third of the window and by default shares information from the headers of each packet captured. Summary information includes source IP address, destination IP address, protocol in use, length of the packet, and information about the packet. By clicking the individual packets, you control what is shown in the bottom two panes. To drill down into each packet, select the packet in the packet list pane to view more details in the middle window, which feeds data into the bottom window.

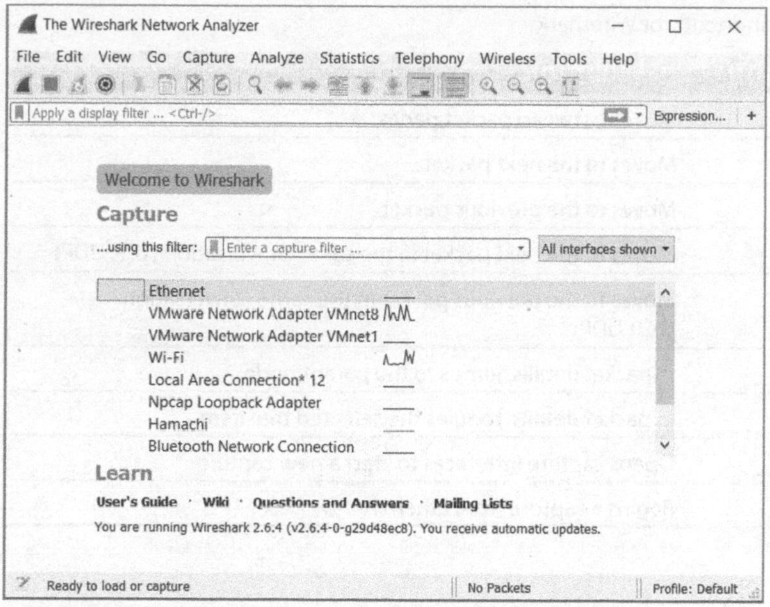

Figure 7.1: Choosing a network interface card for capture

In the packet details pane, you see individual packet size, both on the wire and bytes captured. You also see the transmission medium, protocol, source port, and destination port, and then depending on the type of packet, you may see flags or queries. You can click the > sign on the left to reveal different levels of detail about each packet in human-readable language.

At the bottom is a packet bytes pane. This displays data in hexadecimal code, which makes up the actual digital contents of the packet. It highlights the field selected above in the packet details pane. When you click any line in the middle pane, the hexadecimal code at bottom will be highlighted, giving you an extremely granular view of the data such as a URL that someone visited or contents of an email that was sent.

Under Preferences on the Edit menu, you can change the default layout of Wireshark, choosing exactly what columns you want listed; the fonts, colors, and position/direction of the panes; and what is displayed in each column. Since I learned how to use Wireshark in the default configuration, other than making the font larger and the colors more contrasting, I usually leave all of these preferences alone.

There are also quite a few keyboard navigation shortcuts. Table 7.1 describes the common ones.

Table 7.1: Keyboard shortcuts for Wireshark

KEY COMBINATION	DESCRIPTION
Tab	Moves between packet panes
Ctrl+F8	Moves to the next packet
Ctrl+F7	Moves to the previous packet
Ctrl+.	Moves to the next packet in the same conversation (TCP, UDP)
Ctrl+,	Moves to the previous packet in the same conversation (TCP, UDP)
Backspace	In packet details, jumps to the parent node
Enter	In packet details, toggles the selected tree item
Ctrl+L	Opens capture interfaces to start a new capture
Ctrl+E	Begins a capture from Ethernet

OSI Model

The OSI model was created by the International Organization for Standardization (ISO) to give architects, engineers, and manufacturers a modular way to troubleshoot issues. Certain protocols work at certain layers of OSI. As illustrated in Figure 7.2, the OSI moves in both directions depending on whether someone is either sending or receiving data.

When data is sent across a network, the information is encapsulated as it travels down the OSI layers. When the data is received, it travels up the seven layers and is demultiplexed and delivered to the end user at the upper layers. This process is often likened to using the post office. You write a letter, fold it and put it in an envelope, address it with a destination and receiving address, pay postage, and drop it off at the post office. The post office delivers it to its destination address and the intended person.

Complex problems can be more easily solved when you take this huge process and break it into smaller pieces. Nontechnical end users will turn on their system, log in, open a browser, type in a URL, and enter a username and password to read and compose their email with no clue how it works or what it looks like from a digital point of view. For any type of analysis, it's important to understand what is happening at the different layers of the OSI model. Wireshark will capture and filter traffic on specific fields within supported protocols in manageable-sized .pcap files in real time.

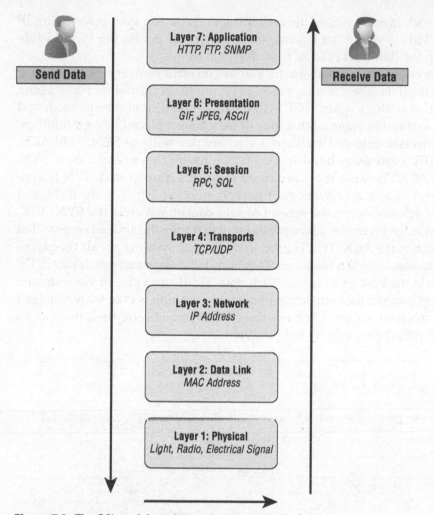

Figure 7.2: The OSI model sending and receiving data

The physical layer is where you start. This is where the transmission of data using electrical signals, light, or radio occurs. Typically you can think of this as being the hardware layer. Devices such as hubs, the actual cables, and Ethernet work at this layer. When forming a hypothesis for correcting issues in your network, the physical layer is the equivalent of "Have you turned it on?" If there is no power, you have no communication, so start troubleshooting the physical layer.

The data link layer (or layer 2) is responsible for the encoding and decoding the electrical signals from the physical layer into bits and bytes and into frames. The data link layer can be subdivided into two sublayers: MAC and Logical Link Control (LLC). The MAC layer controls how a computer on the network gains access to data, and the LLC layer controls flow and error checking. Think of MAC as the MAC address that is burned into the network interface card.

The network layer is where the switching and routing take place using IP addresses. This is where the logical path gets plotted across the World Wide Web, taking the data packet to its final destination.

The transport layer is responsible for end-to-end error recovery. TCP and UDP work to get the data where it is supposed to go, but in very different ways. Using the post office analogy again, TCP is like using return receipt requested, and UDP is the marketing material that may or may not get placed in your mailbox. TCP is connection-oriented architecture where you will see SYN, SYN-ACK, and ACK. TCP's three-way handshaking technique is often referred to as "SYN, SYN-ACK, ACK" because there are three messages transmitted. SYN is synchronize, and ACK is acknowledge. You send a packet, which is the SYN, and the receiver acknowledges the receipt of said packet, which is the SYN-ACK. You acknowledge receivers' acknowledgment that they did indeed receive that packet, which is the ACK. TCP is used to make sure systems get all the pieces they need to reassemble a message. This is called a *three-way handshake*. UDP doesn't care in the least if you receive their data. Think of a video or voice stream. Nothing gets resent if the connection breaks, and nothing is ever acknowledged that it was received. Figure 7.3 shows the ACK of packets and their number so they can be rebuilt properly by the receiver.

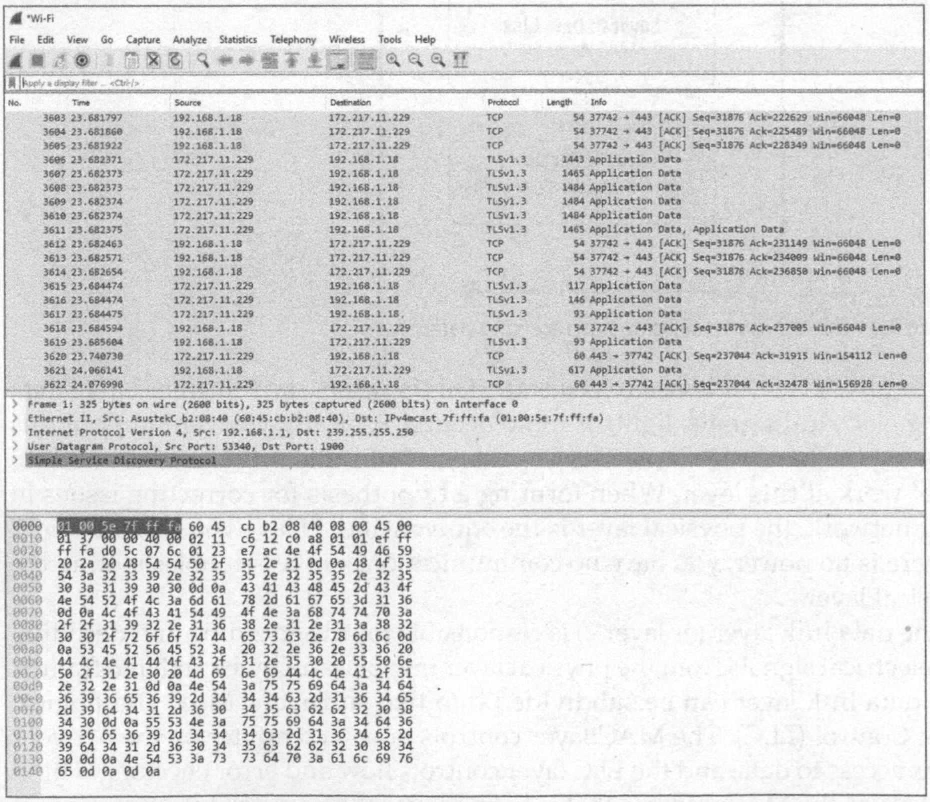

Figure 7.3: Wireshark acknowledgment traffic

The session layer is layer 5 of the OSI model. It's responsible for making, managing, and terminating connections. Layer 6 is the presentation layer, which is in charge of what gets presented to your screen. Encryption and decryption of data happen at layer 6 as well. Finally, the seventh layer is the application layer, which supports the end users and their processes. Quality of service (QoS) works at layer 7 as well as application services such as email and HTTP. QoS is the ability of a network to provide better service to certain network traffic. The primary goal is to give priority to that traffic by dedicating bandwidth to control latency.

Each layer of the OSI model ensures the delivery of data from one place to another. If a layer fails, you end up with an error. With Wireshark's help to diagnos the failing protocol, you can pinpoint where the problem is occurring so you can fix the error.

Capture

One of my favorite ways to teach Wireshark to beginners is to have students download and install Wireshark, bring up a terminal window, and capture the traffic after they launch Nmap. As you learned in Chapter 3, "Nmap: The Network Mapper," good guys as well as bad guys use it. If you can recognize what Nmap traffic looks like and you know that you're not the one running it, then odds are it is someone attempting to map out your network.

LAB 7.1: ZENMAP AND WIRESHARK

NOTE You will need to use three tools to make this lab work: a terminal window, Zenmap, and Wireshark. I am running this lab on a Windows 10 machine where I can open a command shell. You used Zenmap in Chapter 3. You can download Wireshark from www.wireshark.org.

1. Open a terminal window. Run the following command: `ipconfig /all`. Look for the IP address on your Wi-Fi network interface card.

2. Open Zenmap. In the Target field, add the IP address identified in the previous step. In the Profile field, leave the default of Intense scan.

3. Open Wireshark. On the welcome page as you saw in Figure 7.1, identify the Wi-Fi interface that corresponds with step 2. Double-click the Wi-Fi connection. It will start capturing data.

4. Go back to Zenmap and click the Scan button. On a single asset, the Nmap scan may last a to 2 minutes.

5. When the Nmap scan is done, return to Wireshark and click the red box under the word Edit. This will stop the capture, and you now have data to save and analyze.

Continues

LAB 7.1 (CONTINUED)

6. With the Nmap window next to the Wireshark window, you will see traffic in Wireshark you can identify as the Nmap scan. During an Intense scan, Nmap will attempt to resolve DNS.

7. In Wireshark, look at the Protocol column for any DNS traffic. If you cannot find it by scrolling, try clicking the word *protocol* in the top pane. Each column can be sorted in ascending and then descending order just by clicking the column headings.

8. To save the network traffic you just sniffed in Wireshark, go to File ⇨ Save, name the file **nmap**, and click Save.

In any Wireshark menu, items will be grayed out if the feature isn't available. You cannot save a file if you haven't captured any data. Most of the Wireshark menu has the standard File, Edit, View, and Capture options. The Analyze menu allows you to manipulate filters, enable or disable dissection of protocols, or follow a particular stream of data. The Telephony menu is my favorite for analysis of voice traffic. In the Telephony menu, you can build flow diagrams and display statistics.

Capture filters are set before starting a packet capture. Display filters are not. In the Welcome To Wireshark window, you can find the capture filter just above the interfaces list. For instance, if you want to capture traffic only from a specific IP address, the filter would look like this: host 192.168.1.0. To capture traffic over a specific port, the filter would look like this: port 53. Double-click an interface to begin the capture.

Now that you have your first capture started, the top pane is the packet list. The first column shows relationships between packets. Figure 7.4 shows the relationships between the selected packet and other "conversations" you captured. In line 3 under the No. column, you see the first packet of a conversation represented by a right angle, and line 4 continues with a solid line. Lines 5 and 6 start with a dotted line, which signifies that these two captured packets are not part of the conversation started in lines 3 and 4.

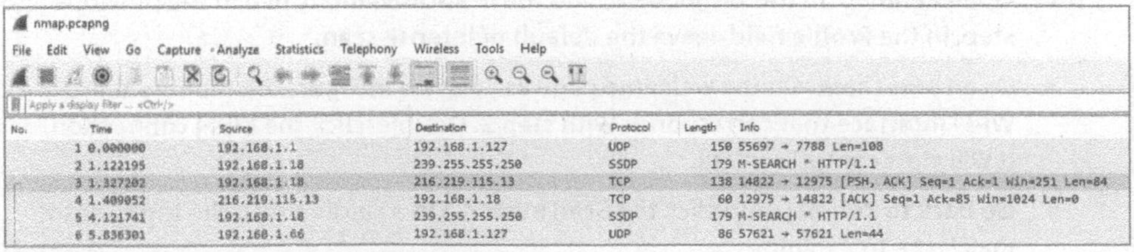

Figure 7.4: Showing conversation relationships

The next pane under the packet traffic is the packet details pane. This pane shows the protocols and fields of the packet selected in the pane above. The protocols and fields can be expanded and collapsed as needed. As you see in Figure 7.5, you can also right-click a packet for options in the packet list pane. Some fields have special generated fields such as additional information that isn't presented in the captured data, which is shown in square brackets. There will be links between packets if a relationship is found. These will be blue and underlined, and you can move from packet to packet.

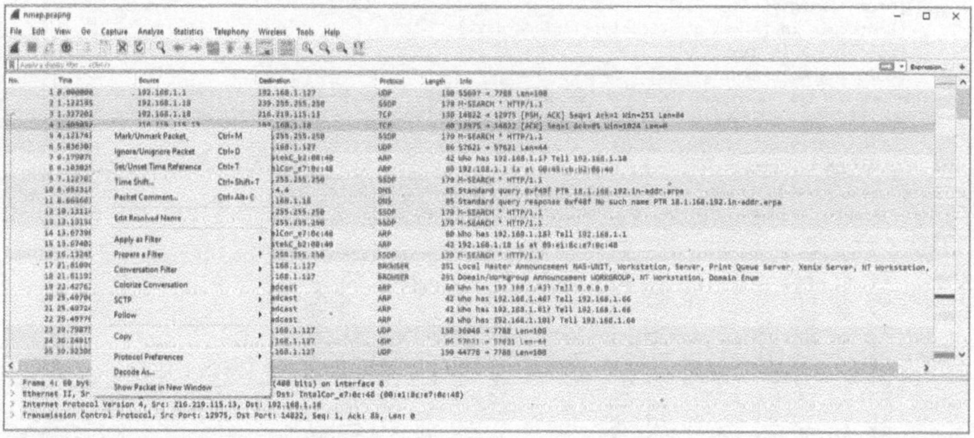

Figure 7.5: Right-clicking a packet

The packets bytes pane at the bottom of the window contains all the hexadecimal code of each packet. Each line of text contains 16 bytes. Each byte (8 bits) of packet capture is represented as a two-digit hexadecimal. In Figure 7.6, you can see the direct relationship between the IP type and the hexadecimal code.

For your second capture, repeat the steps in the preceding lab but instead of doing an Nmap scan, open the browser of your choice and navigate to www. example.com. The Nmap capture was slow compared to this. The second you open the browser, you see an explosion of packets as your home page loads. Navigate to another site that you usually log into, like an email account or a bank. Log in as you usually do, but watch your Wireshark traffic as you complete that task.

Since I have explained how to take a capture, it is important for me to discuss where to take a capture. If you are in a large enterprise environment and there was an issue with network performance, the placement of the network sniffer is important. Place Wireshark as close to the employees and/or customers to identify any traffic issues from their perspectives. If people are complaining about a certain server on the network, you can move Wireshark in proximity to that server to find the problem. One best practice is to put Wireshark on a laptop and move around your location while you're tracking down these problems.

```
∨ Frame 23: 150 bytes on wire (1200 bits), 150 bytes captured (1200 bits) on interface 0
    > Interface id: 0 (\Device\NPF_{40E84EA5-77BC-411E-935B-64559BCD6A68})
      Encapsulation type: Ethernet (1)
      Arrival Time: Nov 16, 2018 21:02:01.356987000 Mountain Standard Time
      [Time shift for this packet: 0.000000000 seconds]
      Epoch Time: 1542427321.356987000 seconds
      [Time delta from previous captured frame: 4.301045000 seconds]
      [Time delta from previous displayed frame: 4.301045000 seconds]
      [Time since reference or first frame: 29.798750000 seconds]
      Frame Number: 23
      Frame Length: 150 bytes (1200 bits)
      Capture Length: 150 bytes (1200 bits)
      [Frame is marked: False]
      [Frame is ignored: False]
      [Protocols in frame: eth:ethertype:ip:udp:data]
      [Coloring Rule Name: UDP]
      [Coloring Rule String: udp]
∨ Ethernet II, Src: AsustekC_b2:08:40 (60:45:cb:b2:08:40), Dst: Broadcast (ff:ff:ff:ff:ff:ff)
    > Destination: Broadcast (ff:ff:ff:ff:ff:ff)
    > Source: AsustekC_b2:08:40 (60:45:cb:b2:08:40)
      Type: IPv4 (0x0800)
  > Internet Protocol Version 4, Src: 192.168.1.1, Dst: 192.168.1.127
  > User Datagram Protocol, Src Port: 36048, Dst Port: 7788
  > Data (108 bytes)

0000   ff ff ff ff ff ff 60 45   cb b2 08 40 08 00 45 00
0010   00 88 00 00 40 00 40 11   b6 94 c0 a8 01 01 c0 a8
0020   01 7f 8c d0 1e 6c 00 74   16 a6 00 00 00 01 00 00
0030   00 60 bc 87 a5 f9 37 01   ae 2f f1 12 6e b0 54 7e
0040   16 a7 f1 43 2f c4 9c 2f   70 11 14 1d a3 3c f9 d6
0050   0f 42 22 eb 40 cb 6e df   82 f3 f0 30 01 7b cb e0
0060   b7 5a 55 7e 88 91 ad 48   cb ce 74 d3 ee 3c 44 1d
0070   3b f1 19 42 9c 98 7d ae   3b f9 7c e6 bb 91 46 37
0080   36 92 3b 12 bf 6a 89 c1   b5 c6 76 e0 0b 8e f2 bb
0090   4b 71 63 09 31 75
```

Figure 7.6: Hexadecimal representation

Filters and Colors

Wireshark uses display filters to concentrate on interesting packets while hiding the boring ones. You can select packets based on protocol, value, or comparison. To filter packets based on protocol, type in the protocol you want to narrow down to, as shown in Figure 7.7. Press Enter to accept the filter selection. When you're using a filter, it only changes the view, not the contents. The capture file remains intact. To remove a filter, click the clear button, which is the X to the right of the filter.

You can compare the values inside packets as well as combine expressions into far more specific expressions. Every field inside a packet can be used as a string, such as tcp. A tcp string will show all packets containing the TCP protocol. Once you have chosen the strings you want to knit together, you choose the appropriate operator. Table 7.2 lists commonly used filters.

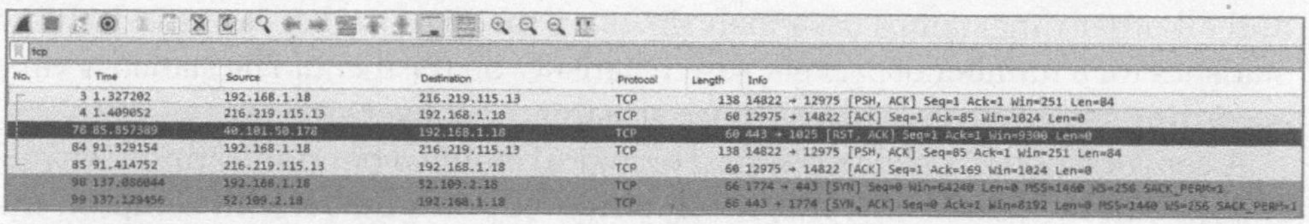

Figure 7.7: Sorting packet capture based on TCP traffic

Table 7.2: Filter operators

ENGLISH	OPERATOR	DESCRIPTION	EXAMPLE
eq	==	Equal	ip.src==192.168.1.0
ne	!=	Not equal	Ip.src!=192.168.1.0
gt	>	Greater than	frame.len>16
lt	<	Less than	frame.len<64
match	~	Field match	http.host matches
contains		Field contains	tcp contains traffic

Colorizing the traffic can be an effective filter to locate and highlight packets you may be searching for. You can choose to color packets that indicate errors, anomalies, breaches, or evidence. Wireshark has predefined coloring rules in the Edit menu under Preferences. Your coloring rules are placed at the top of the list by default, so your rules will trump any that come after.

For temporary colors, right-click a packet, go to Colorize Conversation, and slide down the list of types of traffic. To colorize the conversation, choose the protocol and select the color you would like that conversation to be. For example, you can color all IPv4 traffic blue and all Ethernet traffic red. This color rule will stay in effect until you restart Wireshark. You can also mark packets by right-clicking them. They will be shown with a black background, regardless of coloring rules. Marking a packet is helpful while analyzing a large capture, almost like a bookmark holding your place.

If you right-click a packet, you also have the ability to create packet comments. This is an excellent way to leave information that you have discovered, document a hypothesis, or communicate with other team members about network traffic you suspect is causing an issue.

Inspection

When you start inspecting and comparing packets in a packet capture, you'll notice the second column is based on time. Most computer systems start counting at 0, and Wireshark is no different. The first column is set to a time value of 0, and all other timestamps base their times on that first packet capture. To view statistics for a number of packets, select Statistics on the menu. The statistics vary according to protocols, address, port, streams, or conversations.

A conversation is a pair of physical or logical entities communicating. Conversations can include MAC, ARP, ICMP pings, or port numbers. To compare the conversations in the packet capture, go to the Statistics tab, and then inside that menu, go to Conversations. The default tabs across the top of the Conversation dialog box will show you the data broken down into Ethernet, IPv4, IPv6, TCP, and UDP. Each line shows the values for exactly one conversation. To add other conversation statistics, click Conversation Types in the lower-right corner. When working with a large file, sorting on the bytes transferred between hosts enables you to find the most active communication based on packets or duration of conversation. In Figure 7.8, notice the column for IPv4 conversations has been sorted to show the most active conversation between source and destinations.

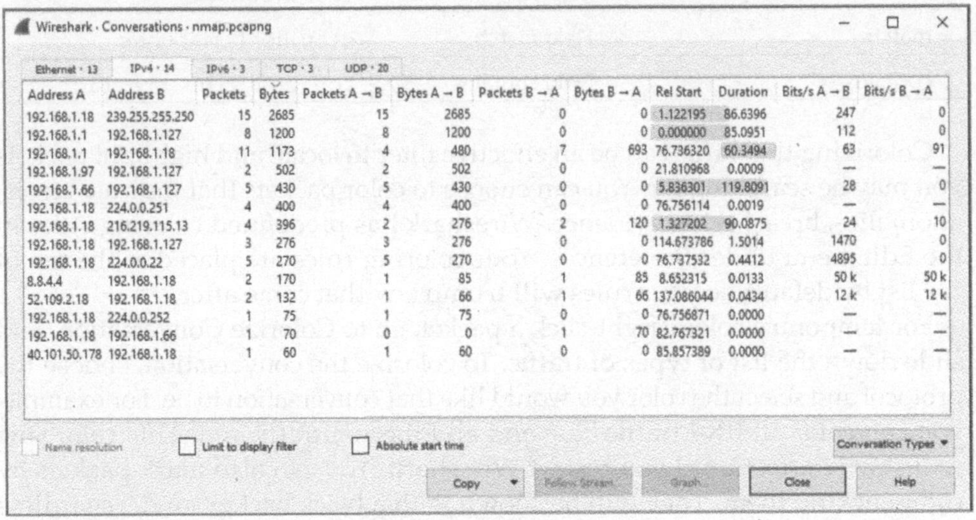

Address A	Address B	Packets	Bytes	Packets A → B	Bytes A → B	Packets B → A	Bytes B → A	Rel Start	Duration	Bits/s A → B	Bits/s B → A
192.168.1.18	239.255.255.250	15	2685	15	2685	0	0	1.122195	86.6396	247	0
192.168.1.1	192.168.1.127	8	1200	8	1200	0	0	0.000000	85.0951	112	0
192.168.1.1	192.168.1.18	11	1173	4	480	7	693	76.736320	60.3494	63	91
192.168.1.97	192.168.1.127	2	502	2	502	0	0	21.810968	0.0009	—	—
192.168.1.66	192.168.1.127	5	430	5	430	0	0	5.836301	119.8091	28	0
192.168.1.18	224.0.0.251	4	400	4	400	0	0	76.756114	0.0019	—	—
192.168.1.18	216.219.115.13	4	396	2	276	2	120	1.327202	90.0875	24	10
192.168.1.18	192.168.1.127	3	276	3	276	0	0	114.673786	1.5014	1470	0
192.168.1.18	224.0.0.22	5	270	5	270	0	0	76.737532	0.4412	4895	0
8.8.4.4	192.168.1.18	2	170	1	85	1	85	8.652315	0.0133	50 k	50 k
52.109.2.18	192.168.1.18	2	132	1	66	1	66	137.086044	0.0434	12 k	12 k
192.168.1.18	224.0.0.252	1	75	1	75	0	0	76.756871	0.0000	—	—
192.168.1.18	192.168.1.66	1	70	0	0	1	70	82.767321	0.0000	—	—
40.101.50.178	192.168.1.18	1	60	1	60	0	0	85.857389	0.0000	—	—

Figure 7.8: Wireshark conversations sorted by IPv4 protocol

There is another tool in Wireshark that logs anomalies found in a capture file: the Expert Info tool. The idea behind this tool is to provide a better understanding and display of notable network behavior. Both novice and expert users can solve issues quickly rather than combing through every packet manually. Expert info, as you see in Figure 7.9, is considered a hint.

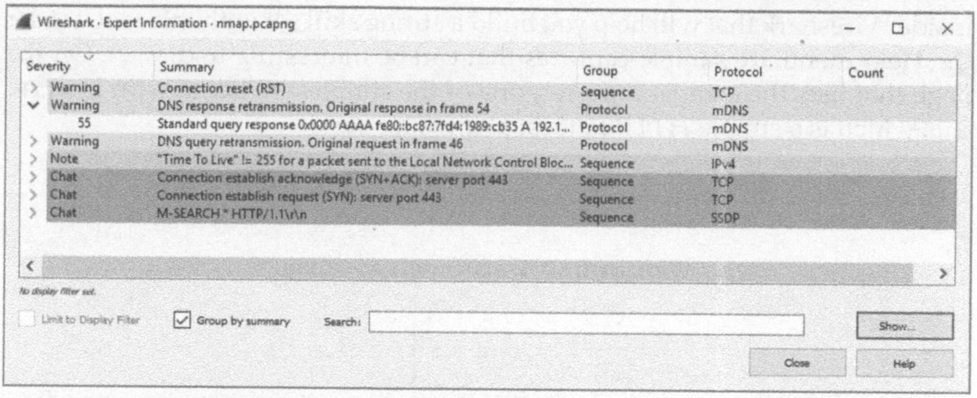

Figure 7.9: Expert Info tool color-coded "hints"

Table 7.3: Expert Info severity levels

LEVEL	COLOR	EXPLANATION
Chat	Blue	Informational, usual workflow
Note	Cyan	Normal errors
Warning	Yellow	Unusual errors
Error	Red	Serious problem

Every Expert Info type has a specific severity level. Table 7.3 lists the different Expert Info severity levels.

You can configure a graph of the captured network packets. You can configure the I/O graph to see the overall traffic as well as highs and lows in your traffic, which is typically based on a per-second, per-packet rate. You can use this to rectify problems, and you can even use it for monitoring. By default, the y-axis will set the interval to 1 second, and the y-axis will be packets like you see in Figure 7.10. Click any point on the graph to focus on that packet in the background. There are three different styles of graphs you can use: line, impulse, and dots. If you are graphing multiple items, you can choose different styles for each graph.

After capturing network traffic on your own system, the Nmap scan, and web browser traffic, if you want to branch out and look at other, more-complicated traffic but you don't have access to a more complicated network, there is a link inside Wireshark that will help you build a strong skill set with this tool. Under the Help menu are sample captures that can be interesting to dissect. On the page that lists the sample captures, one of the simplest to begin with is HTTP. cap, which is a simple HTTP request and response.

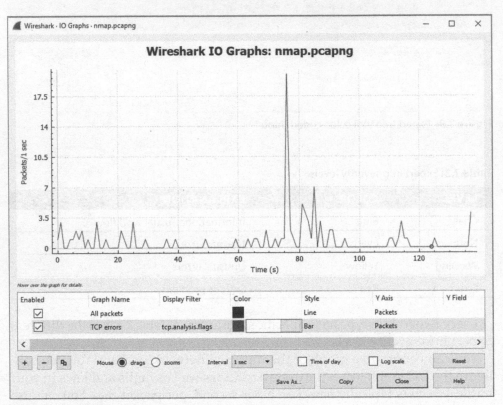

Figure 7.10: Graphing all packets versus just TCP errors

# CHAPTER 8

Access Management

WHAT YOU WILL LEARN IN THIS CHAPTER:

➤ Authentication, Authorization, and Auditing

➤ Least Privilege

➤ Single Sign-On

➤ JumpCloud

Let's take a trip through an airport. You have to produce identification to authenticate you are who you say you are. Then you have to provide a ticket to an agent to access the boarding area. Your belongings are screened to make sure you're not bringing any malicious contraband with you into a secured area. When you board the plane, they scan your ticket to prove you gained access to the aircraft. Now the airline can track and audit if and when you traveled. This is fundamental access management. Now take the same concept and apply it to a networked environment.

With all these layers of access management, how often do we hear of people getting past security? What other layers of security are in place at an airport that you have not even considered? As a security professional, you become acutely aware of those layers of defense in depth. You always have to be thinking strategically and protectively and asking targeted questions. What if someone is impersonating another on my network? What if someone has too much access? What if someone does access the network but has brought ransomware along?

Access management makes system or network administrators think about how people log into their computers and network. Most users don't realize there is a difference between logging in with domain credentials versus logging directly into an asset. Many users don't realize there are different levels of access. They believe what you see is what you get (WYSIWYG).

Access management is the process of identifying, controlling, managing, and auditing authorized users' access to any asset you manage. Typically in IT, asset management (AM) is used in conjunction with identity management (IM). IM creates and provisions different users, roles, groups, and policies where AM ensures that the security guidelines, procedures, and policies are followed.

There are many different organizations selling IM/AM solutions today. Picking a solution is not easy. You have to keep in mind scalability, performance, and usability. Close-sourced solutions can hamper your ability to adapt applications to your specific requirements and total cost of ownership becomes high. Open-source management can give you freedom to make good business decisions, customize it for unique situations, and have low or no maintenance fees, but it can be difficult to implement. Not only do you have to manage IM/AM, you have to add least privilege into the equation. The practice of least privilege is limiting access rights of users to only what they need to get the job done. Josh Franz, a security consultant at Rapid7, says, "Simply put, if you don't have identity access management in your company, you do not have security. All the security controls in the world won't stop an attacker if everyone on your network is a domain admin."

AAA

Authentication, authorization, and auditing (AAA) are often used together in cybersecurity when it comes to how someone gains access to a system. Authentication and authorization are critical topics often confused, but they are different from each other. Authentication is confirming who you are, while authorization means verifying what you have access to. Authentication is usually a username or ID and a password but could also be something you have like a token or something you are like a fingerprint.

Based on your security policies, you and your organization may need different levels of authentication.

- Single-factor—easiest authentication, usually a simple password to grant access to a system or domain.

- Two-factor—two-step verification that results in more security. When you visit the bank to withdraw money from an ATM, you need both a physical card and a personal identification number (PIN).

- Multifactor—the most secure type of authentication to grant access, using two or more techniques from different categories.

Authorization happens after you have been authenticated. In the two-factor analogy, after using the ATM card and PIN, you get access to your money, and only your money. Authorization determines your ability to access what systems and which accounts are you able to withdraw money from. This is a key component to access policy.

Auditing (some say the third *A* is accounting) is used to make sure the controls put in place are working. Auditing is used to support accounting. Auditing is the logging of events that have significance such as who has logged in and logged out or who attempted some type of privileged action. Monitoring can help make sure that there are no malicious activities happening in the environment. If you are looking to prove someone did something on your network, audit and security logs are the absolute best files to maintain that someone or something performed an action in a networked environment.

Another important part of auditing and accounting is nonrepudiation. Nonrepudiation means that the person authenticated and authorized cannot deny the performance of an action. You do not want a situation where one person claims an action happened and another is in total opposition to the story. A traditional example of nonrepudiation is a signature you received a document. In cybersecurity, nonrepudiation requires the creation of certain artifacts such as the following:

- An identity
- Authentication of that identity
- Evidence connecting that identity to an action

Least Privilege

If you ever take a certification exam, you may see this as principle of least privilege (PoLP) and even principle of least authority (PoLA). It is a concept that reduces the accidental or purposeful attack surface of an organization. There are several ways through access management you can use this concept to protect your ecosystem. In IT, we learn from others' mistakes.

About a decade ago, I was an administrator on a network with about 12,000 machines and 9,000 users. We used Group Policy in Windows to control the working environment. It was a way to centralize management of users' settings, applications, and operating systems in an Active Directory environment. We had someone new to the organization who was full of great ideas but was not aware of or willing to follow the change management procedures we had put in place to safeguard the network.

He changed a major feature in Group Policy that had catastrophic results. In the Event Viewer on a Windows machine you can configure your security logs. He checked the box to not overwrite security logs and pushed it out to 12,000 machines using Group Policy objects. If you've been IT for a while, you might be cringing. Within 24 hours, he had locked out 9,000 users on our network by filling up the allotted log space for successful and failed logon/logoff events. Thankfully, we were able to fix the problem within about 30 minutes after we had figured out what had happened. At first, we had thought we were under attack. Through nonrepudiation, we knew which admin had been logged into the system when the change occurred.

Here are the morals of this story:

- If you're not sure what you're doing, then ask.
- Just because you can doesn't mean you should.
- If you limit who has access to critical systems, you reduce your attack surface.

Most devices have mechanisms built in where you have standard end-user and administrator accounts. Administrator accounts are for users who need full access to all areas of the machine where user accounts are restricted; users can run applications but do not have full administrative access.

One reason this principle works so well is that it will make you do internal research on what privileges at what level are actually needed. Unfortunately, the path of least resistance in many organizations has been the overuse of accounts with deep and far-reaching privilege. The consequences of a network administrator opening an email attachment that launches malware while logged into the domain administrator's account are that the malware will have administrator's privilege on the domain and unrestricted access to the network. If the network administrator is logged into a standard end-user account, the malware only has access to the user's data, and the potential compromise scope is much smaller.

You should default to creating a separate standard user account for every user including administrators, and every account should use at least single-factor authentication. This enables you to control what the users can install and websites they can visit. Too many organizations allow all users on their network administrative privileges, and it creates a massive attack surface. Administrators should always log in using their standard user account and then use the Run As Administrator feature to run those programs they need elevated privileges to use. There are far too many breaches that get traced back to administrators opening email and clicking a link that leads to a malicious download that compromises an asset that spreads through a network and steals everything. Not only do organizations lose intellectual property, but they end up fined for violations of compliance, which can lead to a loss of millions in a single breach.

One of the best ways to start implementing the PoLP is to start with a privileged audit. A user account created to use a database does not need admin rights like a programmer building the database. You do not want to hinder your end users; you want to give them only enough access to perform their required job.

Do an audit of privilege on a regular basis. This is not a one-and-done exercise. It is operational. Who has access to what, and who has changed jobs and retained access to their old permissions?

Start every account as low as possible. Only add higher permissions if needed/requested and only for the time needed. An auditor may need elevated privileges but only for the duration of the audit.

Separation of duties (SoD) is a strategic function of least privilege. You have one person write the check and one person sign the check. By having more than one person accomplish a task, it can help prevent fraud or errors. In the Group Policy story earlier, SoD was part of that process. If the employee had followed procedures for change management, I could have told him why it was a really bad idea.

By implementing least privilege, you can even improve operational performance, reduce the chance of unauthorized behavior, reduce the attack surface, and reduce the chances of malicious software propagating since it might need elevated processes to run. One of the biggest benefits of implementing least privilege is that it makes it easier to meet compliance requirements. Many compliance regulations such as PCI-DSS, HIPAA, FISMA, and SOX require that organizations apply least privilege to ensure proper data management and security.

The Federal Desktop Core Configuration requirements by the National Institute of Standards and Technologies (NIST) say that federal employees must log into PCs with standard privileges. PCI-DSS 3.0 7.2.2 requires assignment of privileges to individuals based on job classification and function.

Single Sign-On

Working in our modern-day environments requires us to log into multiple programs to get our jobs done. We have to log into customer management databases, share resources in cloud applications, check email, and create documentation online. It can be a headache for the average user to remember all those usernames and passwords. To alleviate that issue, we use single sign-on (SSO) applications. SSO is another form of access control between multiple, interrelated software systems.

Benefits of single sign-on can include the reduction of password fatigue or having end users write their passwords on sticky notes and put them on their monitor or under the keyboard. It can save time typing in passwords over and over and ideally reduce help-desk issues of people calling in because they went on vacation and forgot their password and locked themselves out. One of the big criticisms of SSO is the access to many different resources from just one login.

To combat this issue, we have to focus on protecting the "keys to the kingdom" and combine this with strong verification like multifactor authentication.

The CIA triad shown in Figure 8.1 is used to find the right balance for an organization based on priorities. Some organizations like the military's preference toward confidentiality, where organizations such as Amazon might lean toward availability. After all, the military does not want its secrets leaked, and you cannot purchase from a website if the site is down.

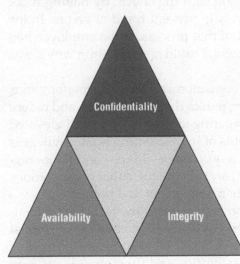

Figure 8.1: CIA triad

Confidentiality is a set of rules that limit access to information, integrity is the assurance that the information is accurate, and availability is giving the right information access to the right people. Network and security IT administrators have to find a balance between protecting the environment and meeting compliance without hindering the workflow of the end users. If you tighten controls too tight, users cannot do their job, but if controls are too lax, it results in a vulnerability. If you're not careful, end users will start saving their credentials in their browser for easy login into their favorite banking or shopping websites. They may even save their corporate credentials, which could be catastrophic if the machine is ever accessed by non-authorized individuals.

As a security leader in your organization, you have decisions to make. The problem with making decisions today is your enterprise will mostly likely change tomorrow. Most of the processes we use in IT are cyclic, always subject to reevaluation. When your security maturity model reaches the point where building and documenting AAA, least privilege, and SSO into your management process, every individual from CEO to the security administrator needs his or her access configuration audited. In Figure 8.2, you see a simple matrix of users' needs when it comes to accessing their network. Once you know what users need to perform their role, it becomes easy to build that role for them.

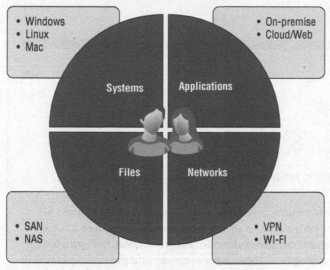

Figure 8.2: Evaluating users' needs in your network

JumpCloud

According to Zach DeMeyer at JumpCloud, "Generally endpoint management solutions have focused solely on managing the system, not including identities and access." JumpCloud is a cutting-edge blend of SSO and management of permissions in a network. Users' identities are at the core of JumpCloud as a directory as a service. You create a central, authoritative version of each identity so employees can use a single set of credentials throughout all the resources they need to access. You can set up password complexity and expiration features to ensure policies are met and then, once set up, bind those users to any of the resources connected to JumpCloud from their host system to applications to networks.

To get started, go to jumpcloud.com and create your user account. Your first ten users are completely free, forever. After that, there is a small charge per user. Once your user account is validated through your email, you have access to the central console where you can set up credentials for platform, protocol, or location. You can use JumpCloud to enforce policies, set password requirements including multifactor authentication, and streamline access to most IT resources. Lab 8.1 shows how to create a user, and Lab 8.2 shows how to create a system.

LAB 8.1: CREATING A USER

1. Open your browser and log into the JumpCloud web interface.
2. On the Users tab, click the green box with the plus sign (see Figure 8.3).

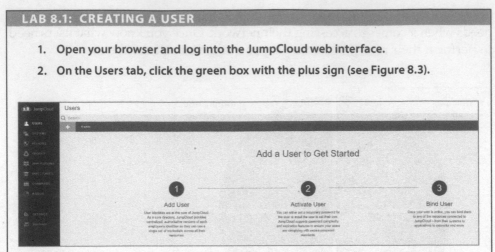

Figure 8.3: How to create a user in JumpCloud

3. Define the new user's first name, last name, username, and email address. If you have audited this user's needs, then you will know if you need to enable admin/sudo permissions or require multifactor authentication. In Figure 8.4, you see the New User dialog box. This is where you can add the initial password for the user.

Figure 8.4: The New User dialog box

4. For each user, you have the ability to add that person to user groups for access permissions, what systems each has permission to sign into, and what directories each needs access to. You will have to build these next to tie them together.

LAB 8.2: CREATING A SYSTEM

1. Open the systems menu, second from the top. Click the green box with the plus sign to open the New System instructions.

2. Mac, Windows, and Linux systems are bound to the JumpCloud platform when you install the system agent. Once it is installed, you can remotely and securely manage a system and the accounts on those systems and set policies. The agent is small and checks in through port 443 and reports event data. *Align the system you need to manage with the platform at the type of New System.*

3. Each of these will have specific instructions and connection keys. In the case of Windows, you have an agent to download as well as a connect key (see Figure 8.5). When you double-click the Windows executable, you will be asked for the key during the install process.

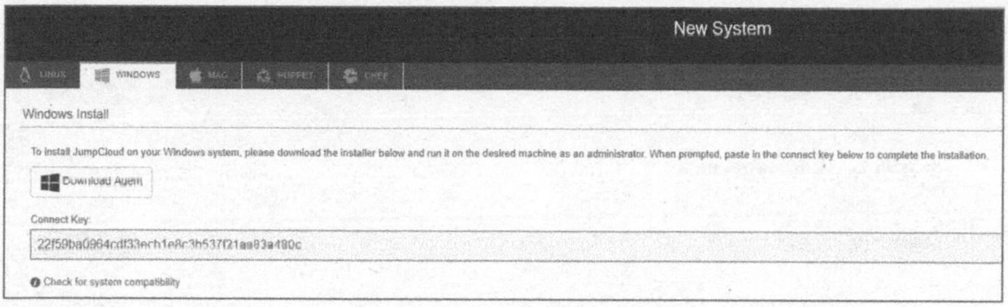

New System

Windows Install

To install JumpCloud on your Windows system, please download the installer below and run it on the desired machine as an administrator. When prompted, paste in the connect key below to complete the installation.

Download Agent

Connect Key:

22f59ba0964cd33ech1e8c3h537f21aa83a490c

Check for system compatibility

Figure 8.5: Download the Windows Agent and use the connect key to complete the installation.

4. Copy and paste the connect key into the install file to bind the JumpCloud agent to your system. In a few moments, you will see the hostname displayed in Systems page.

5. After the asset has successfully checked in, you can apply policies to that asset. By default, Windows has 22 policies you can configure. Figure 8.6 shows a few of them. One best practice is to set up a lock screen.

Continues

LAB 8.2 (CONTINUED)

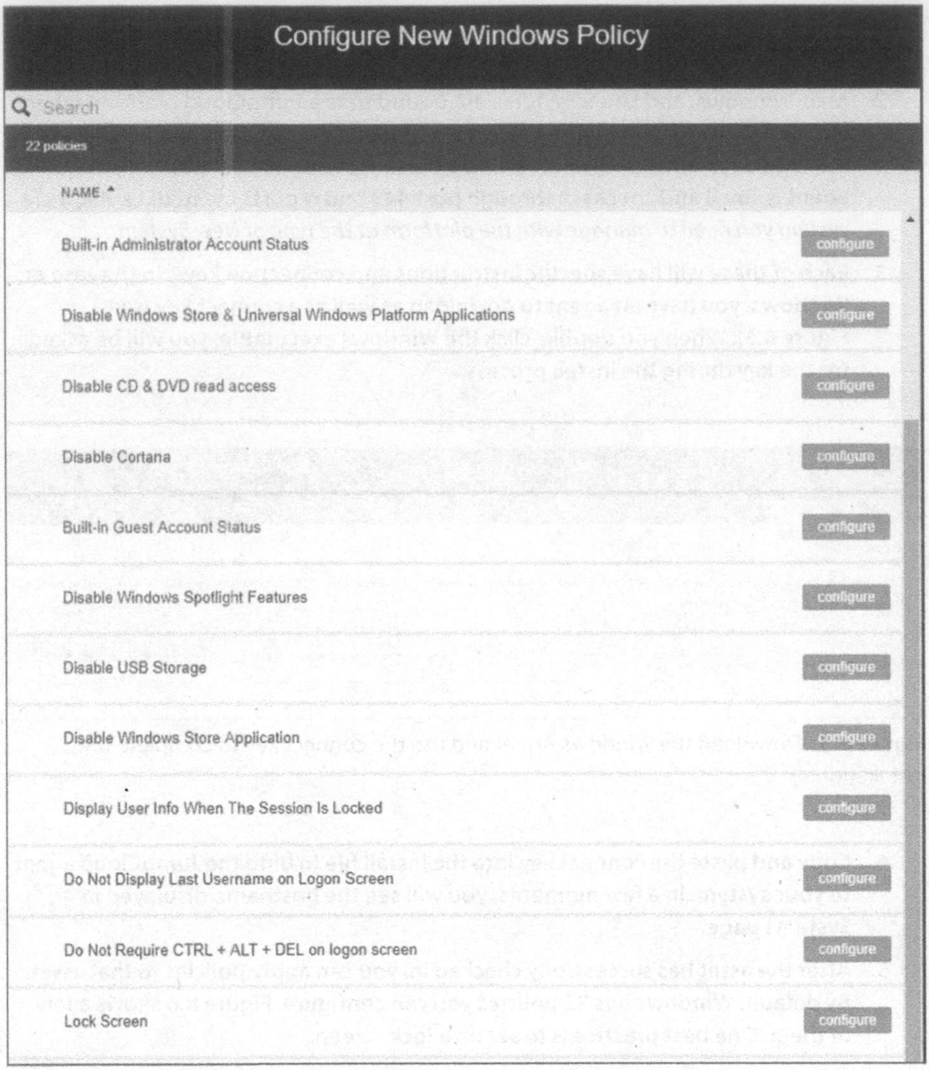

Figure 8.6: Configuring Windows policies

The lock screen can help you not fall victim to donut day. *Donut day* is when you leave your computer unlocked, step away or turn your back for a moment, and someone takes advantage of you being logged in. That person will send an email to everyone saying, "I'm bringing the donuts tomorrow!" Everyone knows you left the machine unlocked. Some organizations I've worked for had a prank where they would change our wallpaper to My Little Pony and called it getting *pwned*. You must lock your computer, and if you forget, a policy can do it for you. It can be an expensive lesson to bring donuts for 250 people. In Figure 8.7, you see the Windows Lock Screen policy and the ability to set the timeout in seconds. Again, you have to balance the CIA triad with usability. I have seen an executive, frustrated with the lockout policy, place a "perpetual drinking bird" next to his keyboard to peck his keyboard and simulate activity so he didn't have to type in his password every 60 seconds.

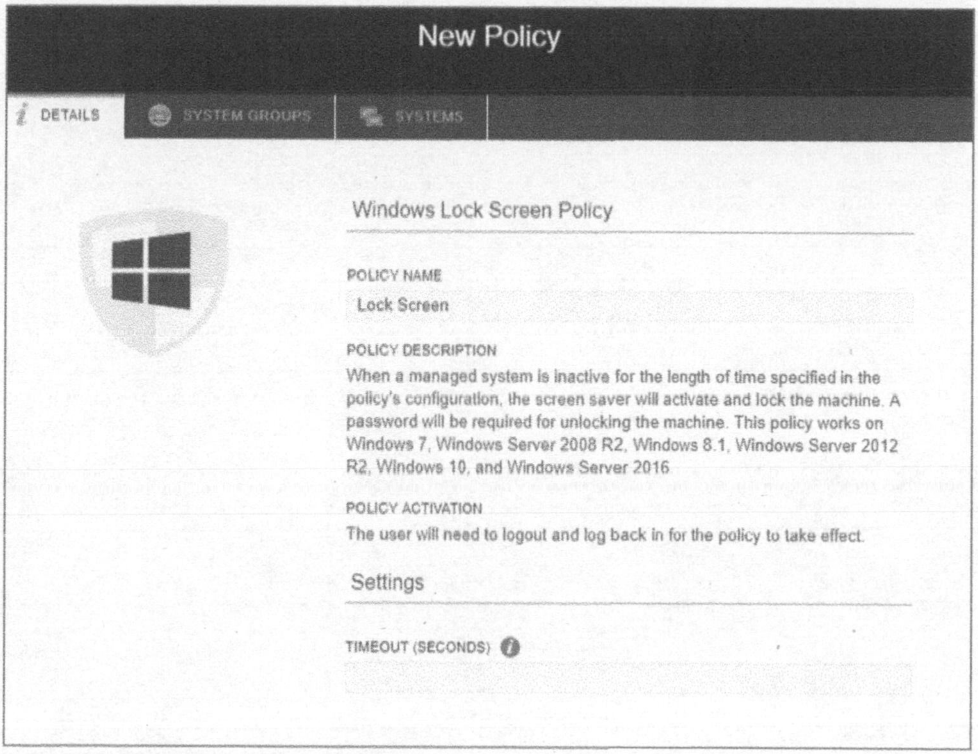

Figure 8.7: Windows Lock Screen policy

Now that you have a user, a system, and a policy, it's time to evaluate groups, applications, and directories. Each of these will have its own impact on the security posture of your organization. With groups, you have the ability to provide your users and admins access to resources while pulling them into a central management portal. To add another layer of security, giving users the ability to use SSO to sign into an application will enhance these processes. Finally, building a directory will allow you to synchronize user accounts and enable JumpCloud to act as a single authoritative directory of users.

The goal is to work your way through the CIS controls. CIS Control 5 is controlling IM and AM. With controlled use of the correct privileges on computers, networks, and applications, you protect information and assets from theft and misuse. It becomes even more important because you have to deal with the monumental outside threat but also insiders doing things they shouldn't be doing. It can be a daunting task, but it is essential.

Managing Logs

WHAT YOU WILL LEARN IN THIS CHAPTER:

➤ Windows Event Viewer

➤ PowerShell

➤ BareTail

➤ Syslog

➤ Solarwinds Kiwi

When I was growing up, my older brother was a Trekkie, a *Star Trek* fan. James T. Kirk, the captain of the U.S.S. *Enterprise*, would make entries into a captain's log. The captain's log has been a form of record keeping since the first captains sailed the seas. The log was used to inform the captain's superiors, either owners of the ship or governmental entities, what was happening while exploring or completing a mission or to record historical facts for future generations. Our networks work the same way. Every device on your network generates some type of log-in some type of language. Some of it is human readable, and some looks like gibberish. Some logs are more useful than others, and we should understand which ones need to be preserved for future analysis. You don't need to log everything, but what you do log should be purposely collected and managed.

CIS Control 6 is the maintenance, monitoring, and analysis of audit logs. Our organizations are evolving quickly, and we have to learn to deal with log data in the big data cloud era. Analyzing audit logs is a vital part of security, not just for system security but for processes and compliance. Part of the process of log analysis is reconciling logs from different sources and correlation even if those devices are in different time zones. If you look at a basic network topology, you will have many types of devices, including routers, switches, firewalls, servers, and workstations. Each of these devices that helps connect you to the rest of the world will generate logs based on its operating systems, configuration, and software. Examining logs is one of the most effective ways of looking for issues and troubleshooting issues occurring on a system or an application.

Synchronization and the ability to correlate the data between these devices are vital to a healthy environment. When I first started in IT, you could get away with occasionally using logs for troubleshooting. Attackers can hide their activities on machines if logging is not done correctly; therefore, you need a strategic method of consolidating and auditing all your logs. Without solid audit log analysis, an attack can go unnoticed for a long time. According to the 2018 Verizon Data Breach Investigations Report, 87 percent of compromises took minutes or less to occur, and 68 percent went undiscovered for months. The full report was based on detailed analysis of more than 53,000 security incidents, including 2,216 data breaches. You can download the full details at verizonenterprise.com/DBIR2018.

Windows Event Viewer

A Windows event log is one of the first tools to use to learn to analyze problems. As a security administrator, you must ensure that local logging is enabled on systems and networking devices. The process that can create an audit log is usually required to run in privileged mode so that users cannot stop or change it. To view logs on a Windows asset through a graphic user interface (GUI) like you see in Figure 9.1, you have to open the Event Viewer.

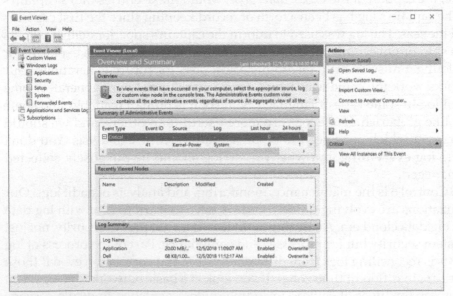

Figure 9.1: Windows Event Viewer displaying logs

Events are placed into three different categories, each of which is related to a log that Windows keeps. While there are a lot of categories, the majority of troubleshooting and investigation happens in the application, system, or security log.

Application   The application log records events related to Windows components like drivers.

System   The system log records events about programs installed.

Security   When security logging is enabled, this log records events related to security, such as logon attempts and resources accessed.

In Lab 9.1 you'll learn how to examine the Windows security logs.

LAB 9.1: EXAMINING WINDOWS SECURITY LOGS

1. On a Windows system, use the Windows+R key combination to open the Run menu.

2. Type **eventvwr** in the Open field and press Enter.

3. There are three panes on the Event Viewer screen. The pane to the left is the hierarchy of log files. The pane to the right shows the actions you can take. For a granular view of the logs, you use the large center pane. Open each level of logs by clicking the arrow to the left of the folder or file in the left pane.

4. Under Windows Logs, click Security. In the center of the page, a list of all security events that have been recorded on this machine is displayed. As you see in Figure 9.2, these are audit successes recorded on this host. To the left, you see actions you can take on these logs, including filtering them for critical events or warnings as well as examining the log properties.

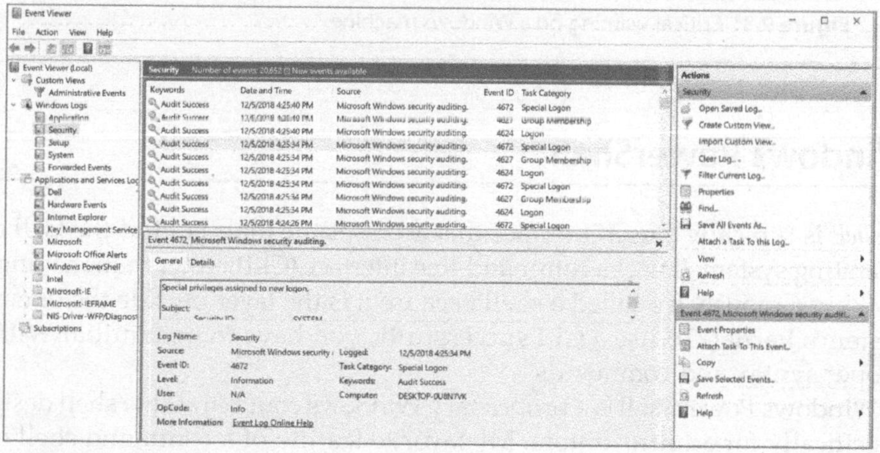

Figure 9.2: Security logs on a Windows machine

Continues

5. When you're familiar with the security logs, open the Application and System folders. These logs will help you understand what applications are running on your machine, what they are doing, and whether they are having difficulties. The System folder is an excellent place to filter critical events such as configuration changes or power loss, as displayed in Figure 9.3.

Level	Date and Time	Source	Event ID	Task Category
⚠ Warning	12/5/2018 4:39:31 PM	DNS Client Events	1014	(1014)
⚠ Warning	12/5/2018 4:24:39 PM	DNS Client Events	1014	(1014)
⚠ Warning	12/5/2018 4:09:40 PM	DNS Client Events	1014	(1014)
⚠ Warning	12/5/2018 11:09:25 AM	Netwtw06	6062	None
⚠ Warning	12/5/2018 11:09:20 AM	DNS Client Events	1014	(1014)
⚠ Warning	12/5/2018 11:08:59 AM	Kernel-PnP	219	(212)
⊗ Critical	12/5/2018 11:08:59 AM	Kernel-Power	41	(63)
⚠ Warning	12/4/2018 9:52:54 AM	DNS Client Events	1014	(1014)

Event 41, Kernel-Power

General Details

The system has rebooted without cleanly shutting down first. This error could be caused if the system stopped responding, crashed, or lost power unexpectedly.

Log Name:	System		
Source:	Kernel-Power	Logged:	12/5/2018 11:08:59 AM
Event ID:	41	Task Category:	(63)
Level:	Critical	Keywords:	(70368744177664),(2)
User:	SYSTEM	Computer:	DESKTOP-0U8N7VK
OpCode:	Info		
More Information:	Event Log Online Help		

Figure 9.3: Critical warning on a Windows machine

Windows PowerShell

A *shell* is typically a user interface that accesses the tools behind the GUI of an operating system. It uses a command-line interface (CLI) rather than moving and clicking a mouse. It's called a shell because it is the layer outside the operating system's kernel. To use a CLI successfully, you have to be familiar with the proper syntax and commands.

Windows PowerShell is a proprietary Windows command-line shell designed specifically for administrators. My favorite feature of a command shell is the ability to speed up the processes by using command-line completion, a lifesaver for those of us who are horrible typists. In the command shell, type a few characters of a command and press the Tab key a couple of times until the item you want appears. Another feature of PowerShell is the ability to save sequences of commands that you might want to reuse in the future. This feature allows you to press the up arrow to cycle through previous commands.

PowerShell introduced the *cmdlet* (pronounced "command-let"). It is a simple, single-function command-line tool built into the shell. A cmdlet is a specific order you give the OS to perform an action like "run this program." There are more than 200 cmdlets that are written as a verb-noun pair. For example, you can type the command `Get-Help`, and this will give you a description of a cmdlet.

Searching logs using PowerShell has an advantage over Windows Event Viewer. You can check for events on remote computers much quicker, which is extremely valuable if you ever do server management. PowerShell will help you generate reports, and since we are all so busy, any automation can help. In Lab 9.2, you'll use Windows PowerShell to review logs.

LAB 9.2: USING WINDOWS POWERSHELL TO REVIEW LOGS

1. On a Windows system, use the Windows+R key combination to open the Run menu. Type in `powershell` and press Enter.

2. To get a list of event logs on the local machine, as shown in Figure 9.4, type the following command:

```
Get-EventLog -List
```

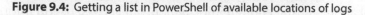

Figure 9.4: Getting a list in PowerShell of available locations of logs

3. To get the system log in its entirety on the local computer, type in the following command:

```
Get-EventLog -LogName System
```

4. The `Get-EventLog` command generates a massive list. To narrow down the view, you can display only the last 20 entries in the system log, as shown in Figure 9.5, by pressing the up arrow and adding the following syntax:

```
Get-EventLog -LogName System -Newest 20
```

Continues

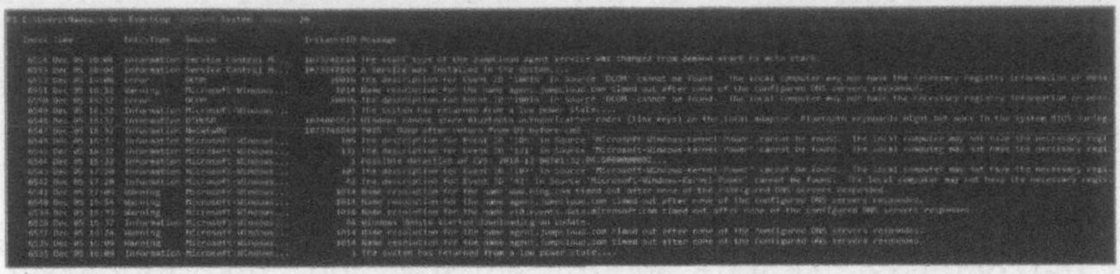

Figure 9.5: Retrieving the index, time, type, source, and message of the last 20 system logs

5. You can specify system log entries related to disk source, as shown in Figure 9.6, by entering the following command:

```
Get-EventLog -LogName System  -Source Disk
```

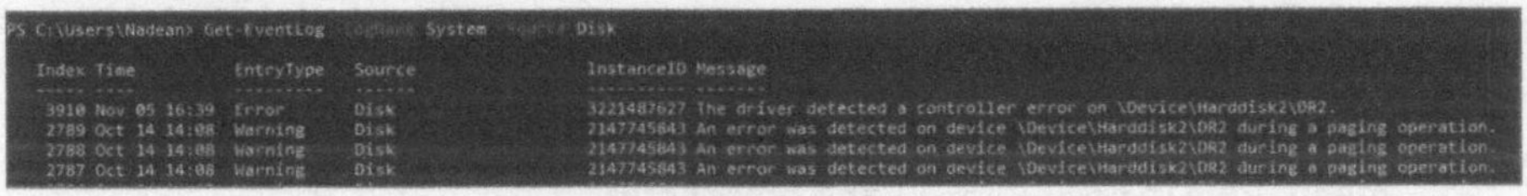

Figure 9.6: Disk errors and warnings in system logs

Windows enables most log files by default, although you might need to define what level of logging you need. Turning on verbose logging, the most detail possible should be done only during a specific event or while trying to track an active, known security incident. If you aren't careful, the volume of logs can take up many terabytes of disk space. Systems have been known to crash because well-meaning system administrators enabled verbose logging for all systems and then forgot to disable it when troubleshooting was completed. Be sure to put a sticky note on your monitor to remind yourself to revert logging levels after you're done troubleshooting.

Great logging is about pulling out the necessary critical events and alerts from an otherwise overwhelming amount of information. The problem for most admins is not about getting enough information, but getting useful information out of an overwhelming deluge of data.

To enable a security audit policy to capture load failures in the audit logs, open an elevated Command Prompt window by right-clicking the Cmd.exe shortcut and selecting Run As Administrator. You could also press Windows+R to open the Run box. Type **cmd** and then press Ctrl+Shift+Enter to run the command as an administrator. In the elevated Command Prompt window, run the following command:

```
Auditpol /set /Category:System /failure:enable
```

As you see in Figure 9.7, you should get a success message that you are now logging all security audit logs. You will have to restart the computer for the changes to take effect.

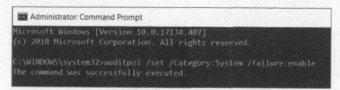

```
Administrator: Command Prompt

Microsoft Windows [Version 10.0.17134.407]
(c) 2018 Microsoft Corporation. All rights reserved.

C:\WINDOWS\system32>auditpol /set /Category:System /failure:enable
The command was successfully executed.
```

Figure 9.7: Elevated command prompt turning on security audit logs

After you have collected the logs you need and so you do not fill up all the storage on your asset, do not forget to run the following command:

```
Auditpol /set /Category:System /failure:disable
```

Searching logs using PowerShell has an advantage over Windows Event Viewer. You can check for events on remote computers much quicker, which is extremely valuable if you ever do server management. There is no need to physically connect to a computer to collect the logs. By using the PowerShell parameter -ComputerName, you can connect and pass a command to the remote computer you choose and collect the information you want. If you want to pull all system logs off the computer named PC1, you can by using the following command:

```
Get-EventLog -ComputerName PC1 -LogName System
```

One of the integral parts of understanding these logs and their access to remote regions of your network is their IP address. The Internet has run out of IPv4 addresses, and the landscape of the Internet is quickly evolving. IPv4 is the technology that allows us to connect our devices to the web with a unique, numerical IP address consisting of 4 octets separated by a decimal with no number over 255. It looks like 192.168.1.0. Sending data from one computer to another and generating logs while doing so requires an IP address on both devices.

But we are in transition. With so many applications and with the evolution of the Internet of Things (IoT), we are starting to see more and more IPv6 addresses in our logging. Google collects statistics surrounding IPv6 adoption globally, and the latest numbers indicate that more than 25 percent of Google users access their resources with IPv6. For home users and small businesses, this may take another few years to become an issue, but nearly all modern devices support this new technology.

What you will start seeing in your logs will be a logical network IPv6 address of 128 bits as opposed to the 32 bits in an IPv4 address. IPv6 is written in hexadecimal as opposed to dotted decimal, and the numbers are grouped together in eight groups of four instead of four groups of three. There are some shortening techniques. For example, if the IPv6 address has a grouping of 0000, it will display as ::. Just be aware, if you ever start to see your source address of your logs displaying 32 hexadecimal characters instead of your usual 12, something on your network is using IPv6.

BareTail

Historically, system administrators would drop down into a shell to run `tail -f` to follow logs in real time. Developed by Bare Metal Software, BareTail is an amazing, free, tiny tool that packs quite an impact. You can monitor your logs in real time in a GUI that allows you to navigate between multiple tabs to organize your streams of logs, highlighting and filtering those parts that are important. You can leave it running, and it refreshes constantly.

When you decide you need a tool to watch the flow of your logs, go to www.baremetalsoft.com/baretail to grab the tool. It downloads as `baretail.exe`, but it does not "install" as a permanent file. You can move this file and run it from any location with extremely flexible configuration options. I usually keep it on a USB.

Once you open BareTail, the first option under the main menu is Open. Click the Open File option to open a dialog box to navigate to the program logs you want to monitor. In Figure 9.8, you see the path to Nexpose to troubleshoot issues or verify confirmed vulnerabilities on your system.

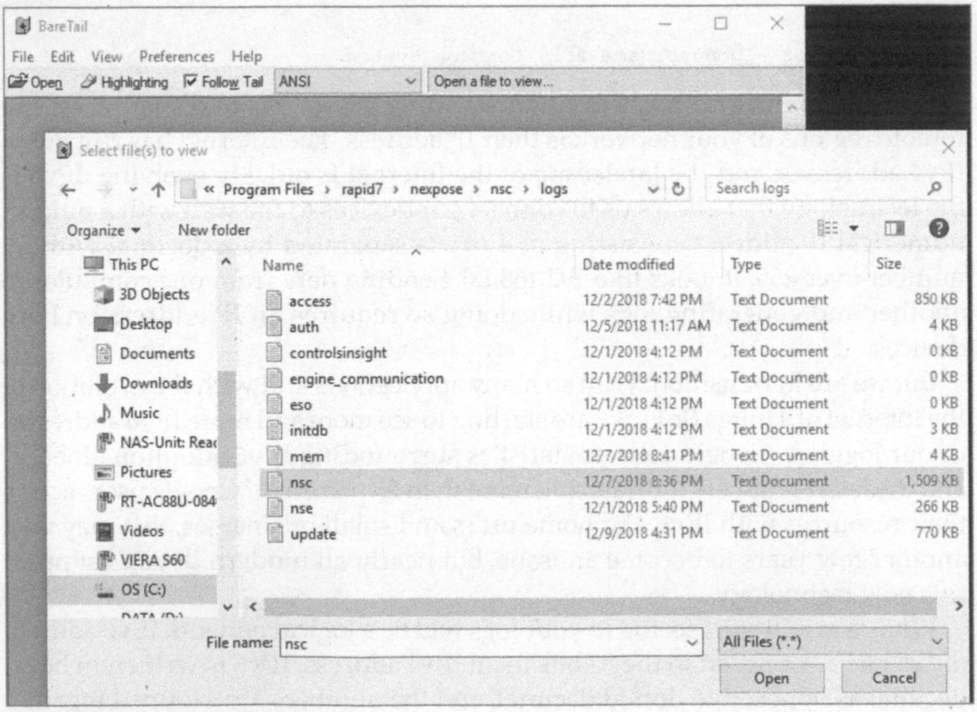

Figure 9.8: Opening a file location to view the log

To look for specific words or *strings*, open the Highlighting menu next to the Open menu. You have the ability to filter, change the foreground color and/or background color, and type into the string location the keywords you are most interested in. In Figure 9.9, you see that in nse.log, I have targeted the word *vulnerable*, and I am ignoring if it is displayed in uppercase or lowercase. In this log, if you scroll down some, you may see Vulnerable or Not Vulnerable when it examines a possible vulnerability on an asset. It will find the word you are searching for inside other words if necessary. When you click OK, the highlighted filters you create will stay activated in the log for as long as you have it open.

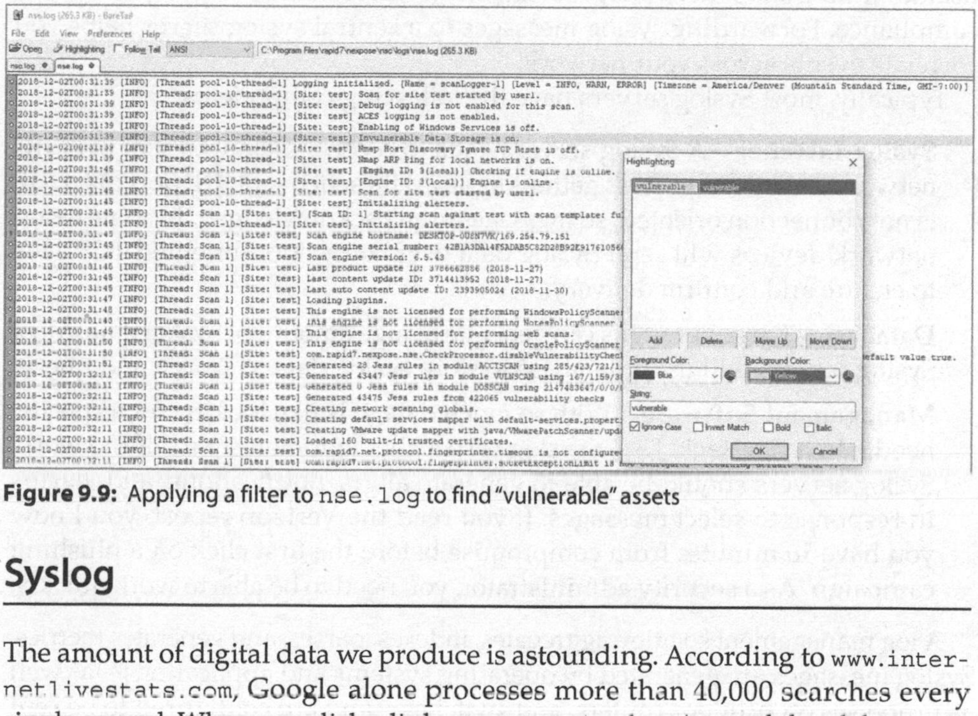

Figure 9.9: Applying a filter to nse.log to find "vulnerable" assets

Syslog

The amount of digital data we produce is astounding. According to www.internetlivestats.com, Google alone processes more than 40,000 searches every single second. When you click a link, you generate a log. Around the globe, every second of the day, computer networks are generating logs. According to the same website, we create 2.5 quintillion bytes of data every single day. Honestly, without searching Google to define *quintillion*, I don't know how many digits that is. So I just Googled it. It's a billion billion, or 18 zeros after the 1.

Some of these logs are routine, and some of these indicate poor network health or a malicious attempt to breach your network. Log files contain a wealth of information to reduce exposure to intruders, malware, and legal issues. Log data needs to be collected, stored, analyzed, and monitored to meet and report on regulatory compliance standards such as HIPAA, FISMA, FERPA, PCI DSS, or the newest global compliance standard focused on privacy, GDPR. This is an incredible and overwhelming task.

Syslog is a way for network devices to send a message to a logging server. It is supported by a wide range of devices. It can be used to log different types of events. Syslog is an awesome way to consolidate logs from many different sources, in different formats, and in massive volumes into a single location. If you don't have a log management strategy in place to monitor and secure connected devices, the results can be difficult to overcome if at all.

Using a syslog server to collect and store syslog messages provides a reliable central repository for log data. Syslog uses UDP communication to send messages to a central collector, also known as a *syslog server*. Syslog messages are used to troubleshoot network problems, establish forensic evidence, and prove compliance. Forwarding syslog messages to a central syslog server helps you correlate events across your network.

Typically, most Syslog servers have the following components:

Syslog Listener   A Syslog server needs to receive messages sent over the network. A listener process gathers syslog data sent over UDP port 514. UDP is not connection oriented, so messages aren't acknowledged. In some cases, network devices will send Syslog data over connection-oriented TCP 1468 to ensure and confirm delivery.

Database   Large networks can generate a huge amount of Syslog data. Most Syslog servers will use a database to store syslog data to search and query.

Management Software   With so much data, it is like looking for a specific needle in a haystack. Use a syslog server that automates part of the work. Syslog servers should be able to generate alerts, notifications, and alarms in response to select messages. If you read the Verizon report, you know you have 16 minutes from compromise before the first click on a phishing campaign. As a security administrator, you need to be able to work quickly.

A log management solution aggregates, indexes, parses, and generates metrics. Syslog messages are generated by operating systems and applications—as well as processes on printers, routers, and switches—and are configured to be sent to your syslog server. If your network includes Windows systems, the syslog server can help you manage Windows event log information.

Logs where there are many login attempts on a single account from diverse geographic locations or other suspicious system activities is a situation any administrator will want to investigate. Proactive, automated detection of unusual activity is critical. Cybersecurity is incredibly dynamic, and we do not know every single potential attack pattern in advance, so monitoring for this type of activity is not an easy task. If you don't analyze your logs to see what's going on, you'll never be able to detect suspicious activity.

A baseline is a starting point you can use for comparisons. Create a baseline that represents normal activity on your system so you're aware when there are anomalies occurring. A few failed login attempts by a user might be considered normal, but hundreds or thousands of failed login attempts might point to a brute-force or malicious attack.

Consolidating and centrally managing all your logs is different from logging each and every event. The big question of what events to record and how much you need to log is a problem best addressed by an audit. With the right coordination, an auditor along with your legal department focused on compliance with a technical CISO's perspective can give consideration as to what the right level of information is. These questions typically need to be answered for every component of your system and be well documented so you are able to easily scale in the future. For most assets, you will probably stick with their defaults. The only major operating system that does not have built-in support for sending syslog is Microsoft Windows. Windows includes PowerShell, and PowerShell can use the .NET Framework to send UDP packets to a syslog server.

Another crucial thing to think about is your data retention needs. How long do you need to keep the logs? Do you need them for troubleshooting? Are there regulatory or audit requirements that require you to keep the logs for a certain period of time?

When I was teaching CISSP for ISC², one of the best tools they gave us to teach with was 250 retired questions. I remember one specifically concerning logs:

> "You are a system administrator. Your organization's security policy states that you keep logs for 3 years. You have kept logs for 5 years. You have been subpoenaed for 5 years of logs. What do you legally have to give the authorities?"

The answer is you have to turn over everything you have. We have to trust that the management team has put security policies in place for a reason. If we disagree with the policy, it is our responsibility as cyber professionals to pursue a discussion with the chain of command until either we understand why the policy is in place or we change the policy. Otherwise, the violation of keeping records too long could open up potential damaging and sometimes legal issues.

Your daily log volume might already be substantial, but it can increase exponentially when a device fails. The resulting log messages could easily quintuple the number of log messages that get generated.

Log files come in a variety of formats. Some formats follow more traditional standards, while others are completely custom. Your log solution should be able to parse and present the data in a comprehensive form in near real time, and it should allow you to define custom parsing rules. Parsing is breaking down a log into smaller, better digestible messages and putting them into their own groups so that you can analyze and even visualize them in order to identify data inconsistencies.

SolarWinds Kiwi

SolarWinds Kiwi Syslog Server has a free edition where you can collect, view, and archive syslog messages. It is easy to set up and configure how it receives, logs, displays, and forwards syslog messages from network devices, such as routers, switches, Unix hosts, and other syslog-enabled devices.

The free version of Kiwi will allow you to get statistics in real time from five sources, with summaries available in the console. You will also be able to receive and manage syslog messages from network devices and view syslog messages in multiple windows.

Just like any other software, you will want to make sure that your system meets the hardware and software requirements and that you've opened the appropriate ports so communication can occur. In Kiwi Syslog Server, you will need Windows 7 or newer, Internet access, and at least 4 GB of disk space. Kiwi Syslog Server uses the ports listed in Table 9.1.

Table 9.1: Ports used by Kiwi Syslog Server

PORT	PROTOCOL	PURPOSE
514 (default)	UDP	Incoming UDP messages
1468 (default)	TCP	Incoming TCP messages
162 for IPv4	UDP	Incoming SNMP traps
163 for IPv6		
6514	TCP	Incoming secure TCP messages
3300	TCP	Internal communication between Syslog service and Syslog Manager
8088 (default)	TCP	Kiwi Syslog Web Access

Source: https://support.solarwinds.com

To download and install this syslog server solution, search in your browser for *Solarwinds kiwi syslog server free*, and it will easily take you to the download file. You will need to supply some information to create an account, and then you will receive the link to download the software. As you see in Figure 9.10, you have a choice to make when you start installing the software. You can choose either Install Kiwi Syslog Server As A Service on your Windows machine or Install Kiwi Syslog Server As An Application on your Windows machine. If you choose to install it as an application, you will be required to log in as a user before you can use the product. I have installed it as a service because it also installs the Kiwi Syslog Server Manager, which you will use to control the service.

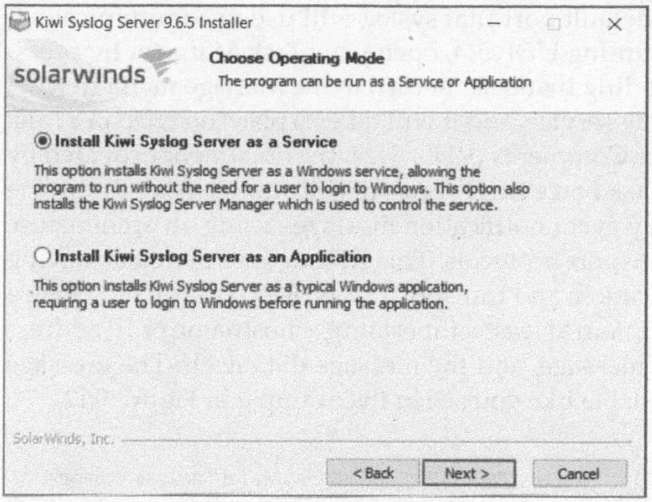

Figure 9.10: Choosing a service or application operating mode with Kiwi Syslog Server

The road map to begin collecting syslog data starts with configuring devices on your network to send the proper logs so that you can start to save, digest, analyze, and be alerted to issues in your environment. In my example, I have collected syslog off a router to give you an idea of what this will look like in Kiwi Syslog Server. In your environment, it will be dependent on what devices you want to send syslog from. You will have to access your device product guide to find out whether enabling syslog can be accomplished through the application GUI or the hardware CLI. Either way, you configure the asset to send logs to one central location.

If you have configured the Kiwi Syslog Server and no logs can be detected from an asset you are attempting to collect logs from, as shown in Figure 9.11, you can test the server to make sure it is actually running.

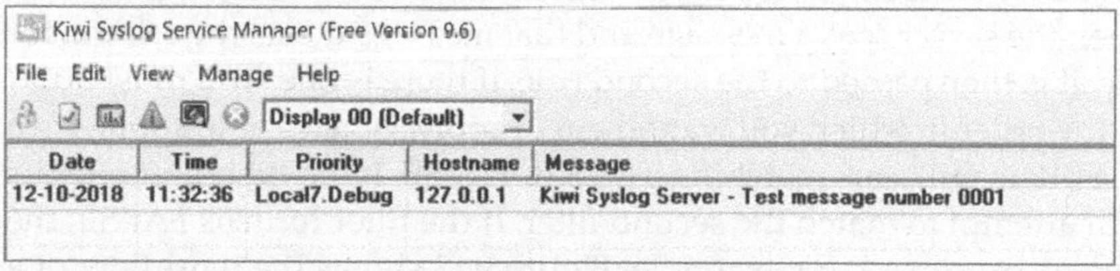

Figure 9.11: Successful test message on Kiwi Syslog Server

If the syslog server does not display the success message, then you'll want to check to see whether the service has initiated properly. Go to the Manage menu to start, stop, or ping the service and see whether it is running. As you learned in Chapter 1, "Fundamental Networking and Security Tools," you can run the netstat -ano command to see whether there are any active network ports using UDP 514, the default port that syslog will use to communicate. If a different process is consuming UDP 514, open your Task Manager by pressing Ctrl+Alt+Delete and ending that task. Return to the Manage menu in Kiwi Syslog Server and restart the service, and it will take its place on UDP port 514.

According to Request for Comments (RFC) 5424, the document provided by the Internet Engineering Task Force (IETF) that specifies and defines the syslog protocol, syslog will convey event notification messages using an architecture that supports different transport protocols. This RFC defines syslog as having three layers: content, application, and transport. There is no rule on how long a syslog will be, but it will contain at least a timestamp, a hostname or IP address of the device sending the message, and the message data itself. The message data is usually human readable like you see in the example in Figure 9.12.

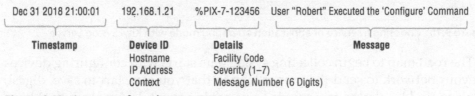

Figure 9.12: Anatomy of a syslog message

Once you have logs flowing into the syslog server, it is time to consider what rules will be applied to the log information. The rules determine what happens when the syslog server sees certain items in a log and what action it takes. You can create rules to log all messages, send an email if something critical occurs, and even run a script if a log contains a certain word. When you begin building your rules, as you saw in Figure 9.12, you will be using filters and actions. In Kiwi Syslog Server, you can have up to 100 rules, and each rule has up to 100 possible filters and 100 possible actions.

If you have ever built rules on a firewall, building rules in a syslog server is similar. When the server sees a message and that message meets the criteria for the first rule, it is then passed to the second rule, if there is one. You must build the rules in the order in which you want them to apply. When a rule applies to a message, the filters will start matching TRUE or FALSE. If the first filter returns TRUE, it will attempt to match the second filter. If the filter returns FALSE, the next message is processed. For example, Figure 9.13 shows the workflow of a rule matching the first filter but not matching the second.

Dec 31 2018 21:00:01   192.168.1.21   %PIX-7-123456   User "Robert" Executed the 'Configure' Command

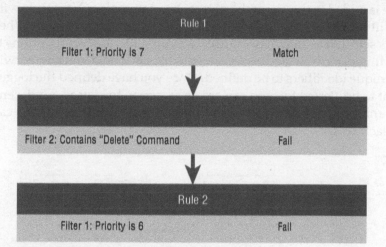

Figure 9.13: Syslog message being filtered by rules

The default rule in Kiwi Syslog Server applies two actions to all messages flowing into the server.

- Display each message on the console
- Log each message to the `SyslogCatchAll.txt` file

Figure 9.14 shows the same message being filtered by a different rule where both filters match so an action is performed. When all actions are performed, the server applies the next rule to the message.

Dec 31 2018 21:00:01   192.168.1.21   %PIX-7-123456   User "Robert" Executed the 'Configure' Command

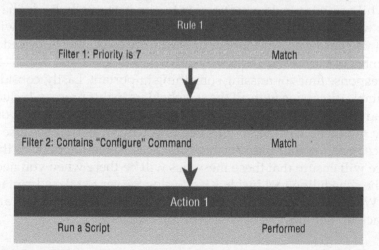

Figure 9.14: Syslog message being filtered by rules and initiating an action

To create a rule, choose the File menu and go to Setup. Click the New button, and a new rule is added to the hierarchical tree. You can replace New Rule with a name that will make sense to the filter and action you want to create. When the new filter is selected as shown in Figure 9.15, you will see several options to filter on, including priority, IP address, or hostname. Each field you choose will have its own unique identifiers to be defined. Once you have defined the logged event you want to be alerted for, you can create an action to play a sound, send an email, run another program, or do all of these things. Multiple actions can be staged for each rule.

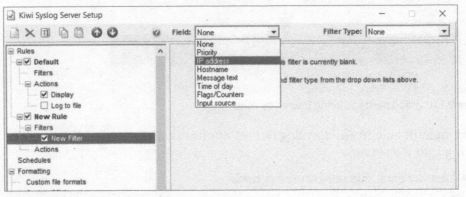

Figure 9.15: Creating a filter in Kiwi Syslog Server

One consideration while building a program with ongoing operational mechanisms is to visit the possibility of alert fatigue. In grade school, we learned about Peter and the wolf. He was the little boy who enjoyed the attention he received when he alerted everyone to a wolf outside the village when one wasn't really there. After a while, no one would pay attention to him. Eventually, he did have a confrontation with the wolf and got eaten. Logs can have the same effect with their alerting. If you have system administrators who are constantly bombarded with a large number of alarms and alerts, they do become desensitized, which can lead to longer response times or missing something important. Lastly, consider having a roundtable discussion with all the stakeholders in this process. Include your network administrators as well as your security team. Decide what your retention policy should be, whether it's dictated to you by an auditor because of your compliance needs or your industry best practices. Retention policies that you put in place will ensure that these messages will be there when you need them. Utilize the scheduling tool inside Kiwi Syslog Server to take advantage of automation. We are all busy with a focus on securing our infrastructure, and forgetting to back up our files can have severe consequences.

Metasploit

➤ Reconnaissance

➤ Installation

➤ Gaining Access

➤ Metasploitable2

➤ Vulnerable Web Services

Software is developed to be the solution for a problem. Metasploit Framework was developed by HD Moore in 2003 when he was only 22 years old. Originally written in Perl with a total of 11 exploits, Metasploit Framework was the answer to a problem he was having. He was spending most of his time validating and sanitizing exploit code. I imagine that for someone as brilliant as HD, this was redundant and boring. He knew there must be an easier way. He couldn't get the project he had in mind approved by the organization he worked for, so he decided to develop it in his free time. Today, we use Metasploit Framework as a platform for creating security tools and exploits, and there is a huge open-source community that supports the effort. In 2009, Rapid7 acquired the project, and HD Moore joined the team as chief security officer.

Now Metasploit Framework is written in Ruby with many, many exploits. In fact, at the time of this publishing, there are more than 3,700. Metasploit Framework is the penetration testing tool of choice of blue teamers and red teamers alike. Blue teamers are the good guys defending the network against malicious intent. Red teamers are the malicious intent. Red teamers are often called *penetration testers*, and they enjoy proving where there are vulnerabilities that can be exploited. For clarification, red teamers are very different than the criminals who use this tool for profit or hacktivism. It is all about intent. In fact, as cybersecurity has matured, there are some people, like me, who consider themselves to be purple. A blend of red and blue, I can defend a network and then periodically hack it as necessary to use this compromised viewpoint of your network as a bad actor would.

Metasploit Framework is not a destination but a journey. That journey begins before you even install the software. Before you get started, you must know that the tools in this chapter are for your personal use on your personal devices. These tools can be used in your business environment only if you have secured permission to do so. Using any of these tools to compromise machines that you do not own is illegal. You must have documentation scoping the range of your penetration test signed by the appropriate entities. This is not the type of scenario where you pass your manager in the hallway and tell him you're about to start this process. If something goes wrong and he doesn't remember the conversation, it could be time to update your résumé and start looking for a new job.

The U.S. federal government has some of the oldest and sometimes problematic cybersecurity laws around the globe. The purpose of cybersecurity regulation is to force companies to protect their systems from cyberattacks like the ones you can create and distribute in Metasploit Framework. Unless you have explicit and written permission to access a computer network or system, do not do it. You must make sure your documentation is correct and signed by the proper authority.

The Computer Fraud and Abuse Act makes it illegal to intentionally access a computer without authorization or in excess of authorization. The original law was passed in 1984 as a reaction to a 1983 movie starring Matthew Broderick called *War Games*. However, the law does not define "without authorization" or "exceeds authorized access," which makes it easy to prosecute and sometimes difficult to defend. The law was crafted to crack down on hacking, and the repercussions can be harsh. First-time offenses of one singular incident of insufficient authorization can result in 5 years in prison and fines.

One of my favorite organizations I have been lucky enough to work with and take classes from is SANS. SANS is an organization of the best-of-the-best instructors teaching a variety of technical and sometimes nontechnical classes. If you search for SANS documentation to use as a template for your penetration test, you'll find a resources download page that has everything from a Metasploit Framework cheat sheet to a rules of engagement worksheet. Inside the scoping worksheet, you will be asked to define security concerns, the scope of what should be tested and not tested, and some type of escalation process should you break something or find evidence of a prior exploit or a currently active compromise.

Reconnaissance

Before you start this Metasploit journey, you have to do your homework. After you have gained permission to legally explore a network, you need to gain as much information about that network. This includes information such as DNS, domains, ports, and services. Start a physical or digital folder for this process. It makes life so much easier when you have to create a report. It also works as a great resource when you start expanding your reach deeper into a network. I use Microsoft OneNote because it is so versatile and keeps everything together in a single location.

Reconnaissance is gathering intelligence about an organization and can take two forms: passive and active. Passive reconnaissance is done to gather as much information as possible without any type of active engagement. The information you gather will be used to attempt successful exploitation of targets. The more information you learn, the better crafted the attacks will be. Passive reconnaissance is completely and totally legal. You can browse the company website just like you were a typical user.

It amazes me how much information is shared on social media websites. Professional social media websites are excellent places to discover employees' names and possibly email structures. If you do decide to conduct a social engineering campaign, it is helpful to know if the employees email accounts are set up using a *first.lastname@companyname*.com structure.

You can visit the websites that most companies use to advertise the jobs they currently have available. When you go to the technical positions section, if organizations are looking for an Active Directory administrator, you can surmise they are using Microsoft infrastructure. If they are looking for someone with a CCNA certification, they are using Cisco network devices. Sometimes organizations will get very specific in their advertisements, and as a red teamer, if I know you're looking for a DBA with Microsoft SQL experience, I know exactly what exploit I will be using against you as soon as I get a foothold in your environment. I mention this since I am making the assumption we are all the good guys or "blue team"— you can work with your human resources department in crafting technical position listings as generically as possible without compromising any company information.

The groundwork you lay when using all the passive reconnaissance will make your penetration test that much smoother and give you strategic options. Nothing you do in passive recon shows up in a security log or an alert, and it cannot be traced back to your IP address. It is completely legal and done every single day by good guys and bad guys alike.

Active reconnaissance involves doing something that can be seen in a security log or an alert, and it can possibly be traced back to you. This is why written permission (or a "Get Out of Jail Free card" as it is sometimes called) is so incredibly important. You start edging close to violating terms of service or even breaking the law when you run a port scan or launch a vulnerability scan on assets you do not personally own. Your goal with active reconnaissance is to build a robust four-dimensional picture of the environment you are concerned with protecting. With active recon, if you can establish a possible a point of entry and gain access, you know where to point your exploits and establish persistence.

Installation

You have many options when it comes to installing Metasploit. There is the Metasploit Framework Open Source, the Framework for Linux or Windows, Metasploit Community, and Metasploit Pro. When you navigate to www.metasploit. com, there is a link on this Rapid7 site to github.com where you can download either the Linux/Mac OS version or the Windows 32-bit version. These installers are rebuilt every single night. These installers also include the dependent software needed like Ruby and the PostgreSQL database that will manage all the information you collect during a penetration test. It will integrate seamlessly with the package manager, so they are easy to update on Linux.

Another option is to download a new operating system called Kali Linux. Kali is an evolution of Debian Linux that is designed and maintained by an organization called Offensive Security. Kali has more than 600 penetration testing programs, including Metasploit Framework as well as some I have already covered in this book, such as Nmap and Wireshark. It also has some tools yet to be covered in this book (like Burp, which is covered in Chapter 11). Kali can run on bare metal as an operating system on a hard drive, or you can boot from it on a USB drive. The most popular way of running Kali is in a virtual environment. I have done all of these, and my personal favorite is running it in a virtual environment. The benefit of deploying Kali in a virtual machine is the ability to take a snapshot. A snapshot is when you preserve the state of a machine at a specific moment in time. It is cyber time travel and a safeguard should you make a mistake. You are able to return to that specific moment in time over and over again.

I covered Nmap in Chapter 3, "Nmap: The Network Mapper," and the Nexpose Community as a vulnerability scanner in Chapter 4, "OpenVAS: Vulnerability Management." Both of these products give you data that can be imported into Metasploit. In this chapter, I cover installing Metasploit Community on a bare-metal Windows machine. The two reasons we are going to be using Metasploit Community are it is free and this is the GUI version.

As security practitioners, we know that practice makes perfect. Once you have Metasploit installed, you have an option of downloading vulnerable systems from the Open Web Application Security Project (OWASP) or Rapid7 to practice different types of exploitation. The Open Web Application Security Project is a not-for-profit organization that focuses on improving security in software. It has many different vulnerable machine downloads so that you can explore exploiting different types of web applications. In future labs and examples in this book, I will be using a vulnerable system called Metasploitable2. Metasploitable2 was purposefully crafted for training Metasploit and has many vulnerabilities to experiment with.

In Lab 10.1, you'll install Metasploit Community on a Windows system.

LAB 10.1: INSTALLING METASPLOIT COMMUNITY

1. Download Metasploit Community from the following website:

   ```
   www.rapid7.com/products/metasploit/download/community
   ```

   NOTE If that link does not work, you can search for *Metasploit community free download*.

2. After you fill out and submit the form for the free license, you will have an option to download the Windows 32-bit, 64-bit, or Linux 64-bit version (see Figure 10.1). Download the appropriate architecture for your Windows or Linux machine. An email containing your license key will be sent to the email you provided on the registration page.

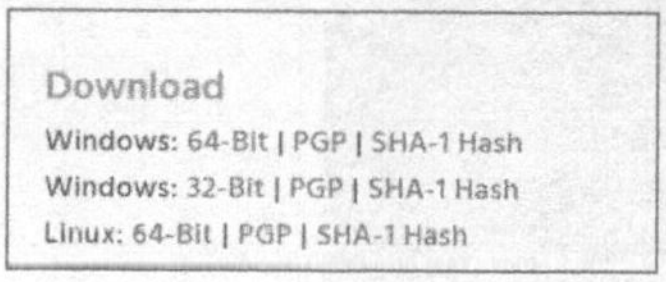

   Download
   Windows: 64-Bit | PGP | SHA-1 Hash
   Windows: 32-Bit | PGP | SHA-1 Hash
   Linux: 64-Bit | PGP | SHA-1 Hash

   Figure 10.1: Select the correct version of Metasploit Community for your platform and architecture.

3. Find and double-click the Metasploit Community .exe file. During the installation, you will get a warning regarding your antivirus and firewall settings, like you see in Figure 10.2. When you are pen testing with Metasploit, it is best practice to use a dedicated asset if at all possible. Do not put Metasploit on a system that you use for personal email, social media, or any financial accounting. It is a bad idea to put QuickBooks financials on a machine you are hacking with. I mention this because I've seen it.

Continues

LAB 10.1 (CONTINUED)

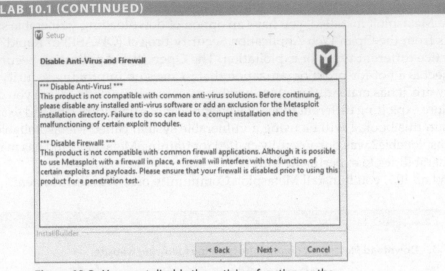

Figure 10.2: You must disable the antivirus function, or the install process might be corrupted.

4. **Metasploit Community naturally binds to port 3790. Leave the defaults for generating a certificate for accessing the software through a browser and complete the install. As the message in Figure 10.3 says, it will take a few minutes for the Metasploit services to start.**

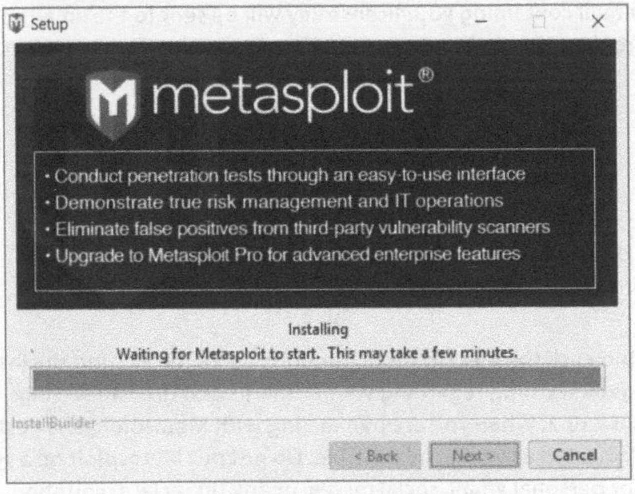

Figure 10.3: Waiting for Metasploit to start

Welcome to Metasploit! The splash screen you see makes for very informative reading. In Figure 10.4, there is an explanation of why there might be a warning regarding an insecure SSL certificate. It also explains that the Metasploit service can take upward of 10 minutes to initialize, and if you get a 404 error, just keep hitting the Refresh button. The URL you will navigate to in your browser is `https://localhost:3790/`. You can use your Start menu and navigate down to the Metasploit folder to open the Metasploit Web UI. You will also have access to updating, starting, and stopping services as well as resetting your password.

metasploit®   **RAPID7**

Welcome to Metasploit

Let's now guide you through configuring your Metasploit instance.

On the next screen, your browser may warn you about an insecure SSL certificate. This is normal, and here is why:

Metasploit runs a web server on your computer with a self-signed localhost SSL certificate that was generated as part of the Metasploit installation and therefore hasn't been signed by a certificate authority. To use Metasploit, you must accept or add an exception for this SSL certificate.

If you just installed or started Metasploit, it may take up to 10 minutes for Metasploit to initialize and for the Metasploit service to start. As a result, you may get a 404 missing page error or a progress dialog on the next screen. If this occurs, please refresh the page until Metasploit is available.

To begin using Metasploit, visit the following URL in your browser:

https://localhost:3790/

Figure 10.4: Metasploit Community splash screen

Please have your license that was emailed to you ready. You are going to need it after you provide your username and password of choice. This credential pair needs to be as robust as possible especially since this software can provide details about your network, operating systems, topology, and software you do not want out in the public. After you create this initial account, you will be asked for the Metasploit license you requested in Lab 10.1. As you see in Figure 10.5, you will need to enter the 16-digit license and activate your license while you are connected to the Internet.

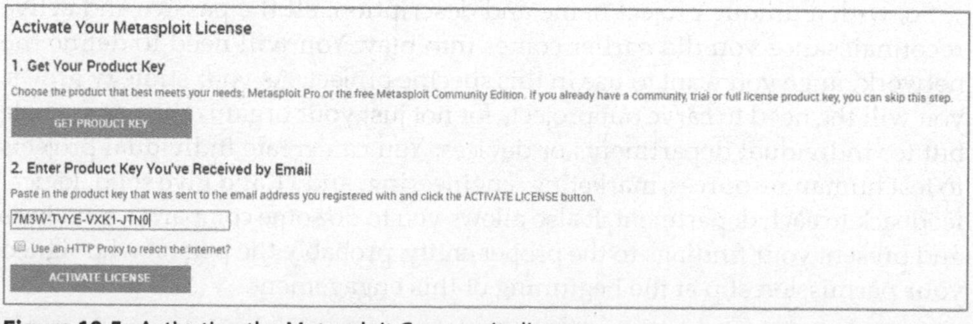

Activate Your Metasploit License

1. Get Your Product Key

Choose the product that best meets your needs: Metasploit Pro or the free Metasploit Community Edition. If you already have a community, trial or full license product key, you can skip this step.

GET PRODUCT KEY

2. Enter Product Key You've Received by Email

Paste in the product key that was sent to the email address you registered with and click the ACTIVATE LICENSE button.

7M3W-TVYE-VXK1-JTN0

☐ Use an HTTP Proxy to reach the internet?

ACTIVATE LICENSE

Figure 10.5: Activating the Metasploit Community license

After successful activation of your license, you are greeted with the Metasploit Community dashboard and the default project. If you click the blue hyperlink named `default`, you will open the overview page of a project. Think of a project as a container that holds all your notes. In Figure 10.6, you see the default project overview. Since you have just installed the software, you see there are no hosts or services discovered. There are no vulnerabilities identified, but there are several different ways to bring in data. You can launch a new scan, import a previous scan, launch an ad hoc Nexpose scan, or if you have the Metasploit Pro version, use a tool called Sonar.

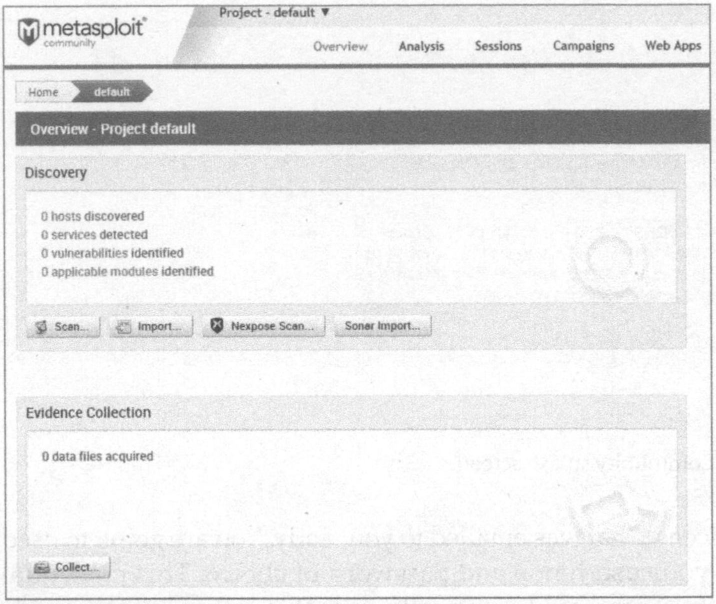

Figure 10.6: Exploring the default project in Metasploit Community

You will have to name the project, and you will want to add a description to remind you why you created this project. The beauty of Metasploit Community versus Framework for the beginner is this ability to create projects through a GUI. It also makes reporting easier when you are done with your penetration test.

So, with a unique project name and description, all the passive and active reconnaissance you did earlier comes into play. You will need to define the network range you want to use in this specific project. As your strategy grows, you will the need to carve out projects for not just your organization as a whole but for individual departments or devices. You can create individual projects to test human resources, marketing, engineering, and IT and give solid, logical feedback to each department. It also allows you to do some comparative analysis and present your findings to the proper entity, probably the person who signed your permission slip at the beginning of this engagement.

When you enter a default network range in the beginning of project creation, it will automatically populate the rest of the campaign. Be careful when you are entering project scope here in the form of IP addresses. If you make a simple mistake in just one octet of an IP address range, you might end up testing and compromising systems that do not belong to you. I normally triple-check my scope in this phase of project creation so I do not have to worry quite so much running modules based on the project definition—I define the IP, triple-check the range, and then check the box to restrict the network range. This is a safe-guard to keep you within your network range. No tasks will be run against a target if their IP address doesn't fall in the network range you have provided.

In Lab 10.2, you'll create a Metasploit Community project.

LAB 10.2: CREATING A METASPLOIT PROJECT

1. Click the New Project button on the Project Listing toolbar. It is a green circle with a plus in the center.

2. When the New Project page appears, you must enter a project name. When you see an asterisk after a field like Project Name, it means that the field is required before you can move to the next step. For the purposes of this lab, name this project MC1.

3. Under Description, enter the following text: **This is my first Metasploit Community project.**

4. Note that there is not an asterisk by the Network Range field. You are not required to enter a network range nor is the restriction to network range checked. This will be a decision you make based on how critical it is for you to stay in scope. The default range is 192.168.1.1–254. For this initial project, that range will be sufficient.

5. Click Create Project.

If you need to edit a project in the future, you can select the project in question from the Project Listing page and click the Settings button in the toolbar, as shown in Figure 10.7. It is not necessary to delete the entire project and start over.

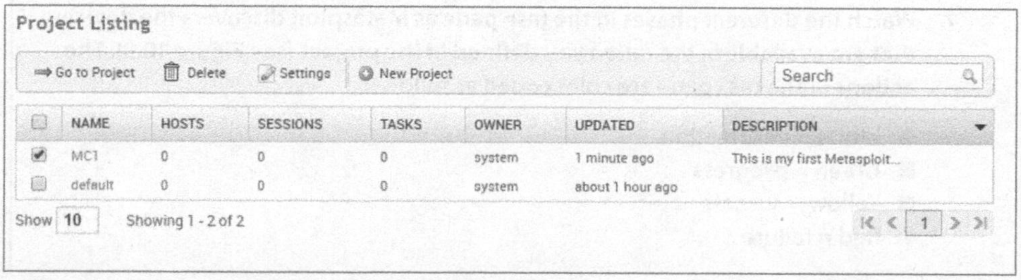

	NAME	HOSTS	SESSIONS	TASKS	OWNER	UPDATED	DESCRIPTION
✓	MC1	0	0	0	system	1 minute ago	This is my first Metasploit...
	default	0	0	0	system	about 1 hour ago	

Figure 10.7: List of projects in Metasploit Community

In Lab 10.3, you'll discover assets that might be vulnerable to attack.

LAB 10.3: DISCOVERING VULNERABLE ASSETS

1. Click the Metasploit Community logo in the upper-left corner of the home page to refresh the page.

2. Open your MC1 project.

3. Click the Scan button in the Discovery window (see Figure 10.8).

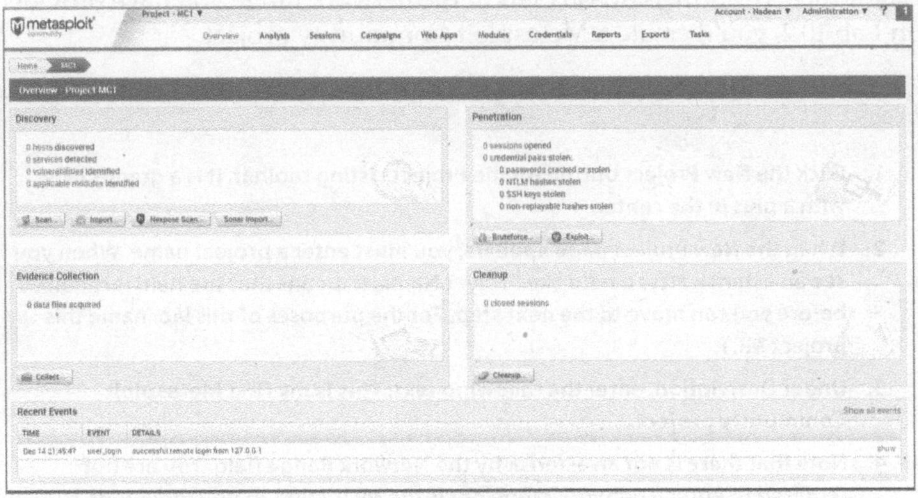

Figure 10.8: Metasploit Community project overview

4. Review the target settings. If you are using a private class A or class B address, you can change the range to align with your personal network.

5. Click the Advanced Options button under the target addresses. Under the advanced options, you can exclude assets from being targeted as well as customize the scan itself. You can also choose the port scan speed depending on how stealthy you are trying to be.

6. Leave all the defaults as they are and click Launch Scan in the lower-right corner of the home page.

7. Watch the different phases in the task pane as Metasploit discovers the devices that are available in the range you defined in the project (see Figure 10.9). The actions in the task pane are color coded as follows:

   ▪ White = information
   ▪ Green = progress
   ▪ Yellow = success
   ▪ Red = failure

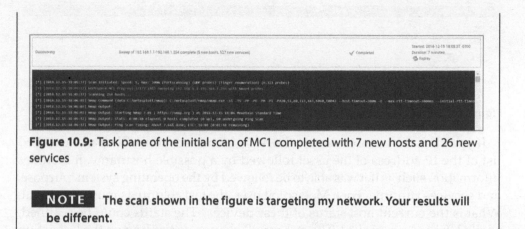

Figure 10.9: Task pane of the initial scan of MC1 completed with 7 new hosts and 26 new services

> **NOTE**   The scan shown in the figure is targeting my network. Your results will be different.

By watching the task pane, you see each of the four distinct phases. The first phase you saw in the discovery scan was the ping. Ping determines if an asset is online. After you know there is a response, then Metasploit runs Nmap to identify the ports that are open and by default will look for commonly open ports such as HTTP and SSH. The third phase that kicked in was looking at key indicators or fingerprints of operating systems and versions. The last action was bubbling that information up into the project.

Gaining Access

An *exploit* is a program that takes advantage of a vulnerability that is on a device. Exploits can be either remote or client-side. A remote exploit will be the type that will focus on services running on network-connected machines that you have decided to target. A client-side exploit is the type of exploit that takes advantage of vulnerability in software you have installed on a computer system. There are software packages that have a reputation for being vulnerable even after you run a patch on them. I have experienced the frustration of patching systems, running a vulnerability scan, and then finding the patch I just used has a vulnerability.

If you look at the data your first scan retrieved by navigating to the Overview page, you will see there are four quadrants. So far, I have done only a discovery scan to try to figure out what is running on my network. As you see in Figure 10.10, the initial scan returned 7 hosts and 26 services with 0 vulnerabilities and 0 applicable modules identified. Let's dig deeper into this example.

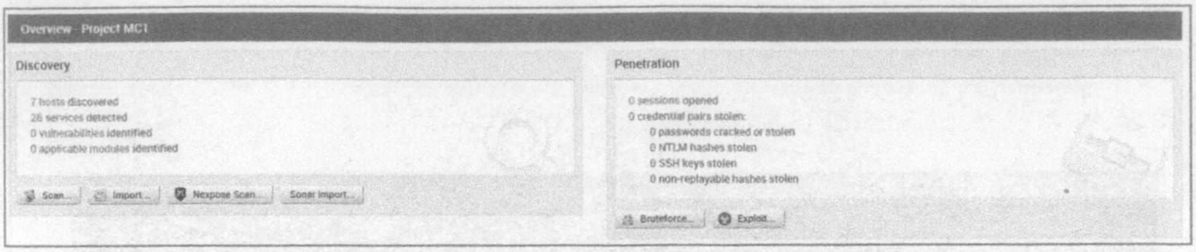

Figure 10.10: Overview after discovery of assets and services on a network

If you click the number next to the hosts identified, you will open a detailed list of the IP address of the asset followed by a possible hostname. It includes information such as if it was able to be followed by the operating system, purpose, and services running. For a Metasploit user, the last column is most important: What is the current host status of these devices? The status could be scanned, shelled, looted, or cracked. The status will change depending on the last action successfully performed on that asset.

- Scanned—A discovery scan or import was completed.
- Shelled—A session was opened.
- Looted—Data, files, hashes, or screenshots were collected.
- Cracked—The password was cracked and is now available in plain text.

Next to Hosts on your project page, you have the Notes tab that tells you the type of data that was retrieved on each asset. The Services tab lists the name and protocol, port number, and current state of each service. The Vulnerabilities tab may populate this project with a few exploited vulnerabilities found during the discovery scan that are considered low-hanging fruit that can be easily exploited. The Applicable Modules tab lists the Metasploit modules that are possible avenues of exploitation. Captured data will help you build a report on what was found in the environment during the discovery and future scans of the selected IP address range. With the paid version, Network Topology will draw a picture of the environment like Zenmap. Zenmap is the GUI Nmap tool that was used in Chapter 3.

Now that you have all this information about the network, the big question is, "What's next?" If you are interested in pursuing a client-side or remote exploit, you will have to investigate which module is best for you to attempt. This is the stage of a penetration test where patience is a virtue. Go to the Modules tab at the top of your project and go down to the Search field.

From the Search Modules dialog box, it is easy to query the operating system or ports. The exploits that have been written for specific vulnerabilities will be ranked by which has the best chance of working. For example, as you see in Figure 10.11, in my environment, I have added an old legacy laser jet printer on my home network that has port 23 open. Port 23 is telnet. Telnet is a network protocol that allows you to log into another device if it is on the same network.

Telnet is hardly used anymore since it is totally lacking in security, but it can still be used if you want to send your credentials in clear text. In my opinion, it's a vulnerability, and it's only on my network temporarily so that I can show you how this works.

	HOST NAME	NAME	PROTOCOL	PORT ▲	INFO	STATE
☐	DESKTOP-0UBN7VK.HomeRT	tcpmux	tcp	1		UNKNOWN
☐	DESKTOP-0UBN7VK.HomeRT	echo	tcp	7		UNKNOWN
☐	DESKTOP-0UBN7VK.HomeRT	discard	tcp	9		UNKNOWN
☐	DESKTOP-0UBN7VK.HomeRT	daytime	tcp	13		UNKNOWN
☐	DESKTOP-0UBN7VK.HomeRT	chargen	tcp	19		UNKNOWN
☐	DESKTOP-0UBN7VK.HomeRT	ftp	tcp	21		UNKNOWN
☐	DESKTOP-0UBN7VK.HomeRT	ssh	tcp	22		UNKNOWN
☐	DESKTOP-0UBN7VK.HomeRT	telnet	tcp	23		UNKNOWN
☐	LaserJet.HomeRT	telnet	tcp	23	**	OPEN

Figure 10.11: Finding open ports in the network

It may take a little research on Metasploit forums, but you can look for a Metasploit module that may work well to compromise port 23 on a laser printer. This is how you start building your repertoire with this tool. As you can see in Figure 10.12, I have searched for *laser jet*. I could have easily searched for *telnet* or *port 23* to see a list of possible options. After I searched for a specific topic, I used the Module Ranking column to sort the modules that have a higher ranking, as shown in Figure 10.12. Now the process of using different modules against different vulnerabilities becomes trial and error.

Home › MC1 › Modules

Search Modules   laser jet

Module Statistics show   Search Keywords show

Found 12 matching modules

MODULE TYPE	OS	MODULE	DISCLOSURE DATE	MODULE RANKING ▼	CVE
Server Exploit		Oracle Event Processing FileUploadServlet Arbitrary File Upload exploit/windows/http/oracle_event_processing_upload	April 20, 2014	★★★★	2014-2424
Server Exploit		MS99-025 Microsoft IIS MDAC msadcs.dll RDS Arbitrary Remote Command Execution exploit/windows/iis/msadc	July 16, 1998	★★★★	1999-1011
Server Exploit		Rejetto HttpFileServer Remote Command Execution exploit/windows/http/rejetto_hfs_exec	September 10, 2014	★★★★	2014-6287
Auxiliary		HP LaserJet Printer SNMP Enumeration auxiliary/scanner/snmp/snmp_enum_hp_laserjet		★★	
Auxiliary		Sybase Easerver 6.3 Directory Traversal auxiliary/scanner/http/sybase_easerver_traversal	May 24, 2011	★★	2011-2474
Auxiliary		Apache ActiveMQ Directory Traversal auxiliary/scanner/http/apache_activemq_traversal		★★	
Server Exploit		HP Jetdirect Path Traversal Arbitrary Code Execution exploit/linux/misc/hp_jetdirect_path_traversal	April 4, 2017	★★	2017-2741
Auxiliary		HP Web JetAdmin 6.5 Server Arbitrary Command Execution auxiliary/admin/http/hp_web_jetadmin_exec	April 26, 2004	★★	
Auxiliary		Apache ActiveMQ JSP Files Source Disclosure auxiliary/scanner/http/apache_activemq_source_disclosure		★★	2010-1587
Auxiliary		Dopewars Denial of Service auxiliary/dos/misc/dopewars	October 4, 2009	★★	2009-3591
Server Exploit		Citrix Provisioning Services 5.6 SP1 Streamprocess Opcode 0x40020006 Buffer Overflow exploit/windows/misc/citrix_streamprocess_get_objects	November 3, 2011	★★	
Server Exploit		Apache Jetspeed Arbitrary File Upload exploit/multi/http/apache_jetspeed_file_upload	March 5, 2016		2016-0710, 2016-0709

Figure 10.12: List of possible exploits to be launched sorted by starred rankings

My personal strategy is to open the higher ranking modules—because at this point, I'm just trying to gain access or get a foothold in the network. By opening the link to the module, you get a detailed description of exactly what the exploit will be doing and possible options to configure the module. These modules were created by subject-matter experts and configured for general best practice. I will try them out of the box first, and then if I have an idea for reconfiguring, I will try different parameters. As you see in Figure 10.13, there is an HP LaserJet Printer SNMP Enumeration module that allows you to possibly enumerate previously printed files. I know that the asset in my environment IP address is 192.168.1.93.

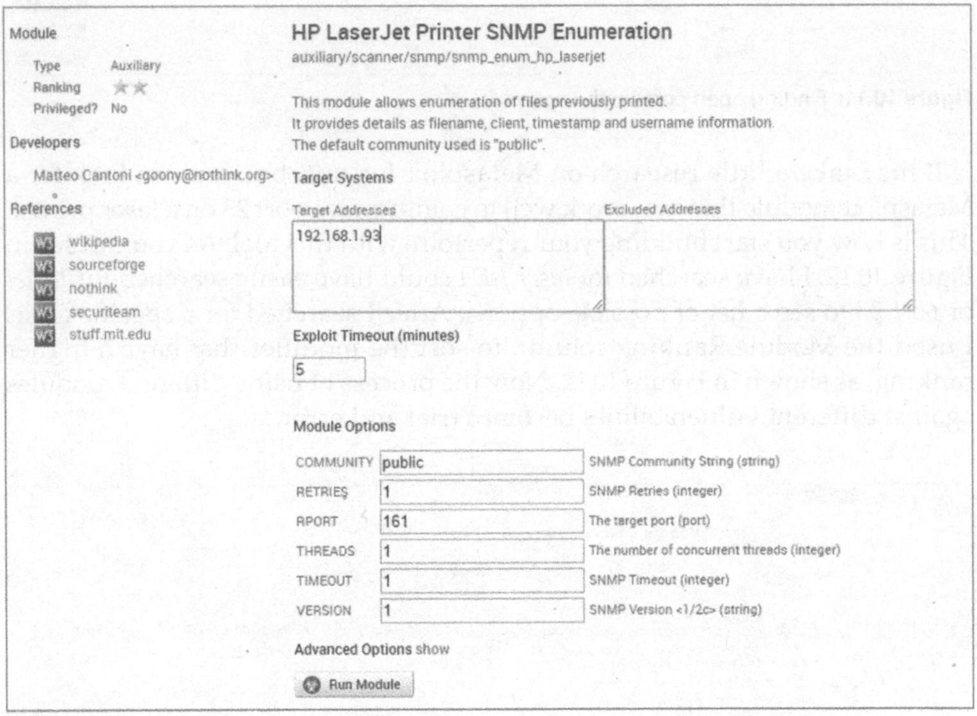

Figure 10.13: Configuring a Metasploit auxiliary module for possible exploitation against a printer

As you can see in Figure 10.14, in less than 5 seconds, the connection was refused and forcibly closed. It's time to move to the next most applicable module.

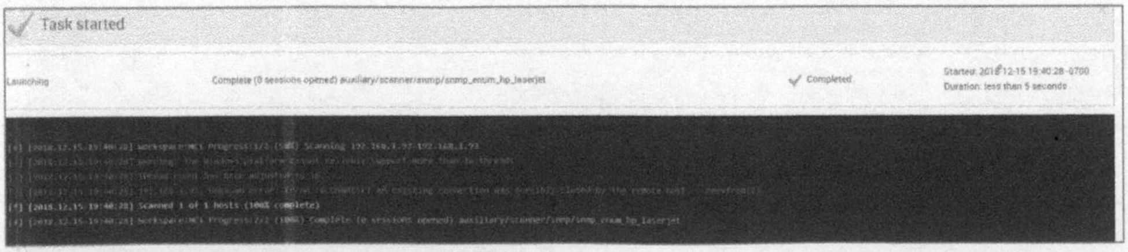

Figure 10.14: Failure of an auxiliary module

Another strategy is to search for operating systems you know exist on your network and, rather than sort by ranking, sort them by date. What are the odds that everything in your network has the newest patches delivered to it on a schedule? Here you are counting on security administrators being incredibly busy and not getting the newest and latest upgrades and patches on their machines in a timely way. Another strategy is to search the web for the best, most frequently used Metasploit modules. In Figure 10.15, you see the exploits displayed by date when searched for a specific platform.

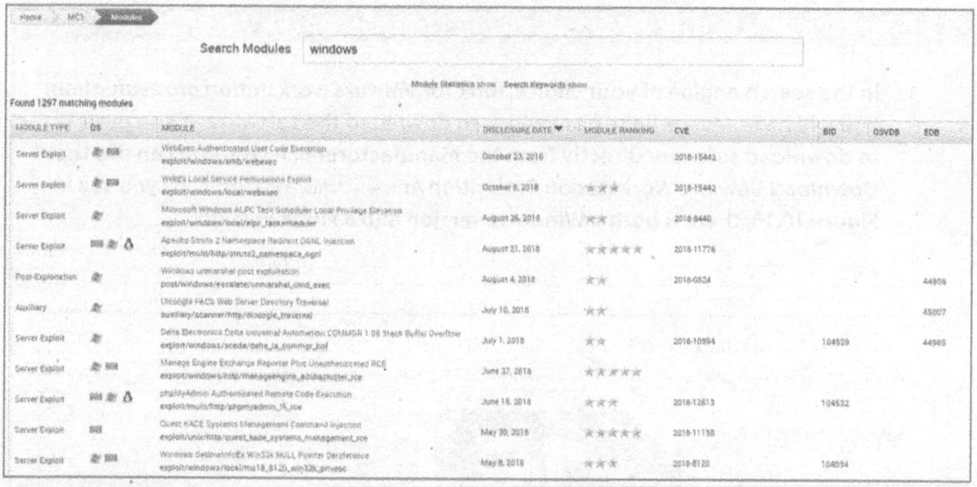

Figure 10.15: Windows server, auxiliary, and post-exploitation exploits organized by disclosure to the public date

Metasploitable2

The initial scan that you conducted in Lab 10.3 was on your personal assets. One of the best ways to experience Metasploit in a vulnerable environment is to use Metasploitable2 in a virtual machine. Metasploitable2 is an Ubuntu 8.04 server that runs on a VMware image. The Metasploitable virtual machine contains a number of purposeful vulnerable services, including the following:

- FTP
- Secure Shell
- Telnet
- DNS
- Apache
- Postgres
- MySQL

To use VMware as your virtual environment, you can get the perpetually free VMware player or the VMware Workstation Pro hypervisor that is fully functional for 30 days. I am using VMware of Workstation Pro on this workstation to create the Metasploitable2 instance. If you prefer VirtualBox, you are more than welcome to use a different virtual host. If you already have VMware Workstation installed, you can skip Lab 10.4.

In Lab 10.4 and Lab 10.5, you will install VMware Workstation Pro to run Metasploitable2.

LAB 10.4: INSTALLING VMWARE WORKSTATION PRO EVALUATION

1. In the search engine of your choice, look for *VMware workstation pro evaluation*. You will have several links from which to download the software. If you prefer to download software directly from the manufacturer like I do, you can use the Download VMware Workstation Pro option at www.vmware.com. As you see in Figure 10.16, there is both a Windows version and a Linux version.

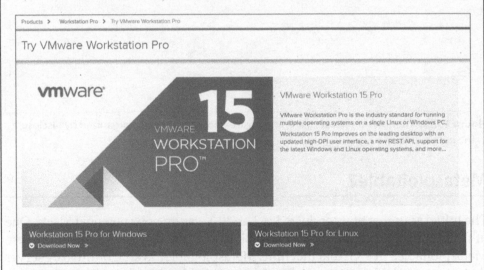

Figure 10.16: VMware Workstation Pro download—Windows or Linux

2. Download the appropriate file for your platform. The .exe file will typically download to your Downloads folder. Install it, and when you're asked for a license, go ahead without one. The installation will take a few minutes.

LAB 10.5: PLAYING METASPLOITABLE2 IN VMWARE PRO

1. Metasploitable2 is created by the Rapid7 Metasploit team in Austin, Texas. By downloading directly from the `Rapid7.com` link, you are getting the latest, greatest, clean version of the machine. In the browser of your choice, navigate to the following website:

   `https://information.rapid7.com/download-metasploitable-2017.html`

2. Fill out the form to download the vulnerable machine and submit. The file link will be available on the next page. When you click Download Metasploitable Now, it will download the `metasploitable-linux.zip` file, which is about 825MB.

3. When the download is finished, unzip the archive. Please do not forget where you unzipped the file. (I have been known to re-unzip a file because I was not paying attention.)

4. Go into VMware Workstation. Click the File menu and select Open. A dialog box will appear, asking you which virtual machine you want to open. You are not going to open the zip file from here. Instead, go into the directory where you unzipped it. There should be a file there called `Metasploitable.vmx`. Open the file that has the description VMware virtual machine, as shown in Figure 10.17.

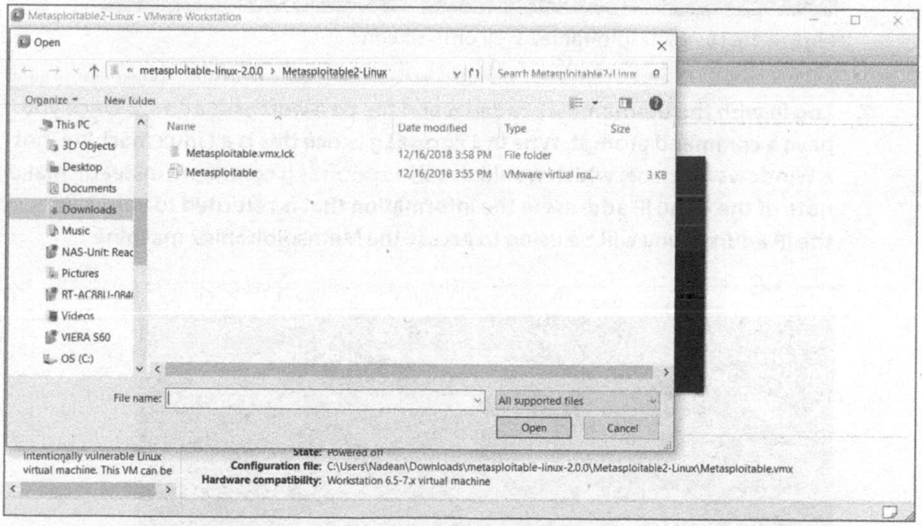

Figure 10.17: Opening `Metasploitable.vmx` in VMware

Continues

5. Your virtual machine should appear on its own tab in VMware. Click OK and power on this vulnerable Linux machine.

6. You may get a dialog box that asks if you moved it or copied it. For the purposes of this lab, click the I Copied It option. Once the machine is loaded, you will see the Metasploitable2 welcome screen, as shown in Figure 10.18. Note that the welcome screen tells you to log in with `msfadmin/msfadmin`, which means that `msfadmin` is used for both the username and the password.

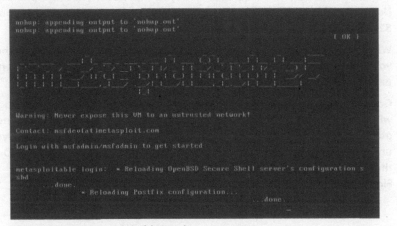

Figure 10.18: Metasploitable2 welcome screen

7. Log in with the username `msfadmin` and the password `msfadmin`. Once you have a command prompt, type in `ifconfig` (since this is a Linux machine, not a Windows machine, which would use the `ipconfig` command instead). Make note of the `eth0` IP address in the information that is returned to you. This is the IP address you will be using to access the Metasploitable2 machine.

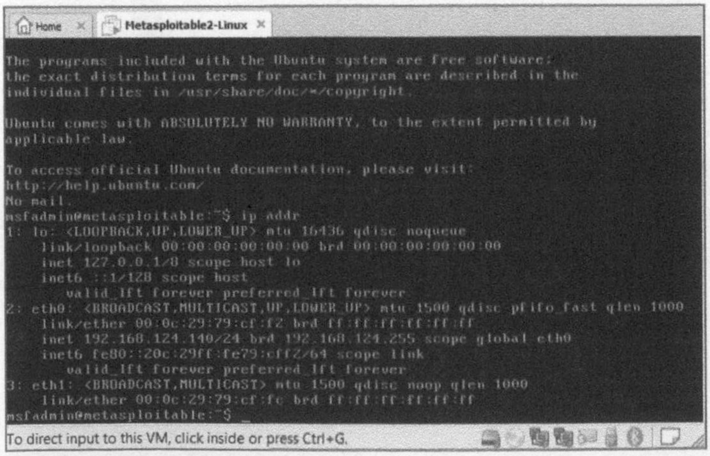

Figure 10.19: `ifconfig` on the Metasploitable2 box

(You could also use the command `ip addr` to get this information.) As you see in Figure 10.19, the `eth0 inet` address is `192.168.124.140`.

8. Create a new project by opening Project and scrolling down to Create Project. Name this project **Metasploitable2** and use the target IPv4 address. Scan the one asset. When the scan has completed, as you see in Figure 10.20, this machine has 33 services.

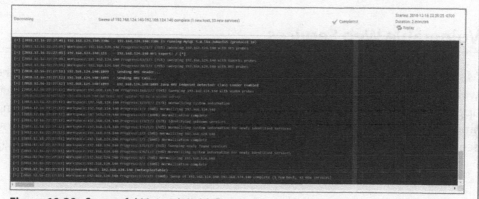

Figure 10.20: Successful Metasploitable2 scan

9. If you open the Analysis tab and sort by port, you will see that Telnet is open on the Metasploitable box. Remember the PuTTY install? Open PuTTY, add `192.168.124.140`, and choose Telnet as your connection type. Click Open. Sometimes you don't even need to brute-force a password. As you see in Figure 10.21, the password is displayed on the welcome screen. On the Services tab, notice that port 22 and 513 are also open. Try using SSH or Rlogin to get into the Metasploitable box.

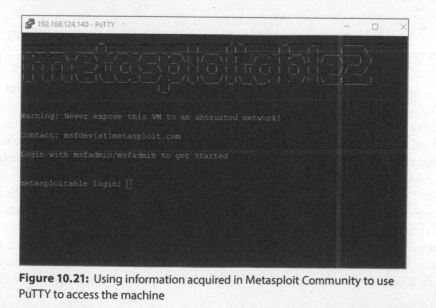

Figure 10.21: Using information acquired in Metasploit Community to use PuTTY to access the machine

You may be surprised at just how easy that was. There are times you might find this type of open service on a switch using a default password. Navigate to the Overview page on the main page, and you should see at least one vulnerability identified, one applicable module identified, and one credential pair stolen and cracked. Open the vulnerability discovered as well as the module that Metasploit Community suggests would be a viable exploit. Open the Credentials tab to find out what service credentials were acquired.

Vulnerable Web Services

Metasploitable2 also has deliberately vulnerable web applications preinstalled. The web server starts automatically when Metasploitable2 is booted. To access the web applications, open a web browser and enter the IPv4 address you have been using since Figure 10.19. I can access mine by browsing to `http://192.168.124.140`. As you see in Figure 10.22, there are web applications that can be accessed from this page.

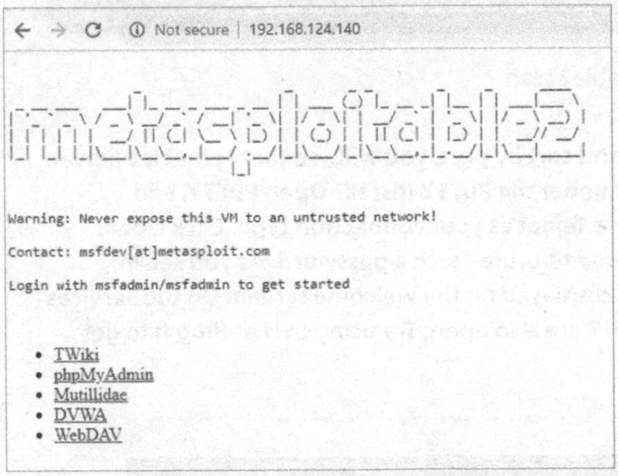

Figure 10.22: Metasploitable2 web application home page

The Mutillidae web application contains all the vulnerabilities from the OWASP Top Ten (see Figure 10.23). If you scroll through the menus starting with the OWASP Top 10, the menus will cascade into subdirectories of vulnerabilities, including form caching and click-jacking. Mutillidae allows the user to change the security level from 0 (completely and totally insecure) to 5 (secure). Additionally, three levels of hints are provided, ranging from "Level 0 – I try harder" (no hints) to "Level 2 – noob" (maximum hints). If the application is damaged by user injections and hacks, clicking the Reset DB button resets the application to its original state.

Damn Vulnerable Web App (DVWA) is a PHP/MySQL web application, and it really is damn vulnerable. As described on the DMVA home page shown in Figure 10.24, its main purpose is to help security professionals test their skills and tools in a legal environment and help web developers better understand the processes of securing web applications.

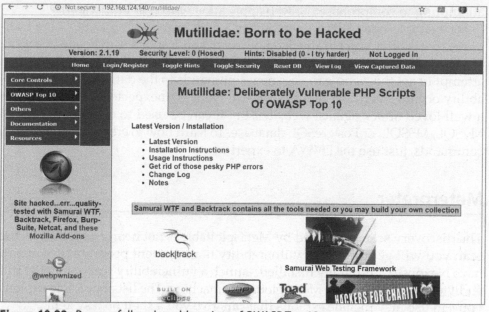

Figure 10.23: Purposefully vulnerable scripts of OWASP Top 10

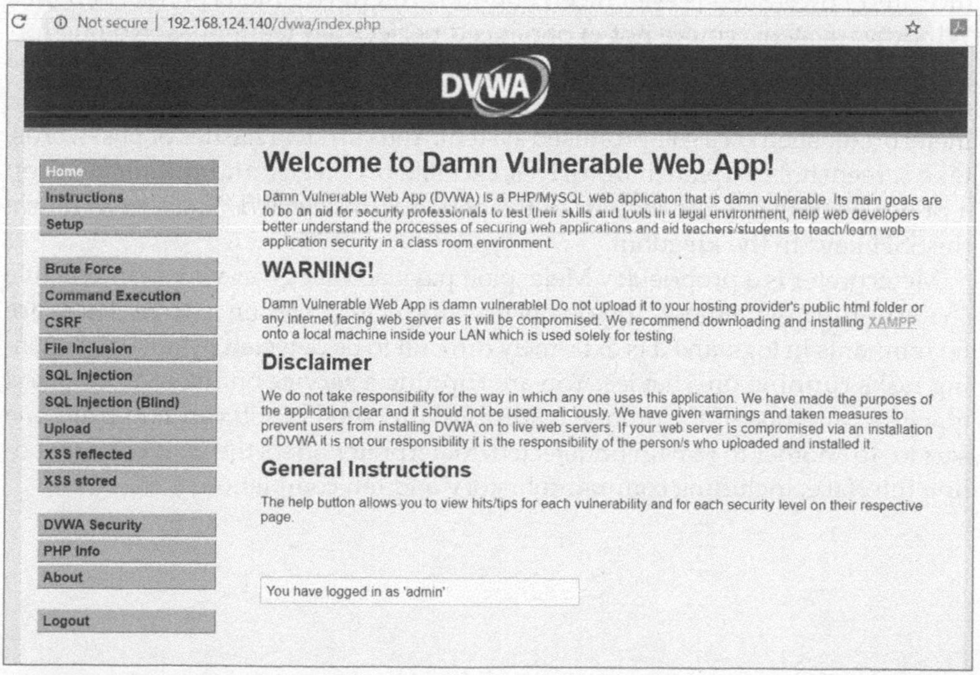

Figure 10.24: DVWA home page

The default DVWA username is *admin*, and the default password is *password*. Once you're inside the DVWA, you have the option of choosing different vulnerabilities and then using this tool to learn about each vulnerability and attempting to compromise the web application with that vulnerability.

For example, one of the vulnerabilities is SQL injection (SQLi). SQLi is a technique that is often used to attack data-driven applications using code injection. This is done by including portions of the SQL statement in an entry field in an attempt to get the website to pass new commands to the database. The vulnerability occurs when user input is not valid and is unexpectedly executed. It is a well-loved attack against websites, but it can be used to attack any type of MySQL, MSSQL, or PostgreSQL database. To learn how to create the rogue SQL commands, just use the DVWA to experiment.

Meterpreter

The discovery scan completed by Metasploitable is not nearly as robust as the scan you will get from your vulnerability management program. If you still have Nexpose Community installed, launch a vulnerability scan using the full audit template against the Metasploitable2 machine. The list of possible exploits you can use may include exploits that can give you a shell on a system.

A successful exploit can give you access to a target system in a multitude of ways. The premier access of choice is a meterpreter shell. A command shell is nice, and PowerShell is even nicer, but until you have a meterpreter shell on a Windows system, you've not experienced perfect red team bliss. No one forgets his or her first meterpreter shell. Teaching Metasploit for the past couple of years, I've had students astounded when they see the power embedded in a meterpreter shell on a compromised system. You can steal hashes of passwords, take screenshots, explore hard drives, escalate privileges, and ultimately drop a proxy pivot to explore the rest of the network undetected. You literally have the SSH keys to the kingdom.

Meterpreter is a proprietary Metasploit payload that gives you an interactive shell running in memory. You do not execute meterpreter on a drive. There are no remnants in logs, and it is extremely difficult to be detected by anyone watching tasks running on a device. You are running a service on the compromised machine, and one of the unique features of this shell is you can hop from one service to another to remain undetected. Meterpreter offers the usual command-line interface, including command history and tab completion.

CHAPTER
11

Web Application Security

WHAT YOU WILL LEARN IN THIS CHAPTER:

➤ Web Development

➤ Information Gathering

➤ DNS

➤ Defense in Depth

➤ Offense: Burp Suite

I was flying on a Delta flight from Atlanta to Denver this past summer and had been upgraded to first class. I recognize that some people hate flying and, like my husband, hate being talked to by strangers on a flight. My normal mode of operations is to smile and say hello and leave it there. If my seat mate says hello back, then conversation may ensue. Otherwise, I'm happy to put my noise-cancelling headphones on and watch a movie. On this flight, I found my flying companion was a web application developer and was flying to Denver to meet with venture capitalists to show them the final product. Of course, being a geek, I'm terribly interested and ask all sorts of questions. To most of them, he answered, "That's proprietary, and I can't share." Toward the end of our trip, he asked me what I did. I told him I work for Rapid7 as a consultant and teach security classes—mostly vulnerability management and Metasploit, but I dabble in application security and incident detection and response. To that, he replied, "What's that?"

That is the mind-set of some web application developers I have met. They are full of wonderful ideas and a vast knowledge of coding, but when it comes to security, not a single clue. How can you deliver an application and not factor in security? What was even more eye-opening was seeing the advertisement during the Super Bowl the following year for the application this guy helped create. My immediate thought was that I hoped he remembered our conversation on the value of the software development lifecycle (SDLC).

Web Development

It takes a lot of work to create really great applications and even more to maintain the evolution of those applications over time. In the past 20 years, the Internet has progressed exponentially. Take, for example, the original Facebook page, which was called www.aboutface.com in 1999. If you use the Internet archive site called the Wayback Machine at www.archive.org, you can see what Facebook looked like two decades ago (see Figure 11.1). What I love about the Wayback Machine is that if you want, you can right-click the website archived and view the page source.

The progression of the Web has led to a need for the evolution of web application testing. Back in the day, a web page was a static page, and the flow of information was from server to browser. Most sites did not require any type of authentication because it just wasn't needed. Any issue you had was as a result of vulnerabilities in a web server. Now what you see are web applications that are dynamic and customized for each user, and the problem is private data being exposed to the public, not just web server files.

Every developer I know says that the foundation of a strong application is the framework and architecture it is built on. Web application architecture is the interaction between applications, middleware, and the databases the application relies on. It is critical that when a user hits the Submit button through any browser that the information is processed correctly. Middleware is the software that provides services to applications besides those offered by the operating system. Any software between the kernel and the application can be middleware. Some describe middleware as "software glue."

You type in a URL, and the browser finds the Internet-facing server that hosts that website and asks for that particular page within that site. The server responds by sending the appropriate files to the browser to execute. Now you get to interact with the website. The most important thing here is the code. The code gets parsed by the browser, which may or may not have specific instructions to tell the browser what to do. The web application framework and architecture have all the components and routines and interchanges needed for the application.

Ultimately, the design of web applications is for usability. You want an application to accomplish goals efficiently. This is critical for many organizations since the majority of global business and our lives are on the Internet. Every application and device today is built with the idea of web-based interaction. You have Amazon for shopping, Instagram to keep up with friends, JPMorgan Chase for banking, and all the email you send using Google or Yahoo!. Even when you have the assurance that these web applications are protected and the

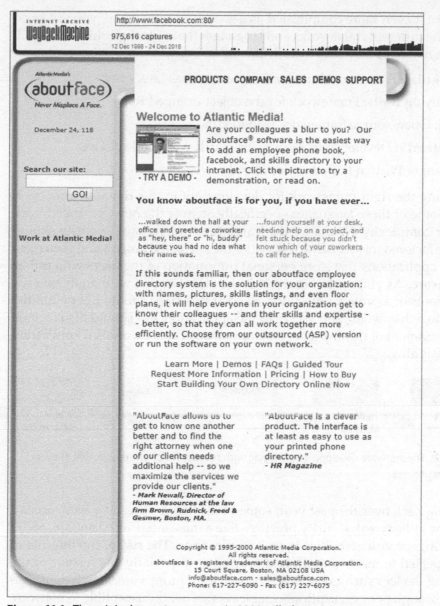

Figure 11.1: The original `Facebook.com` in 2000 called `AboutFace.com`

lock icon appears in the browser and the application states that they are secure because they are using SSL or they are compliant with PCI-DSS, the websites have fallen to vulnerabilities such as SQL injection, broken access controls, cross-site scripting, or request forgery. Even if SSL is being used, which encrypts links between a web server and a browser, there can still be vulnerabilities in the web application.

To make it even more complicated as a security professional, you are faced with all the different frameworks and languages that web applications are built with. The most popular ones include the following:

- **Angular:** Framework built by Google and uses JavaScript
- **Ruby on Rails:** Framework for the object-oriented Ruby
- **YII:** Open-source framework using PHP5
- **MeteorJS:** Developed in `Node.js`, primarily for mobile devices
- **Django:** Written in Python for complex websites

Choosing the right framework for development in this dynamic process is critical. Some of these languages specifically answer the need for speed, scalability, or complexity. No matter the framework or language, security should always be factored into the SDLC, no matter the size of the project, and even more so in the applications that store personal information of the users who utilize that software. As you see in Figure 11.2, the SDLC begins with analyzing the requirements of a project. Questions asked at this stage should not be limited to the who, what, when, and where of the application, but should also include a risk assessment of the impact of a compromise of this theoretical application you're designing.

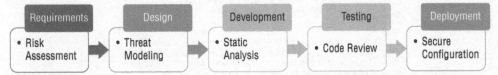

Figure 11.2: The software development lifecycle with security functions embedded at every stage of the process

Looking back over the past year, some of the biggest breaches were accomplished by either weak security practices like a misconfigured database, social engineering, or vulnerabilities in web applications. The rise of the Internet of Things has led to many complicated problems—especially when some of the life-saving devices such as pacemakers or insulin pumps are shown to be vulnerable through poor encryption—and leaves software susceptible to malware infection. Even the cars we drive have to be evaluated on the size of their attack surface and network architecture. If your automobile offers features like Bluetooth, Wi-Fi, cellular network connections, keyless entry, or radio-readable tire pressure, monitoring systems can offer a security vulnerability to gain an initial foothold into the car's network.

There are many reasons for problems in securing web applications. One of the major problems is the lack of developers' security awareness, as mentioned at the beginning of the chapter. Add to that the customization of web applications by in-house staff, the threat actors developing new web attack techniques, and time constraints where you have to get a web application to production as soon as humanly possible. This all leads to serious threats to both the company hosting the web application and the users who share their credit card information on them.

Information Gathering

Web application testing starts very much like the penetration testing discussed in Chapter 10, "Metasploit." You must get authority to test a target, and validation of ownership is critical. With web application reconnaissance specifically, you have a few other resources to utilize, such as Whois and DNSdumpster.

In Lab 11.1, you'll be validating the owner of the web application you are testing.

LAB 11.1: VALIDATING TARGETS

1. Whois is a protocol for searching Internet registration databases for domain names and IP addresses. Open your browser and navigate to `https://www.whois.icann.org`.

    Make sure you are going to the correct site. Some clones of Whois are trying to sell you something. As you see in Figure 11.3, ICANN's WHOIS Lookup gives you the ability to look up a domain owner.

Figure 11.3: ICANN WHOIS for domain lookup

2. Where the form asks you to enter a domain, type in `www.example.com`. In Figure 11.4, you see that `www.example.com` is a domain that has been owned by the Internet Assigned Numbers Authority (IANA) since 1992.

Continues

Raw WHOIS Record

```
% IANA WHOIS server
% for more information on IANA, visit http://www.iana.org
% This query returned 1 object

domain:       EXAMPLE.COM

organisation: Internet Assigned Numbers Authority

created:      1992-01-01
source:       IANA
```

Figure 11.4: ICANN WHOIS domain lookup results for `www.example.com`

3. **Open another tab in your browser and type in** `https://dnsdumpster.com`.
   DNSdumpster is a free domain-research tool that can discover other hosts
   associated with the initial domain you looked up with Whois. You have to
   know the entire web application landscape in order to protect it. As you see in
   Figure 11.5, you get a wealth of information about `www.example.com`.

Figure 11.5: DNS server reconnaissance and researching domains including host (A), mail (MX), and TXT records

4. With both tabs open, compare the registered owner with the DNS servers hosting the site. If they are the same, feel free to proceed with the rest of your test. Just a side note, my favorite part of the DNSdumpster site is toward the bottom of a search. It will map the domain for you.

5. Are any of the devices you are testing connected to the Internet? Open a third tab and navigate to `www.shodan.io`.

   Shodan is the search engine to use if you are looking for specific types of IoT, including webcams, routers, or servers mostly running HTTP/HTTPS, FTP, SSH, Telnet, SNMP, IMAP, SMTP, and SIP. Shodan users can find all sorts of fun things connected to the Internet. Everything from traffic lights, control systems, power grids, security cameras, and even a nuclear power plant or two have been found. Many of these IoT devices still have their default configuration on them, such as `admin/admin`, and the only software needed to connect is your web browser. In Figure 11.6, you see the search for `www.example.com`. Shodan.io crawls the Internet for publicly accessible devices. With your search, you will get 10 results unless you create an account. If you sign in, you can get up to 50.

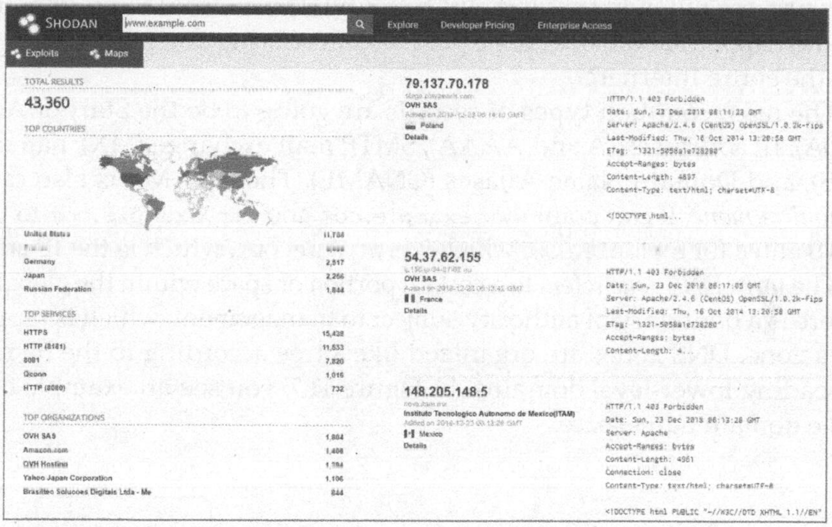

Figure 11.6: Top countries, services, and organizations that have a publicly exposed server with `www.example.com` in their details

6. Type **telnet** in the search bar.

   It is quite scary when you find a Shodan result with username/password credentials in the banner. Remember, *do not touch these devices unless you have permission to do so.*

DNS

I believe having a solid understanding of the hierarchical naming system for anything connected to the Internet will make your security tasks easier. DNS stands for Domain Name System. Since 1985, DNS has been an essential component of the Internet. It provides a global, distributed directory service. It coordinates information with domain names assigned to a numerical IP address. It is much harder for us as humans to remember the four octets for every website we want to visit. It is much easier to remember www.example.com.

There are 4,294,967,296 IPv4 addresses. It would be very difficult to build and maintain a database of all those IPv4 addresses in just one place. With the addition of the 340,282,366,920,938,463,463,374,607,431,768,211,456 IPv6 addresses, it is mind-boggling. It is estimated there are 7.7 billion people on Earth. That is more than a trillion IP addresses assigned to every single person on this planet. We need a way to track all these addresses. Actually, we have to delegate this process to a system.

The DNS is going to share the responsibility of assigning domain names and mapping those names by designating authoritative name servers for each domain. A name server is going to respond to questions asked about names in a certain zone. This server should only respond to questions about domain names that are specifically configured by a network administrator. This allows this process to be distributed and be fault tolerant. Could you imagine what would happen should one single point of failure bring down the naming system for the entire Internet?

The most common types of records are going to be the Start of Authority (SOA), IP addresses (A and AAAA), SMTP mail exchange (MX), name servers (NS), and Domain Name Aliases (CNAME). The CNAME is also called the *canonical name*. It can point www.example.com and ftp.example.com to the right DNS entry for example.com, which has an A record, which is the IP address.

The term *DNS zone* refers to a certain portion or space within the global system. There is a boundary of authority subject to management, which is represented by a zone. DNS zones are organized like a tree according to the hierarchy of cascading lower-level domains. In Figure 11.7, you see an example of a DNS zone domain namespace.

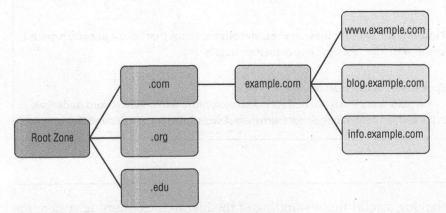

Figure 11.7: The domain namespace of example.com

A DNS zone transfer is the process where a DNS server passes part of its database to another DNS server. There is a master DNS server and one or more slave DNS servers so you can have more than one DNS server able to answer questions about a particular zone. A basic DNS zone transfer attack is to pretend you're a slave DNS server and ask the master for a copy. A best practice is to restrict zone transfers. At the minimum, tell the master the IP addresses of the slaves so they don't share information with an impersonator.

Defense in Depth

If you have ever toured a well-engineered medieval castle, you have walked through a defense in depth. The ultimate goal is to keep the bad guys out. You have to cross a moat and get through the outer portcullis, and the castle itself is usually in a well-defended place on a cliff somewhere with high walls and arrow slits in the wall for archers. Individuals who do web development should think about their processes of defense in the same manner.

The personal information and intellectual proprietary information need to be hosted in the most innermost, protected area of the castle so that if attackers get over the moat, they still have not been able to get the keys to the kingdom. There are several mechanisms you can put in place that will protect web applications. Most web applications use the authentication, session management, and access control triad to reduce their attack surface. They have interdependencies, providing overall protection. Any defect in any part of the triad could possibly give an attacker access to the data.

Authentication is the most basic where you have to prove you are who you say you are by logging into a site. After you log in with a strong password or multifactor authentication, the authenticated person's session must be managed. This is usually done with some sort of token. When a user gets a token, the browser submits it to the server in each subsequent HTTP request. If the user is not active, the token will ideally expire requiring that user to log in again. Access control is put in place to make and enforce who has access to what. If this has been deployed correctly, it will know if this user is authorized to perform an action or access the data he or she is requesting.

Even using this triad, no web application or technology has proven to be invulnerable. New threats and techniques pop up every day that add a dynamic element to defense. Bad guys attack and we move to defend. Anyone who is in a development role must realize that you can maintain security in your web applications during the actual development of those tools. A good rule of thumb is to assume all input to be hostile. Input validation is done so that only properly formed data can be placed in a web application field. The next time you pull up a form, check to see whether you can add letters in the field for a ZIP code. That field should accept numbers only, as well as only a certain number of numbers.

Encryption is another defense mechanism whether it's protecting data in transit or data at rest. You must implement an authentication plan, but the data those services shared must be encrypted in some way. An open, unsecured web service is a hacker's best friend, and there are algorithms that can crawl the web looking for this.

Another development-focused security tool to implement is exception handling. Think of the last time you mistyped your username and password. Did the error tell you it was your username or your password? Ideally, it should be generic. If the error message was that your password was incorrect, hackers now know that the username was correct and to focus their efforts on your password. In any case, the exception or error should reject or fail closed. An application that fails securely will prevent operations from happening that shouldn't.

Lastly, don't forget auditing and logging as well as quality assurance and testing. Logs often record suspicious activity and can provide individual accountability. If you can, hire a third-party service that specializes in penetration testing or vulnerability scanning. In college, one of the best practices was to have another person read your thesis. You become immune to your errors. You know what you meant to say, but did you say it right? Getting someone with expertise to give your application a test can make the difference between a multimillion dollar breach and no breach at all.

I'm lucky enough to call Chris Roberts, the Sidragon himself, a friend. I would hate to be unlucky enough to call him an enemy. Physically imposing, even when wearing a kilt and sporting a foot-long blue beard, he is one of the best security researchers out there and one of the nicest guys you'll ever meet. He says, "There are those of us in the know, we know what is going on and there are too many organizations out there saying, 'Oh, we are perfectly safe,' but we do have a hell of a lot of people who are unaware." We have to learn and evolve.

Burp Suite

Burp Suite is a Java-based web penetration testing graphical tool developed by PortSwigger Web Security. It has become an industry-standard suite of tools used by security professionals. There are three versions: the community edition that can be downloaded freely and the professional and enterprise versions that have a trial period. Burp Suite helps you identify vulnerabilities and verify attack vectors that are affecting your web applications. In its simplest form, Burp Suite can be used as a proxy server, scanner, and intruder.

While browsing a target application, penetration testers can configure their Internet browser to route traffic through the proxy server. Burp Suite then captures and analyzes each request to and from the target web application. This allows the interception, inspection, and possible modification of the raw traffic. Penetration testers can pause, manipulate, and replay individual HTTP requests to analyze potential parameters or injection points. Intruder can perform automated attacks on web applications. The tool can configure an algorithm that makes malicious HTTP requests as well as test for things like SQL injection and cross-site scripting (CSS). Certain injection points can be specified for manual as well as automated fuzzing attacks to discover potentially unintended application behaviors, crashes, and error messages. Fuzzing is a technique that allows you to test software by putting invalid or unexpected data into the computer program and monitor the behavior.

In Lab 11.2, you will be installing Burp Suite Community Edition.

LAB 11.2: INSTALLING AND CONFIGURING BURP SUITE COMMUNITY

1. To download the Burp Suite Community Edition, go to `https://portswigger.net/burp/communitydownload`. **As you see in Figure 11.8, there is a Windows edition as well as the plain JAR file.**

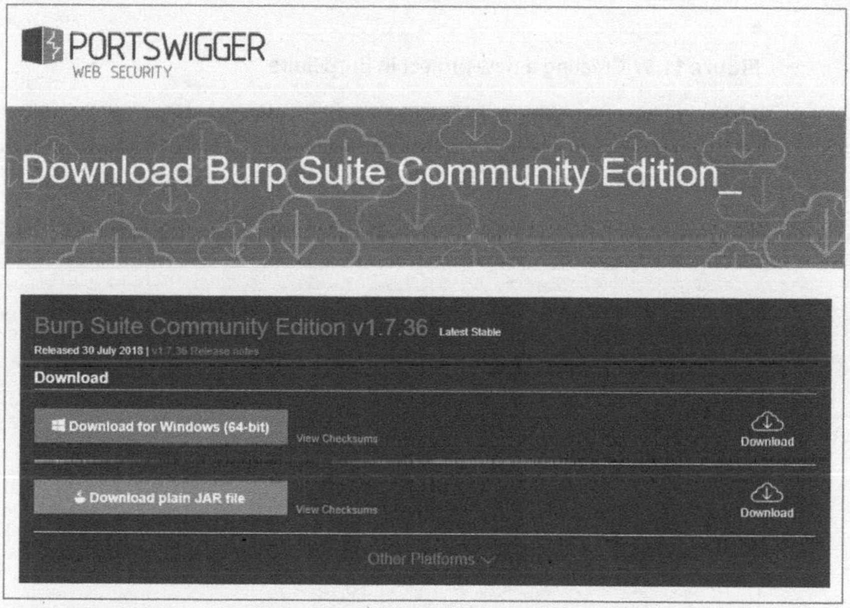

Figure 11.8: PortSwigger Web Security page for downloading Burp Suite Community Edition

2. Download the executable, open your Downloads folder, double-click the proper file, and follow the directions until you finish.

3. Navigate to the start menu, and search for Burp Suite to open the software. Load the Burp Suite defaults for your initial project and then click the Start Burp Suite button in the lower-right corner (see Figure 11.9).

Continues

LAB 11.2 (CONTINUED)

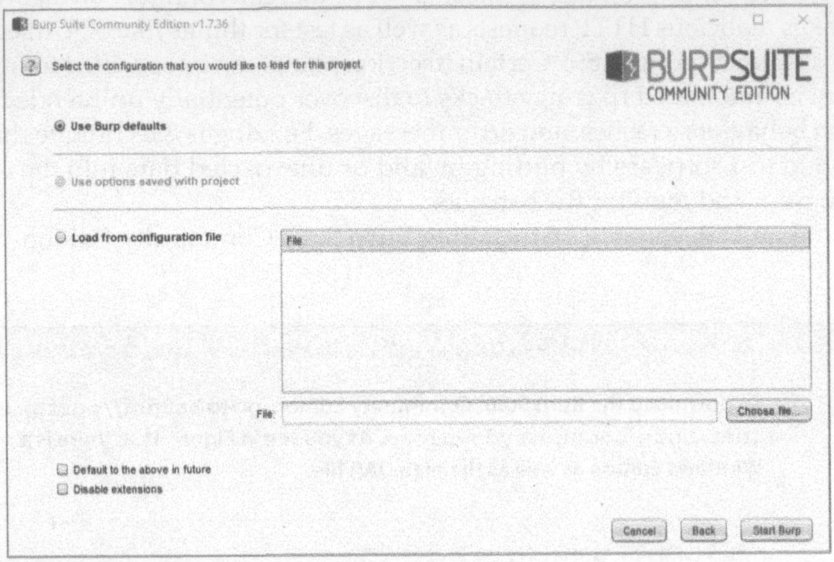

Figure 11.9: Creating a new project in Burp Suite

4. **After you have the temporary project loaded, click the User Settings tab to adjust any display settings. For example, you can change the font size and font as well as how you want HTTP messages to display, character sets, and HTML**

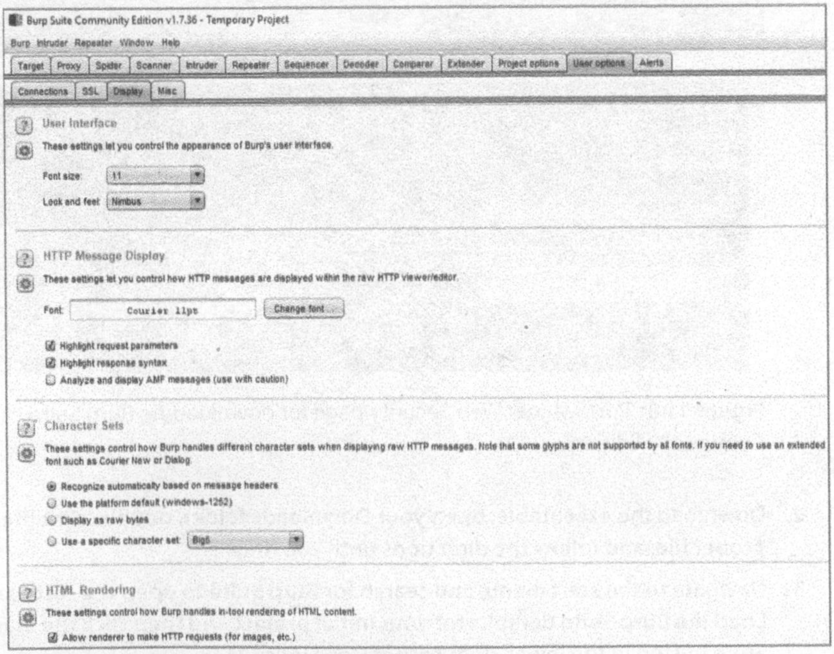

Figure 11.10: Configuring Burp Suite Community

rendering. As you can see in Figure 11.10, these settings will select how Burp Suite handles in-tool rendering of HTML content.

Next, you need to configure the proxy listener to make sure it is active and working. This will allow your browser to work with Burp Suite to serve as an HTTP proxy and have all HTTP/S traffic pass through Burp Suite. This will allow you to operate as a "man in the middle" between your browser and target web applications.

5. Under the Options subtab as seen in Figure 11.11, in the Proxy Listener section, you should see an entry in the table with the checkbox selected in the Running column, and 127.0.0.1:8080 showing in the Interface column. Click the Intercept tab and verify that "Intercept is on." Burp Suite now can intercept the traffic between you and your HTTP destination.

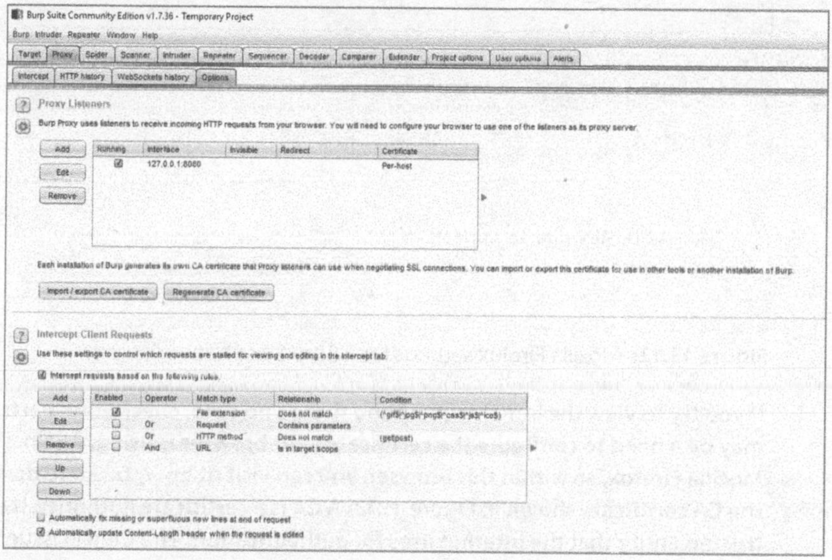

Figure 11.11: Configuring your browser to listen for traffic over the Internet

6. Open your browser and visit www.example.com. Burp Suite should show you each request you have made in the form of raw data. If you have raw data, click the Forward button to cycle through each request the browser has made for more data.

If the listener is not running, then Burp Suite was not able to open the default proxy listener port over port 8080. You will need to edit the port number of the listener to the proper port number for your device in Burp Suite or configure the browser of your choice to interact with Burp Suite. When using Burp Suite, I use Firefox as my browser because of the extensibility and ease of configuration. Go to the Firefox menu and select Preferences and then Options. Under the General tab, open Network Settings. As you see in Figure 11.12, you should configure the manual proxy to be 127.0.0.1 over port 80 and use this proxy for all protocols.

Continues

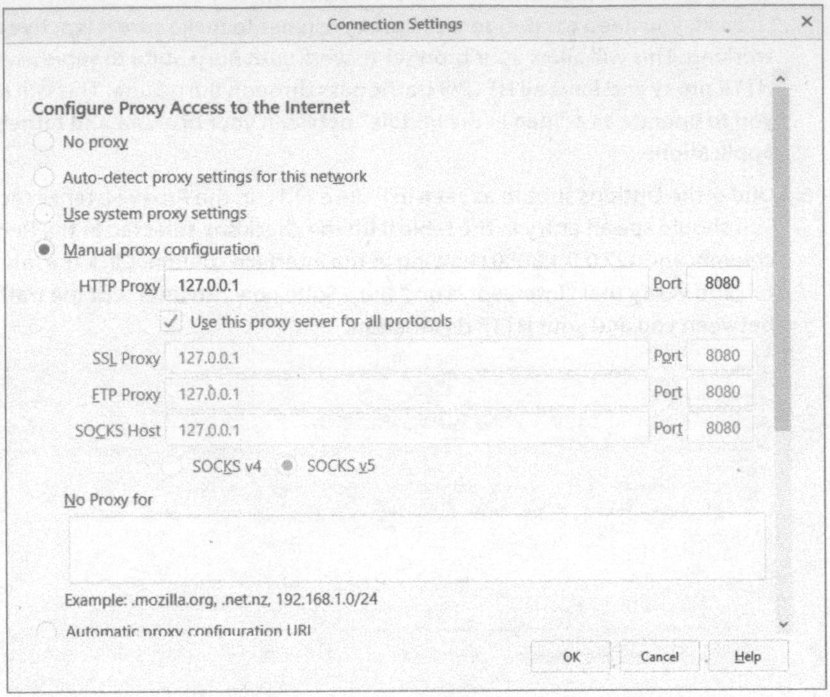

Figure 11.12: Mozilla Firefox settings for a Burp Suite network proxy

7. If you try to view the initial request and there's no data, check your alerts. There may be a need to configure the certificate your browser is using. Again, I prefer Mozilla Firefox, so within this browser, you can visit `http://burp` to download the CA certificate shown in Figure 11.13. A CA is a certificate authority. It is a trusted entity that the Internet uses for authentication. The CA will issue the SSL certificate that web browsers are going to use to authenticate content.

Figure 11.13: `http://burp`

8. Once you have the certificate downloaded, you will need to bring it into the browser. In Figure 11.14, you see the options for bringing the SSL certificate into Mozilla Firefox to be used by Burp Suite. According to Marissa "Reese" Morris, senior director of Firefox at Mozilla, "In the case of Burp Suite, the CA allows professionals to test their encrypted services for vulnerabilities."

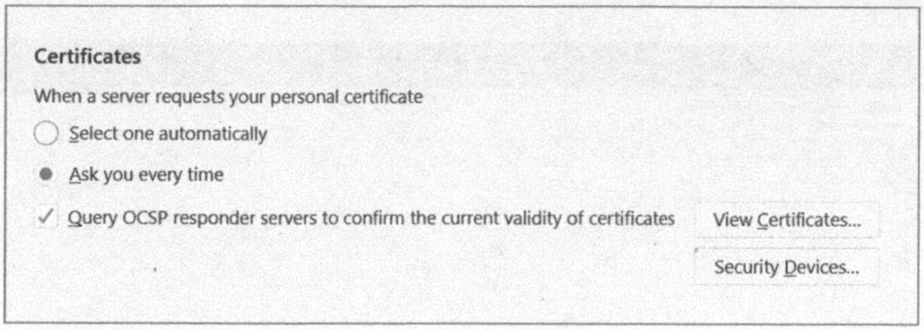

Certificates

When a server requests your personal certificate

○ Select one automatically

● Ask you every time

✓ Query OCSP responder servers to confirm the current validity of certificates   View Certificates...

Security Devices...

Figure 11.14: Loading the CA certificate into Firefox Preferences located under Privacy And Security

With only a little bit of effort, anyone can start using the core features of Burp Suite to test the security of his or her applications. Burp Suite is very intuitive and user-friendly, and the best way to start learning is by doing. These next steps will get you started with running Burp Suite and using some of the basic features.

The Proxy tool is the core of the product acting as a web proxy server. A proxy server is a server that sits between a web browser and a real server. As you request a file, connection, or web page, the proxy server examines the request for many reasons, such as control, simplification, or anonymity. In Burp Suite, the purpose is to inspect and possibly modify the raw traffic as it passes in both directions.

In Lab 11.3, you will be using core features of Burp Suite Community Edition.

LAB 11.3: USING BURP SUITE TO INTERCEPT HTTP TRAFFIC

1. Navigate to www.whatismyip.com to take note of your actual IP address. Knowing your true IP address is critical for any type of technical support across a network or connecting to an external device.

2. Each HTTP request made by your browser is displayed in the Intercept tab. You can view each message, and edit it if required. You then click the Forward button to send the request on to the destination web server. In fact, you may have to hit Forward many times until the page loads to cycle through all the requests.

   In Figure 11.15, you see the successful capture of information between the Firefox browser welcome page and Burp Suite. Click through each of the message editor tabs to see different ways to view the data. There will be the raw data, then more specifically the header content, and finally, hexadecimal.

3. While you're still in the Proxy tab, go to the HTTP History tab. Here you will have a table of all HTTP messages that have been intercepted. If you select an item in the table, you can go between the request and response.

Continues

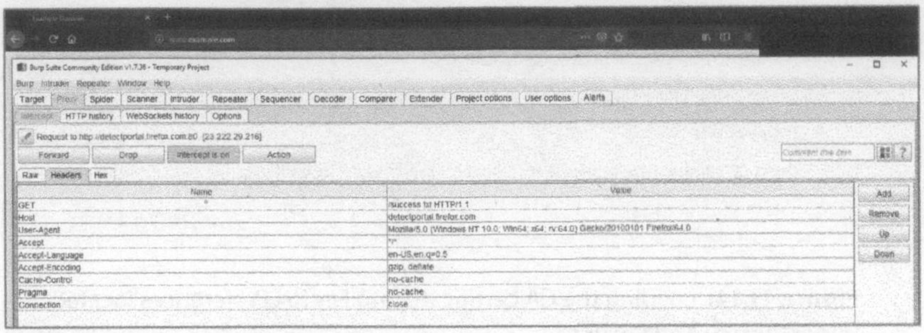

Figure 11.15: Web traffic captured over 127.0.0.1:8080 in the header view

4. Next, click a column header in the History table to sort the data. If you click it again, it will reverse the order whether it's numerical or alphabetical. In fact, you can use the column headers to sort data in any page.

5. As you're doing your analysis of web traffic in the HTTP History page, you can click the number in the first column to add a color. You can also right-click a row to add a comment for future reference.

Another key part of the user-driven workflow is the ability to take the same information and process it in different ways. You can right-click any entry representing traffic in the HTTP history and, if available, do a vulnerability scan of that request using the Burp Scanner. As you see in Figure 11.16, you also have the ability to take traffic and use it over and over again, making minute modifications of the request and reissue it over and over using the Repeater. With Sequencer, you can analyze the randomness in a token that is returned in the response that you receive.

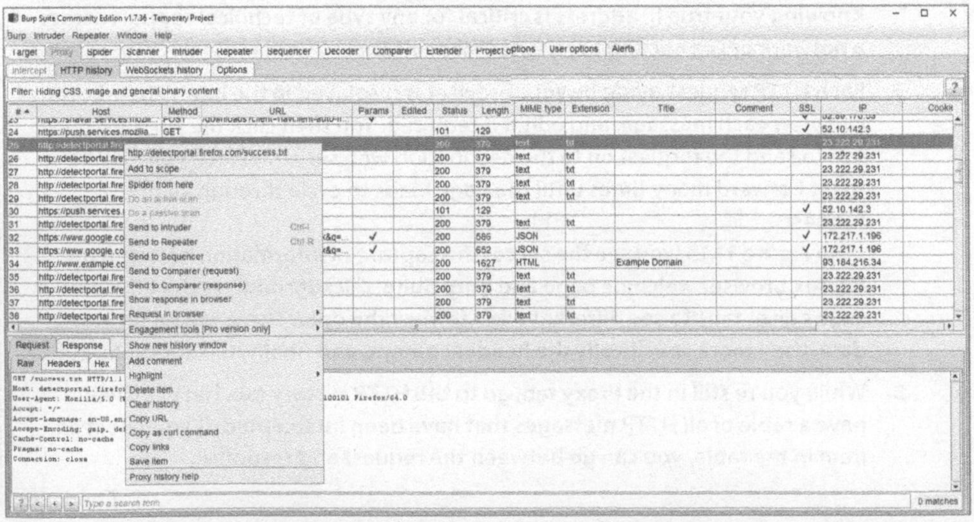

Figure 11.16: The channels you can take in analyzing individual HTTP requests in Burp Suite

Web application vulnerabilities will offer a huge amount of risk to an organization, especially to enterprise systems. Too many of the vulnerabilities are a result of lack of data validation, and bad actors can leverage that to misuse the application. Make a checklist and check everything. Best practice says check the outgoing, internal, and mail links. Test your forms for default values, and test your cookies to make sure they are deleted properly. Test HTML and CSS so there are no syntax errors and so that other search engines can crawl your site easily. Test the content and navigation as well as the database for integrity and response time.

A web application penetration tester will tell you it will be an arduous process and you are going to run into roadblocks. Deadlines will be a huge issue since everything is needed now, if not yesterday. Plan your work, know what is expected of the process, and create the best process for your organization.

# CHAPTER 12

Patch and Configuration Management

WHAT YOU WILL LEARN IN THIS CHAPTER:

➤ Patch Management

➤ ManageEngine Desktop Central

➤ Configuration Management

➤ Clonezilla live

I had so much fun this past October at the Wild West Hacking Fest (WWHF) in South Dakota. Conferences are a great way to connect to people who share the same interests as you, and when you get all that intelligence and weirdness in the same room, it's just phenomenal. I've been to BlackHat, DefCon, and BSides, but the WWHF by far has been the most hands-on con I've ever had the pleasure of attending. Any conference you attend and find yourself with James Lee (aka Egypt), the author of many Metasploit exploits, and Johnny Long, the original Google Dork, sitting across the table from you working on the same hack is a conference that you put on your agenda for the next year. Ed Skoudis was the keynote speaker and was able to give us the backstory to WebExec, the vulnerability in Cisco's WebEx client software. Ed's team at CounterHack discovered the vulnerability in July 2018 and worked with Cisco's PSIRT team to remediate. He was able to discuss the advisory at the conference on October 24, the day of his keynote speech.

One of the best things about the WWHF is that all the talks are online. If you can't get to South Dakota, you can still listen to all the talks given by subject-matter experts. Ed's keynote topic was the "Top 10 Reasons It's GREAT to Be a PenTester." Number 9 was Java and Adobe Flash. They are incredibly vulnerable, and so many organizations do not have a solid patch-management program. In fact, Magen Wu, senior associate at Urbane Security and my favorite red-shirted

Goon at DefCon, says that in her experience of small to medium businesses, only one business in five has a well-documented patch-management policy in place. That's not good.

Patch management is a vital area of systems management. As your security model matures, it becomes necessary to develop a strategy for managing patches and upgrades to systems and software. Most software patches are necessary to fix existing problems with software that are discovered after the initial release. A great many of these are security focused. Other patches might have to do with some type of specific addition or enhancement to functionality of software. As you see in Figure 12.1, the patch management lifecycle is similar to the vulnerability management lifecycle I discussed in Chapter 4, "OpenVAS: Vulnerability Management."

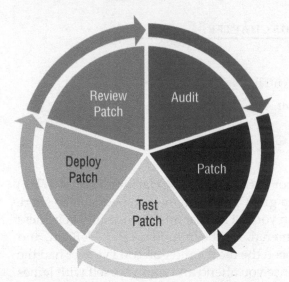

Figure 12.1: The patch management lifecycle

Patch Management

I believe there are two deadly attitudes in cybersecurity: "This is how we have always done it" and "It will never happen to me." On March 14, 2017, Microsoft issued a critical security bulletin for the MS17-010. This vulnerability, nicknamed EternalBlue, was an exploit written by the National Security Agency (NSA) and was leaked to the general public by the Shadow Brokers hacker group exactly one month later. EternalBlue exploits a Microsoft SMB vulnerability and, in short, the NSA warned Microsoft about the theft of the exploit allowing the company to prepare a patch. Too many people did not install the patch, and in May of the same year, the WannaCry ransomware virus used the EternalBlue exploit to infect these vulnerable systems. More emergency patches were released by Microsoft. Again, many people did not patch, and in June, NotPetya malware swamped the globe, focusing on the Ukraine in June 2017.

Have you ever watched a horror movie and thought to yourself, "That was your first mistake . . . that was your second . . . and third . . ."? If organizations had been paying attention in March, they would have been fine. If they had paid attention in April, they would have learned how to circumvent the exploit. Again, in May and then again in June, patches could have been run and problem averted. The exploit is still a problem today and has morphed into many variations, targeting the cryptocurrency industry with malware called WannaMine. *Cryptojacking* is a term we use to define the process where malware silently infects a victim's computer and then uses that machine's resources to run very complex decryption routines that create currency. Monero is a cryptocurrency that can be added to a digital wallet and spent. It sounds fairly harmless, but thinking back to the CIA triad, you are losing your CPU and RAM resources to the malware, and it can spread across your network. If you think of the volumes of processing power and bandwidth it will consume in your organization, you definitely don't want this infection.

The lesson learned is that we must keep our systems up-to-date. In your patch management program, you will have to include operating system patches and updates for Microsoft, Apple, and Linux as well as third-party applications such as Chrome, Firefox, Java, and Adobe Flash. You may have other software or firmware on your network. If you have a system with software, you must have security policy outlining when to patch systems. If you take the risk of not patching, you will leave your systems vulnerable to an attack that is preventable.

The patch management lifecycle will start with an audit where you scan your environment for needed patches. After you know which patches are needed and before you roll out those updates to the entire organization, test those patches on a nonproduction system. If you do not, you take the risk of breaking something with what should have fixed it. If you are able to identify issues before a global production rollout, your operations should not be impacted. Once you know what patches are missing and which patches are viable, install them on the vulnerable system. Most of the time, this is done with Windows Update. Most enterprise-sized organizations will use some type of patch management software solution.

Focusing on your most vulnerable systems like those running Windows operating systems, as well as highly vulnerable third-party programs like Adobe Flash, Adobe Reader, and Java, is one of patch management's key concepts. Starting with your most risky yet mission-critical devices allows you to allocate time and resources where they will be best utilized and will provide the most risk mitigation.

Depending on the size of your organization, how many people you have on your cybersecurity team, the hours they can devote to patch management, and how many systems need to be kept up-to-date, you may want to utilize third-party patch management software. For Microsoft patching specifically, Microsoft includes a tool called Windows Server Update Services (WSUS) with all Windows Server operating systems. WSUS may be sufficient, unless you are using other third-party applications like Adobe Flash or Java. There are several open-source tools available, but I have used and like the ease of deploying Desktop Central by ManageEngine.

ManageEngine Desktop Central is web-based, desktop management software. It can remotely manage and schedule updates for Windows, Mac, and Linux, both in local area networks and across wide area networks. In addition to patch management, software installation, and service pack management, you can also use it to standardize desktops. You can use it to keep your images current and synchronized by applying the same wallpapers, shortcuts, printer settings, and much more.

Desktop Central is free for small businesses and supports one technician across 25 computers and 25 mobile devices. Its professional and enterprise versions make it scalable as your business grows. The free edition still gives you access to all the essential features of the software, and it is easy to set up.

In Lab 12.1, you'll be installing Desktop Central by ManageEngine.

LAB 12.1: INSTALLING DESKTOP CENTRAL

1. Browse to `https://www.manageengine.com`. In the upper-right corner of the screen, open the search field by clicking the magnifying glass. Type **Desktop Central**. The Download link will be one of your options.

2. Choose the appropriate architecture, either 32 bit or 64 bit. The file should automatically download to the Downloads folder. Before you leave the page, should you need to register for free technical support, you can do that here.

3. Navigate to your Download folder. Find the `ManageEngine_DesktopCentral` executable and double-click it.

4. During the install process, you will get a warning to define exceptions for the `c:\ManageEngine` directory. Antivirus could possibly interfere with database files. Check to make sure your antivirus is turned off during installation.

5. DesktopCentral also uses port 8020 by default for the web server port. If you are using port 8020 for another service or software, you can change it during this process. Keep the rest of the defaults and finish the installation. It will take a few minutes.

6. Once the installation finishes, double-click the new icon on your desktop to start DesktopCentral. To open the DesktopCentral Client, open your browser to `http://localhost:8020`. Figure 12.2 shows the login page.

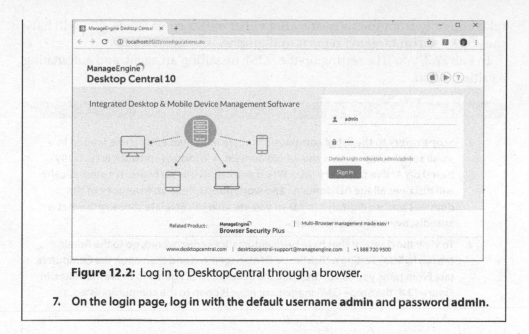

Figure 12.2: Log in to DesktopCentral through a browser.

7. On the login page, log in with the **default username admin** and password **admin**.

The patch management process begins with the installation of an agent. Once the agent is downloaded and installed from the Scope of Management (SOM) page, it will scan the system it is installed on, and you can view the missing patches. At that point, you can either install patches manually or automate and schedule the patching process. As you see in Figure 12.3, which is a screenshot

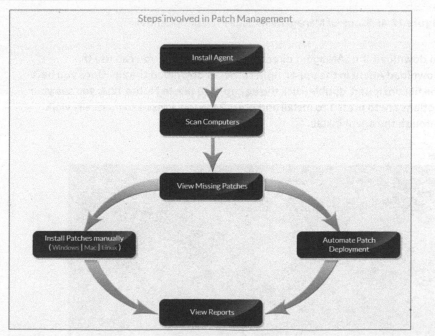

Figure 12.3: Patch management processes in DesktopCentral

taken directly from the software, after either of those processes, you will have the ability to run targeted reports and graphs.

In Lab 12.2, you'll be setting up the SOM, installing an agent, and automating a critical patch.

LAB 12.2: INSTALLING DESKTOP CENTRAL AGENTS

1. Scope refers to the list of computers that are managed and can be limited to a small set of computers or the whole domain. A Windows network is typically based on Active Directory (AD). When you install this software, it automatically will discover all the AD domains and workgroups. Take an inventory of the domains and workgroups in AD so you are able to correlate those with what is autodiscovered in the next step.

2. To view the domains that have been automatically discovered, go to the Admin tab, go to SOM Settings, click Scope Of Management and then open the Computers tab. From here, you can orchestrate the installation of agents to those machines. In Figure 12.4, the Scope Of Management page is open to the computers listed.

Figure 12.4: Scope Of Management page in DesktopCentral

3. To download the LAN agent directly from the console, you can use the Download Agent in the upper-right corner to download the zip. Once you have the file unzipped, double-click the `setup.bat` file. In Figure 12.5, you see your options are to press 1 to install and press 2 to stop. Press 1 to manually walk through the agent install.

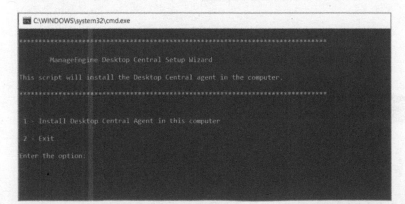

Figure 12.5: Downloading and installing the agent manually to a Windows system

4. Refresh the Computers page, and the system you added the agent to should appear. Navigate to the Home menu and click Patch Management. From here, you are able to see exactly what patches are installed and which ones are missing as well as graphics on system health and missing patches based on severity. Figure 12.6 shows the example Windows machine missing a Java Runtime patch, which happens to fall into the Top 20 Vulnerabilities.

Figure 12.6: The Dashboard page of Patch Management in Desktop Central

5. On the left side of the console, under the Dashboard icon, click the Patches icon directly underneath. In the list on the right is a breakdown of patches that are needed. You can install, download, or decline a patch as well as see detailed information linked to this patch, including the patch ID and bulletin ID. You can click a link to learn more about the specific patch that is necessary to the health of the system. Figure 12.7 shows the Java vulnerability information and what system is lacking the patch and platform.

6. Click the patch ID of the vulnerability you want to patch and then click Install Patch. In Figure 12.7, you see the Install/Uninstall Windows Patch page based on the operation type with the scheduler and deployment settings. If you have any critical patch vulnerabilities, check them and deploy immediately. You could also choose to deploy a patch after a specific number of days to make sure it is stable.

Continues

LAB 12.2 (CONTINUED)

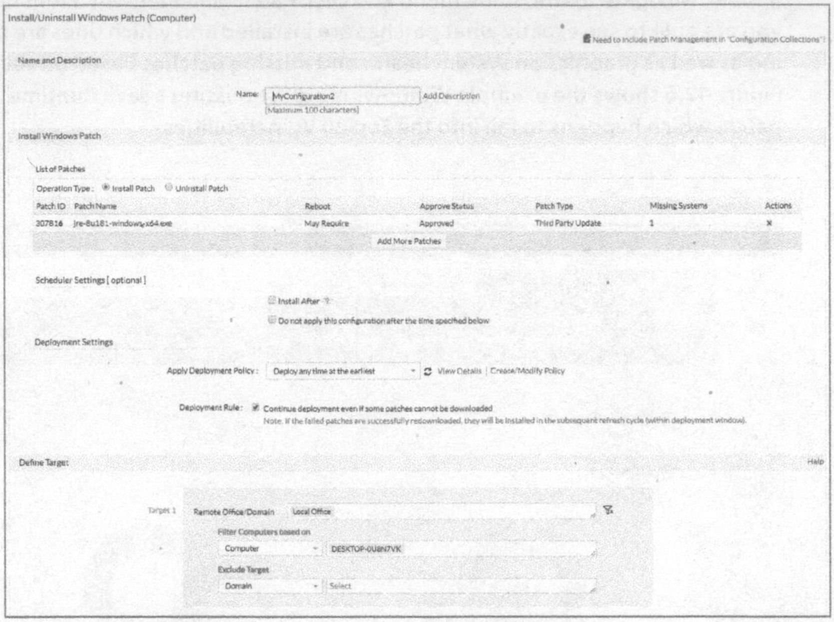

Figure 12.7: Install/Uninstall Windows Patch configuration

The target machine will get a pop-up message, stating that the DeskCentral Administrator is applying packages to your machine. The console shifts to the Deployment page where you can watch the current status of the patch move from Yet To Be Applied to In Progress to Succeeded. As shown in Figure 12.8, you'll get the details of the patch process configuration and execution status as well as summary in graph form.

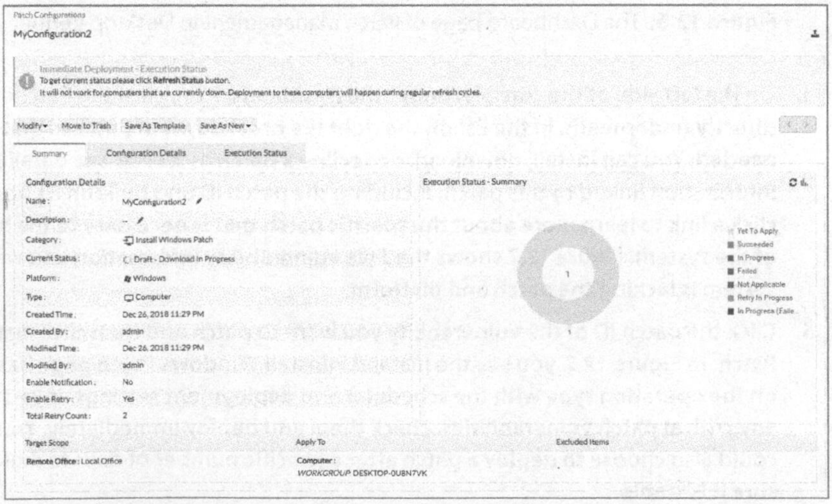

Figure 12.8: Deployment execution status for patch management of a Java vulnerability

The time between the discovery of a vulnerability and the action an IT administrator should take to protect the environment from that vulnerability should be as short as possible, especially on assets that are mission critical. That philosophy can possibly cause issues where rapid patch management causes a problem with change management and quality assurance testing. It will be a balance evaluating the risk of an unpatched system with the possibly of breaking systems in the process of fixing it. Creating a patch management program where you document your strategy for establishing, documenting, and maintaining the changes is the beginning. The next level in your security maturity model should be configuration management. You must have a hardened baseline.

Configuration Management

In 2010, I was hired for a Department of Defense (DoD) contract to help deploy the technical assets for the newly formed Air Force Global Strike Command (AFGSC) with Lt. General Klotz in command. The AFGSC mission was to manage the U.S. Air Force (USAF) portion of the U.S. nuclear arsenal. With a newly formed team of 10, the decision was made to split up the team based on our strengths, and I ended up in the lab with someone who was to become one of my very best friends, newly retired Master Sergeant Robert Bills. He is the type of IT guy who does IT for the fun of it. His call sign in the lab was Crazy Talk because sometimes solving the problem was so obvious it was crazy.

When we walked into the lab, the process was to take a Windows XP, Windows Vista, or Windows 7 .iso of an operating system, burn it to a DVD, and image a single machine. After imaging, patching, joining to the domain, adding the appropriate software, and then forcing group policy on the system, it could take 7 to 10 days to get just one machine ready for the end user. Over the next two years, we developed a system using master images, an old 40-port Cisco switch, and a whole lot of cable to scale down the deployment process to about 45 minutes per machine with a hardened gold image built especially for the division it was intended for.

Some administrators refer to a golden image as a master image that can be used to clone and deploy other devices consistently. System cloning is an effective method of establishing a baseline configuration for your organization. It requires effort and expertise to establish and maintain images for deployment. However, the ability to push a tested and secure system image to your devices can save countless hours per tech refresh. In fact, our images were so good, the other technicians in other divisions would take them to the field to reimage machines that were having issues rather than troubleshoot the problem. It took less time to image them than to fix them.

To start this process in your organization, build an inventory of every server, router, switch, printer, laptop, desktop, and mobile device in your environment that is going to be connected to the network by using some of the tools we have already explored. Ideally, the inventory list should be dynamically and automatically collected. Manually entering an inventory list into a spreadsheet is not scalable and opens up opportunities for human error. This should include the location, hostname, IP address, MAC address, and operating system. For servers, identifying the function and services running on those systems is also helpful.

After you have an inventory of systems, you need to configure the image you will use in the future for all servers and workstations. I have worked with small to medium businesses whose idea of provisioning a laptop for a new user is to order one from New Egg, open the box, hand the new employee the machine, and let him or her set it up. If you accept the default options on a Windows machine, how many vulnerabilities are sitting there out in the open?

Security is about balance. Considering the CIA triad, use caution when securing a workstation. Some organizations lock down their systems so hard they make it difficult for end users to do their job. Some organizations do nothing to preconfigure a system and leave themselves vulnerable. There are a couple of free tools you can use to compare a configuration to a predetermined template.

Microsoft has a Security Configuration and Analysis tool that is free. It is a stand-alone snap-in tool that users can add to import one or more saved configurations. Importing configurations builds a specific security database that stores a composite configuration. You can apply this composite configuration to the computer and analyze the current system configuration against the baseline configuration stored in the database. These configurations are saved as text-based .inf files.

In Lab 12.3, you'll be adding the Security Configuration and Analysis (SCA) tool to a Microsoft Management Console (MMC).

LAB 12.3: ADDING THE SCA TO THE MMC

1. Open your Microsoft Management Console by going to the Start menu and searching for *MMC*.

2. Under File, scroll down to Add/Remove Snap In. You will have many choices to add to this customizable console.

3. Navigate down to Security Configuration And Analysis, click to select this tool, and click the Add> button in the middle of the screen (see Figure 12.9). Add the Security Template add-in too.

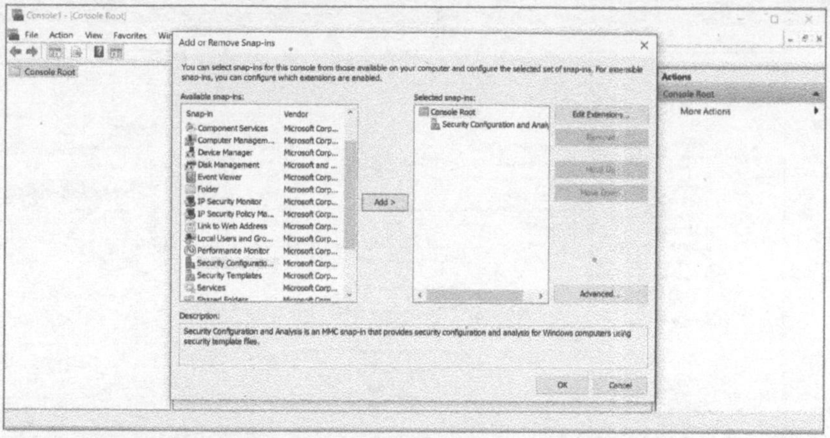

Figure 12.9: Building the Security Configuration And Analysis MMC

4. Save the MMC using the Save As button. (As you can see In Figure 12.10, I have saved this customized MMC as SecurityConfig.) Click the OK button.

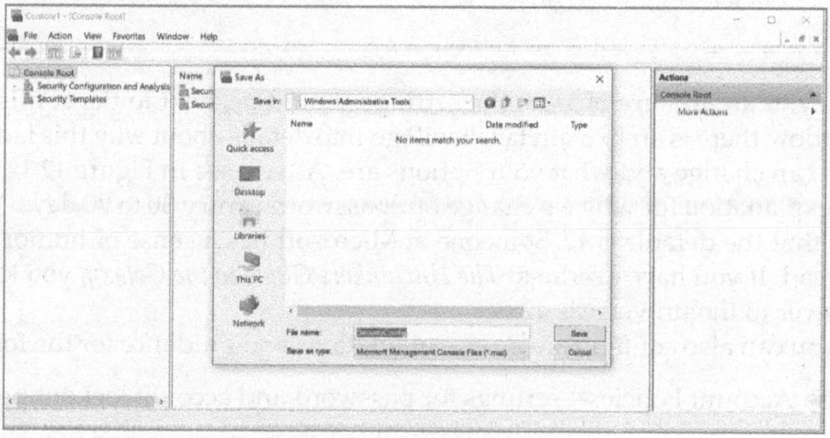

Figure 12.10: Saving the SecurityConfig MMC for future use

5. On the left side of the screen, find the Security Templates snap-in and use the arrow to open each menu through the console tree. When you get to the template path, right-click the path. Choose the New Template command from the shortcut menu. When prompted, enter a name for the template that you are creating. You can see what the newly created template looks like in Figure 12.11. Drill down into each policy to configure appropriate settings for your environment.

Continues

LAB 12.3 (CONTINUED)

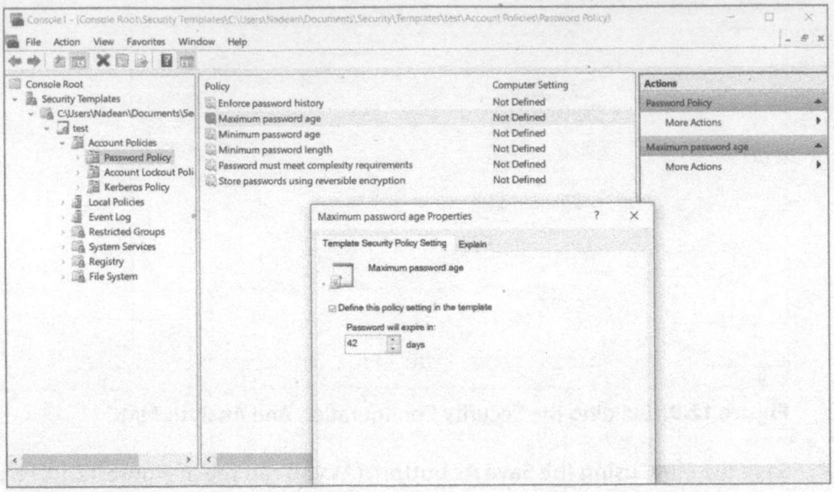

Figure 12.11: Configuring the test security template's Maximum Password Age policy

If you are unsure of what the settings should be, next to the configuration window there is an Explain tab. It will go into details about why this is a feature you can change and what your options are. As you see in Figure 12.12, there is an explanation for why we change our passwords every 30 to 90 days. You also see that the default is 42. Someone at Microsoft has a sense of humor or likes to read. If you have ever read *The Hitchhikers Guide to the Galaxy*, you know the answer to the universe is 42.

You can also configure and see explanations and guidance for the following:

- Account Policies—settings for password and account lockout policy
- Event Logs—manage controls for Application, System, and Security events
- File Systems—manage file and folder permissions
- Local Policies—user rights and security options
- Registry—permission for registry keys
- System Services—manage startup and permission for services

You can use the Security Configuration And Analysis tool to configure a computer or to analyze a computer. For an established Windows machine, you will want to perform an analysis. To do so, right-click the Security Configuration And Analysis option, and select the Analyze Computer Now command from the shortcut menu. When prompted, enter the desired log file path, and click OK.

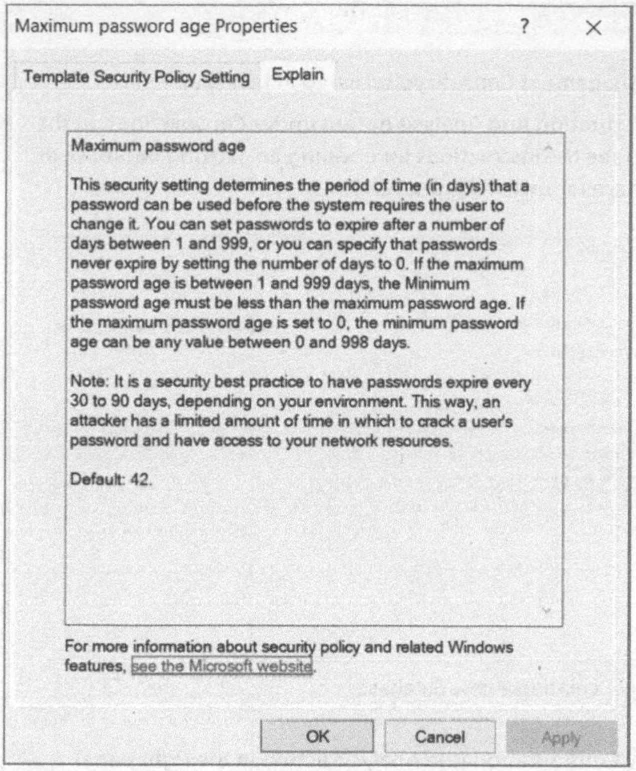

Figure 12.12: Microsoft explanation of password-policy best practices

You can compare the template settings against the computer's settings. As you analyze the comparison, pay attention to the icons associated with the policy setting. A green icon indicates that the setting is defined within the template, and the PC is compliant with that setting. A gray icon indicates that the setting is undefined in the template, and a red icon indicates that the setting is defined within the template, but the machine is not compliant.

As stated earlier, a security template is a plain-text file that takes an `.inf` extension. This means it's possible to copy, edit, and manipulate security templates using nothing more than a text editor. It is better to work from an existing template file. So, always begin working on security templates by opening an existing template; then always use the Save As command to save it under a new name. If you use the Save command but find you have made a mistake in the configuration, you have nothing to restore. From experience, it is much easier to save the original and change the next template to keep working templates working and leave default templates in a restorable state.

In Lab 12.4, you'll be analyzing a system with a configuration `.inf` file.

LAB 12.4: COMPARING A HOST TO AN .INF FILE

1. Open the Microsoft Management Console you created in Lab 12.3.

2. Click the Security Configuration And Analysis option under Console Root. In the middle workspace, you see the instructions for opening an existing database or how to create a new one, as shown in Figure 12.13.

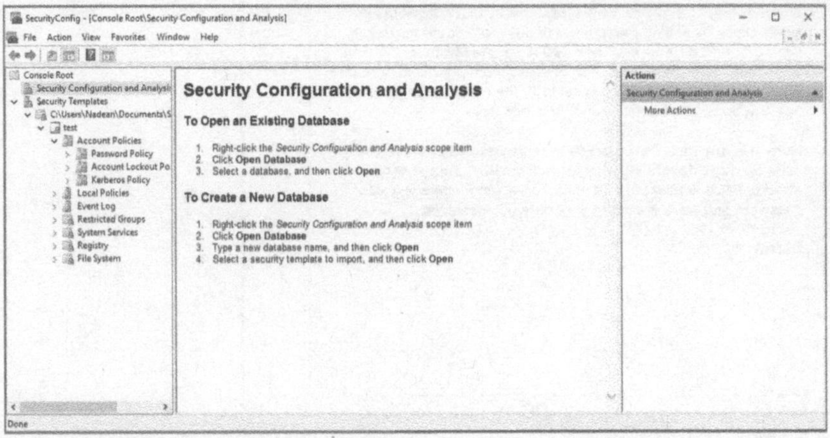

Figure 12.13: Opening or creating a new database

3. Right-click the Security Configuration And Analysis action in the right panel and select Open Database.

4. Type in a new database name and click Open in the Import Template dialog box. Select the template you modified in Lab 12.3 and then click Open (see Figure 12.14).

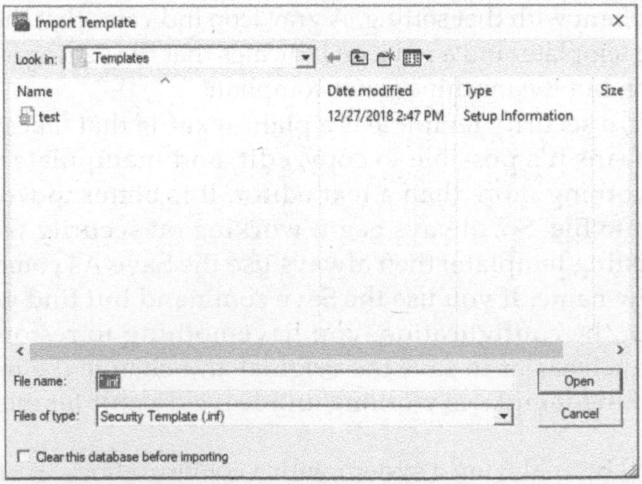

Figure 12.14: Opening the template created in Lab 12.3 with modifications

> 5. To analyze your system and compare the new `.inf` file to your existing system, right-click Security Configuration And Analysis and choose Analyze System Now in the Management Console. You also have the option of configuring the system to the `.inf` file. The log file should display automatically, showing what was reconfigured successfully.

Microsoft also has a Security Configuration Toolkit, published in late 2018, that offers the ability to compare current group policies with a Microsoft-recommended Group Policy or other baselines, edit them, and store them. As you see in Figure 12.15, the toolkit is available to download. Currently supported operating systems include Windows 10, Windows 8.1, Windows 7, Windows Server 2008, Windows Server 2008 R2, Windows Server 2012, Windows Server 2012 R2, Windows Server 2016, and Windows Server 2019.

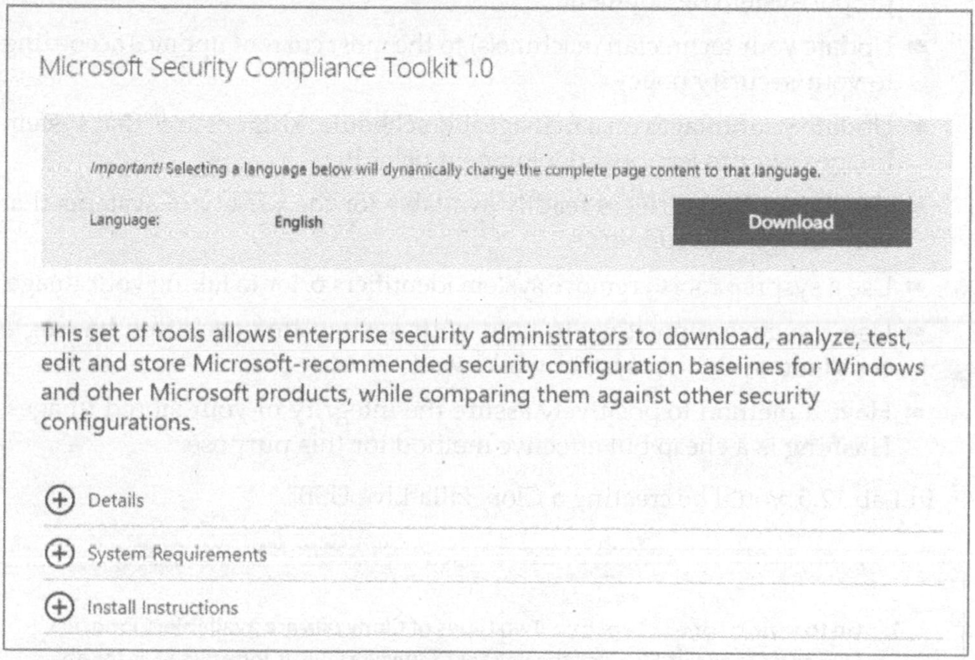

Microsoft Security Compliance Toolkit 1.0

Important! Selecting a language below will dynamically change the complete page content to that language.

Language: English   Download

This set of tools allows enterprise security administrators to download, analyze, test, edit and store Microsoft-recommended security configuration baselines for Windows and other Microsoft products, while comparing them against other security configurations.

⊕ Details

⊕ System Requirements

⊕ Install Instructions

Figure 12.15: Microsoft Security Compliance Toolkit 1.0

Now that you have the asset configured with all the proper policies and patched, it is time to prepare it for cloning.

Clonezilla Live

Using any of the freely available imaging solutions like Clonezilla is an efficient way to create a fully configured and patched system image for distribution on your network. Clonezilla can be implemented from a server or a bootable device and permits users a variety of options based on their needs. One of the more flexible options of this solution can be deployed using a portable drive. This drive can contain prestaged images for on-site deployment. Sometimes you will have a situation where a machine will not boot to the network or it is against regulations to move an ailing asset and using a portable drive is ideal.

If you have an on-site technician lab, you can create an effective cloning system using a server machine, one or more technician machines, and a network switch to facilitate deployment to multiple systems at once. Many environments have this equipment sitting unused on a shelf. In practice, this simple setup has been shown to be able to image and deploy more than 100 systems in a single week.

Some best practices to consider when deciding to clone systems versus original media installations include the following:

- Use an established checklist for pre- and post-imaging actions to ensure proper system deployment.

- Update your technician machine(s) to the most current updates according to your security policy.

- Update your images on a manageable schedule. This ensures that system images require less post-deployment patching.

- Have important drivers readily available for the variety of systems that your image will support.

- Use a sysprep tool to remove system identifiers prior to taking your image.

- Use a secure repository to hold your system images; often having a stand-alone cloning system works well.

- Have a method to positively assure the integrity of your stored images. Hashing is a cheap but effective method for this purpose.

In Lab 12.5, you'll be creating a Clonezilla Live USB.

LAB 12.5: CREATING A CLONEZILLA LIVE USB

1. **Go to** www.clonezilla.org. **Two types of Clonezilla are available: Clonezilla Live and Clonezilla SE. Click the link for Clonezilla Live. (Clonezilla SE is for an enterprise, where Clonezilla Live is for a single backup and restore. I personally have had multiple USBs in action at the same time.)**

2. **For a USB flash drive or USB hard drive install, find the document link for this type of boot media.**

3. **There are several methods to format a USB drive so that it is bootable. I have used Rufus USB creator and found it to be very lightweight, fast, and user friendly. Follow the directions to download and install Rufus. Run the** Rufus. exe **and download the Clonezilla Live** .iso **file for the architecture you are running.**

4. Plug in your USB flash drive or USB hard drive. Rufus will auto-detect the device. Under boot selection, make sure that `.iso` is selected and then choose Select.

5. Navigate to the location where you downloaded the Clonezilla `.iso` and choose that file and double-click to open it.

6. Review the options, volume label, and cluster size. As you see in Figure 12.16, I usually leave the defaults.

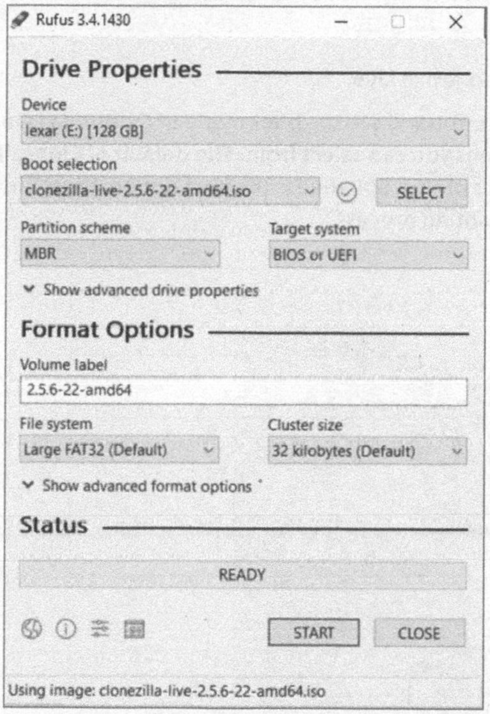

Figure 12.16: Configuring Rufus with the Clonezilla .iso

7. Click Start. You will get a warning that all data on the drive will be erased. Click OK, and the status bar will let you know what Is currently happening on that drive. You may think nothing is happening, but as long as the timer in the lower-right corner is running, the USB is being formatted, partitioned, and `.iso` loaded. The status bar will turn green and display "Ready" when it has completed.

Once you have built your Clonezilla Live USB, you can boot your target machine with it. You may have to edit the BIOS of the machine to be able to boot to USB. Set USB as the first priority when you edit the BIOS. With Clonezilla Live, you are able to save an image and restore that image. In Clonezilla Live, two accounts are available. The first account is "user" with sudo privilege, and the password is "live." A sudo account will allow users to run programs with the security privileges of a superuser. Sudo means "superuser do." The second account is an administration account "root" with no password. You cannot log in as root. If you need root privilege, you can log in as **user** and run `sudo -i` to become root.

In Lab 12.6, you'll be creating a Clonezilla Live image.

LAB 12.6: CREATING A CLONEZILLA LIVE IMAGE

1. Boot the machine via USB Clonezilla Live.

2. The USB is the software host. You will see the boot menu of Clonezilla Live. Figure 12.17 shows the options you can select from. The default of Clonezilla Live with the default settings of VGA 800×600 is the best option. Press Enter, you will see Debian Linux booting process.

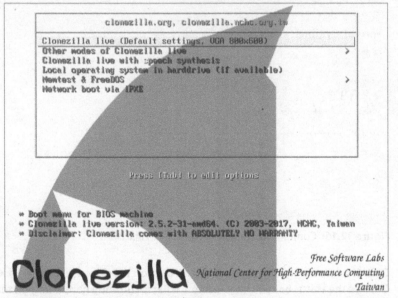

Figure 12.17: Clonezilla Live boot menu

3. The next configuration page has you choose language and keyboard by using the up and down arrows to select the correct option. (As you can see in Figure 12.18, I chose "Don't touch keymap" to keep the layout of a QWERTY keyboard.) For the purposes of this lab, leave the defaults as they are and press Enter and then Start Clonezilla.

4. Choose the `device-image` option from the next step. This will allow you to work with disks or partitions by creating an image.

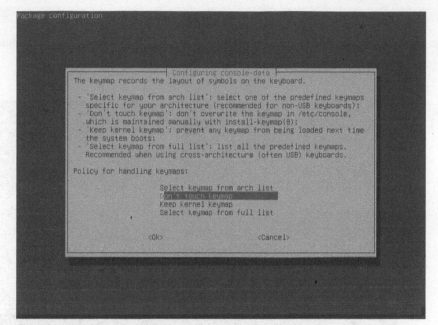

Figure 12.18: Preparing the Clonezilla Live environment

5. **Choose the** `local_dev` **option to assign** `sdb1` **as the image home, as shown in Figure 12.19. Wait for the instructions to insert the USB into the machine and then wait 5 seconds before pressing Enter.**

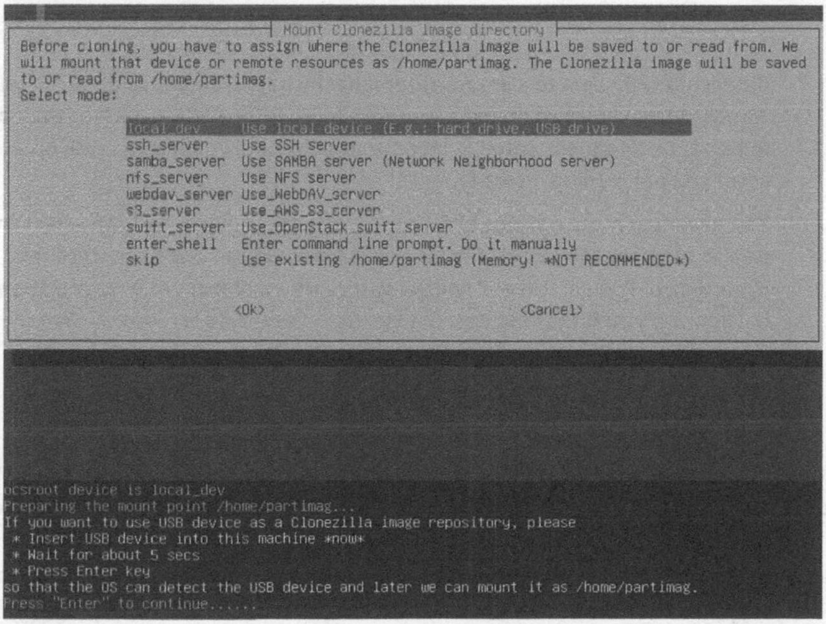

Figure 12.19: Assigning where the Clonezilla image will be saved or read from

Continues

6. Select `sdb1` as the image repository, keep the Beginner mode, and then choose the `savedisk` option to save the local disk as an image, as shown in Figure 12.20.

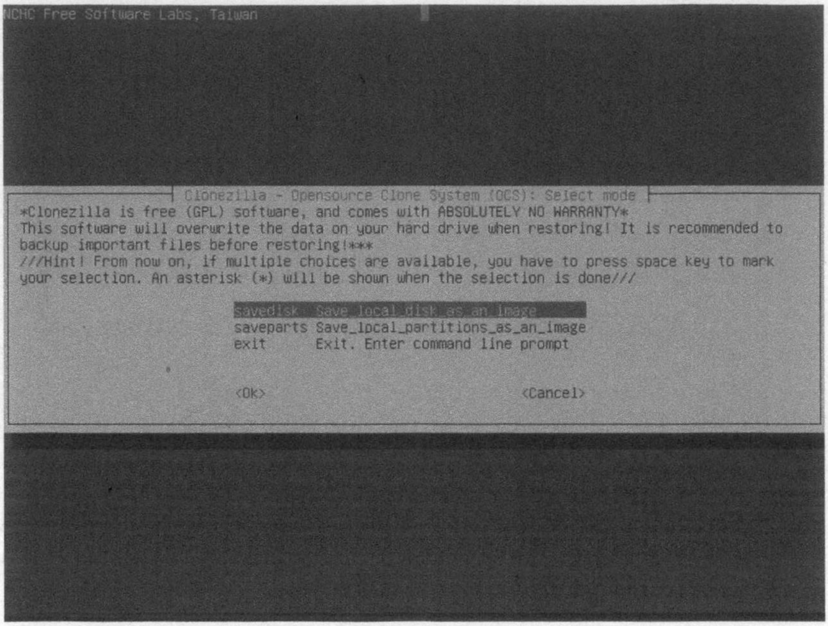

Figure 12.20: Saving the current disk to an image

7. Clonezilla will name this image automatically based on day and time. If you want, you can edit this image name with more information, such as the operating system, and press Enter. Select the source disk, which is the disk on the asset you are cloning. Press Enter.

8. You have two more options before the clone takes place. You can select the option to check the cloned file for errors, and you can opt to encrypt this cloned disk. The default will check the disk for error but not encrypt. There is no backdoor if you forget the passphrase. Now Clonezilla is ready to save the disk image after you have made those choices. Press Enter.

When in doubt, keep the defaults except at the end of the cloning configuration. When everything is finished, choose `-p poweroff` as your final selection because this will shut off the machine. If you are not paying very close attention at the end of this cloning process, it could restart the entire process since you are booting with a USB, and you'll end up right back at step 1 of configuring the clone. (Yes, that has happened to me many times.) You won't forget to properly eject the USB and accidentally corrupt it.

To restore the image, follow steps 1 through 5 in Lab 12.6. At that point in the process, you should choose `restoredisk` instead of `savedisk`. Choose the image name you just cloned and then the destination disk where you want to deploy the image.

With Clonezilla SE, I've been on a team that imaged over 100 new machines a week. When I was teaching at Fort Carson, we had two classrooms with 18 computers each and 36 laptops that we recycled the image on every month. I would harden the OS and then load all the files that students would need for the CompTIA, ISC2, Microsoft, and Cisco classes. The certification boot camps we taught were either 5 days or 10 days, or for CISSP, 15-day classes. Class ended Friday at 5 p.m., and the next class started Monday at 8 a.m. We needed to be fast and as efficient as possible. Remember, my job is to make your life easier, and these are tools that will help.

# CHAPTER 13

Securing OSI Layer 8

WHAT YOU WILL LEARN IN THIS CHAPTER:

➤ Human Nature

➤ Social Engineering Attacks

➤ Education

➤ The Social Engineer Toolkit

> "The definition of insanity is doing the same thing over and over again and expecting a different result."
>
> *Quote attributed to Albert Einstein*

> "There are three kinds of men: The ones who learn by reading, the few who learn by observation. The rest of them have to pee on the electric fence for themselves."
>
> *Will Rogers*

Most people think that cyberattackers are going to use high-tech, very advanced techniques to hack into their accounts and infect their systems. The simple truth is that the easiest way to hack a system is through human hacking or social engineering. Kevin Mitnick, world-renowned social engineer says, "Companies spend millions of dollars on firewalls and secure access devices, and it's money wasted because none of these measures address the weakest link in the security chain: the people who use, administer, and operate computer systems." It takes only one person clicking one link and downloading one malicious exploit.

Human Nature

We are funny creatures, we humans. We have put men on the moon and nearly wiped out polio on the face of the earth, but when faced with the elevator not coming as fast as we like, we press the button over and over thinking it might speed things up a bit. If I am waiting at the elevator with you, I have already made several assumptions about you and your need to get where you're going as quickly as possible. First impressions are very important in social engineering. You have approximately 8 seconds before people will have a solid impression of who you are, and it is difficult to overcome a first impression.

Social engineering is practiced every day by everyone in every walk of life. If you have ever had a job interview, you attempted to social engineer the interviewer into giving you the job. If you have ever had a first date, you were attempting to make someone like you enough to go on a second one. Social engineering is when person A attempts to manipulate person B into doing what person A wants person B to do. It doesn't have to be malicious or evil. It could simply be a marketing company trying to sell you a car you don't really need. It could be a political candidate campaigning for your vote or a magazine telling you what you should wear. Social engineering is using influence by whatever means necessary to get what you want. It could be a vote, a sale, a vacation, or your administrative credentials.

In cybersecurity, this is done through any type of social interaction whether in person, over the phone, or over the Internet. The absolute best defense is training and education. If you can recognize that someone is attempting to influence you, you become hyperaware to the attempt. If you look at the results of the DEFCON Social Engineering Capture the Flag (CTF), it is obvious that the winners employ the "6 Principles of Persuasion" laid out by Professor Robert Caildini. In his research and what he believes to be the science behind getting people to say "yes" are six fundamentals that guide human behavior:

- Reciprocity
- Scarcity
- Authority
- Consistency
- Liking
- Consensus

Reciprocity is defined as being an exchange for mutual benefit. You scratch my back, and I will scratch yours. You may have heard this in Latin as *quid pro quo*. In IT social engineering, I have seen this as a simple, "Please click this link and fill out this survey for a $5 gift card." As a pen testing campaign against an organization, it works extremely well unless your end users are aware of attacks like these. If you are the one creating the attack, be the first to make an offer and make sure it is meaningful.

A used car lot is the epitome of social engineering. "Someone was here an hour ago, and they really want this car." Scarcity creates a sense of urgency. People want more of the things they cannot have. With any type of social engineering, the timing is key, but especially with scarcity. I have seen this used in password reset emails. What do people stand to lose if they do not do as you ask? They lose access to their files, they can't do their job; now they can't pay the rent, and they're homeless. A little extreme, but it does create a sense of urgency.

A few years ago, I was an adjunct instructor teaching a computer class for a nursing school. The chancellor had asked all the professors to wear a white doctor's coat, even if we were not teaching medical classes. At the time, I thought it was a little odd until I went to pick up a prescription for my daughter. Even the pharmacist assumed I was in a position of authority and had me come to the head of the line. Then it clicked. The students had been conditioned to recognize the doctor's coat to be the authority figure. If someone wears a uniform, people will naturally follow the lead of that person. It is important to signal to others what makes you a credible, knowledgeable authority before you try to influence them.

Greg Foss, senior researcher at Carbon Black, told me of a time that he was conducting a penetration test and consistency was the theme of his experiment. He had created a Google phone number, created a voicemail mailbox message, and called his target at a time when he knew the target was not going to be around. He left a message to have that person call him back because he needed to help the individual with a problem that person was having. They played telephone tag a few times, which built a foundation of trust and consistency with the target.

There are three major components to the principle of liking. We like people who are like us—we naturally gravitate to them. We like people who pay us compliments, and we like people who have the same goals as we do. We like them even more if they are willing to help us get us to our goal. One of the fun things to try to do with social engineering is to have someone form a goal of his or her own volition that we have actually orchestrated. The very first thing you should do in a job interview is find some commonality with the interviewer, and in your mind-set, the interviewer is a friend, not an adversary. Now the goal for that person is to woo you to the organization, and you are now interviewing that person.

One of the best tools we have in social engineering is to smile. Smiling has been shown to be a psychological signal of altruism. Altruism is the concept that you want to help others because of a concern for their happiness, not your own. Smiling even makes you look younger, giving you a mini facelift because it lifts your cheeks, jowls, and neck. Every time you smile, dopamine, endorphins, and serotonin throw a little party in your brain. For most people, smiles are contagious, so they respond to a smile with a smile of their own, having their own little brain party, making you seem likable and competent. Try it. The next time you have to deal with a difficult person, make eye contact and smile.

As for consensus, marketing and politicians do this all the time. Ninety percent of dentists recommend this toothpaste. If you're a good and intelligent person like us, you will vote this way. When individuals don't have a strong opinion, they can be easily swayed and follow others. In cybersecurity, it can be dangerous for people to trust but not verify.

"Trust, but verify" is an old Russian proverb. The phrase became popular during the late 1980s when U.S. President Ronald Reagan was negotiating nuclear disarmament with the Soviet Union's General Secretary Mikhail Gorbachev. I believe it fits the mind-set of a cybersecurity professional. When an outcome matters more than a relationship, you have to trust, but verify. In IT, safety and security are of utmost importance with outcome-critical parameters. If a relationship matters more than an outcome, then this philosophy doesn't fit as well.

To add to Professor Caildini's six principles of persuasion, when you are crafting a social engineering campaign, there are six human truths I have learned over the past 20 years. These have helped me social engineer both professionally and personally.

- Most people want to be helpful.
- Humans want instant gratification.
- Never use the words "obviously" and "but."
- The brain wants ease and order and dislikes change.
- Most people, including my students, have a limited attention span.
- Humans respond to beauty and emotion.

Men have dominated my cybersecurity classes over the past 20 years. I have not kept up with the numbers, but in my personal experience, I'm lucky to have one female in up to 20 men in a technical class. Men dominate the ranks of developers, administrators, researchers, and hackers. Chris Hadnagy of Social-Engineer.org and one of my favorite authors says, "Unfortunately, there is a chauvinist consensus that females don't get security. The truth is, as social engineers, women do better. We've seen hacktivists like Anonymous and LulzSec use females as part of their attacks."

David Kennedy, founder of TrustedSec and DerbyCon, says because of this attitude in our culture, women aren't thought to be technical or disingenuous. He also says it is helpful to have a Southern accent. A Southern accent is synonymous with warmth and hospitality, whereas a New York accent can be fast and harsh. It is my goal one day to participate in the Social Engineering CTF in Vegas. As a technically adequate female who was born and raised in Louisiana, I feel that I have a bit of an advantage, especially if I ask for help. I have had the doors held for me in a secure location because I had my arms full of books, ignoring the RFID badge reader and the mantrap.

Humans want instant gratification. We are hardwired to want what we want without any delay or denial. It's evolutionary. Humans survive when they take the smaller reward but skip the bigger yet delayed reward. If you have children, experiment with them. They can have this one marshmallow now, but if they can wait 5 minutes, they can have two. Mine never wait for two.

I met Deidre Diamond about a year ago when she gave the keynote at EC Councils Hacker Halter conference in Atlanta. In her keynote, she said we have to choose our words with care. There was a list of several words you ought not to use, but the two that burned into my brain are "obviously" and "but." Try using "obviously" in a sentence and not sound condescending. If you are attempting a role that is arrogant or patronizing, by all means it might work for you. She also suggested using "and" instead of "but." No one hears anything past "but." "I love this idea, but can we do this instead?" That sentence sounds a lot different than "I love this idea, and what do you think about this instead?" "But" will start an argument or stop the conversation. "And" will engage.

The brain wants ease and order and dislikes change. I think this becomes even more pronounced the older we get. If you are attempting a social engineering campaign, you have to build it around something that is believable and not out of the ordinary.

Most people, including my students, have a limited attention span. When I was studying for my CompTIA Certified Technical Trainer certification, my instructor told the class that we had 20 minutes to engage students with a lecture before they started thinking about what was for dinner or what movie they were going to this weekend. If you need someone's attention for more than 20 minutes, you will have to change the delivery. In training, we can show a video or give a hands-on exercise. In penetration testing, you don't normally want a long personal engagement. You want to get in, do what you need to do, and get out.

Humans respond to beauty and emotion. I believe this is self-explanatory. People are attracted to what they find beautiful or what makes them feel great emotion. The movie *Oceans 8* made me chuckle when Rhianna social-engineered the video security engineer with a compromised site about the Wheaten breed of dogs. I'm not sure I could drop a Meterpreter shell as fast as she did in the movie and turn on his webcam, but yes, that's exactly how it's done. Appeal to your targets' interests, what they feel is beautiful, and you have a great start to a campaign.

Human Attacks

Before I talk about different type of social engineering attacks, I would like to take a quote from Chris Hadnagy's book, *The Science of Human Hacking*. He says, "A professional social engineer's goal is to educate and assist rather than humiliate to win." The whole purpose of this chapter is for you to understand the way most people make decisions and how to help organizations educate their end users how to recognize if someone is trying to take advantage of them for gain. Education and training is one of the most important things you can do to secure your organization, but unfortunately, one of the first things to get cut out of a budget.

If you are doing any social engineering campaign, just like any penetration test, it must be documented and permission must be given. You also have to be careful with any type of impersonation. I had a student take my Metasploit class as a result of a decision he made to internally phish his organization and impersonate a three-letter agency. The campaign was discovered because the comptroller of the company he worked for was married to an agent for this three-letter agency. She made a phone call to ask him if the agency was indeed being audited.

Phishing is one of the most popular ways to gain access into an organization. Through open-source intelligence (OSINT), you know who works for the organization and the positions they are in. You know from different press releases what the company is excited about. Sometimes penetration testers use phishing for knowledge and sometimes for gain. If we are able to compromise a system with stolen credentials from a phish because we successfully extracted information from an end user, we can attempt to elevate those privileges to administrative levels, just like a bad actor would. The purpose of this type of phishing test is to leverage what we can find into what else we can find. Phishing will often take advantage of things going on either within the organization or other popular current events or disasters.

Vishing (voice phishing) is still popular, which surprises me. I never answer the phone. In fact, most people will text me if they are about to call me. Vishers use the telephone to gain access to personal or financial information. One vish I have seen in the news lately targets older people with college-age grandchildren. With enough OSINT, criminals know enough to impersonate the grandchild and call the grandparent because they've gotten into trouble and need them to send money. If the grandchild is off to school, odds are the parents are not in constant contact. Smishing (social media phishing) sends a text message to a mobile phone to attempt to gain access to personal information with the same intention as phishing or vishing.

Education

Criminals are familiar with human nature. They will use whatever is in their arsenal to attack your organization and the people who work with you. No one who interacts with others is immune. You must educate your end users to

- Be very suspicious of any phone calls, visits, or email messages that they did not initiate. If you get requests for information about other employees, try to verify the identity of the requesters. If it's legitimate, they will provide credentials. If they have malicious intent, they will usually give up and try to find easier prey.

- Do not ever reveal personal or financial information in email, and do not respond to email solicitations requesting this information. This includes clicking the links sent in an email. Banks will never ask for your PIN. The IRS will never call you.

- Pay close attention to the URL of a website linked in the email or SMS message. Malicious websites may look very similar to a legitimate site. If you know the URL of the site they want you to visit, type it in yourself. Do not click the link.

- If you are unsure whether an email request is legitimate, forward it to your IT incident and response team. Do not use contact information provided on a website connected to the request.

- Install and maintain antivirus software, firewalls, and email filters.

- Block ads and pop-ups whenever possible. When you click an ad, you are susceptible to a number of attacks like downloading malware or clickjacking.

Another of my favorite resources is Lance Spitzner, director of SANS Security Awareness. He says, "People are not the weakest link today, they are the most common attack vector." One of the biggest takeaways that SANS offers to everyone are its OUCH! newsletters. If you have not subscribed, then I highly recommend you put this book down long enough to Google *SANS OUCH!* OUCH! is a free security-awareness newsletter designed for everyone, not just IT professionals. These newsletters are published every month in multiple languages and are scrupulously reviewed by other SANS instructors. You can go back several years or search for a specific category.

A couple years back, I was tasked with coming up with some security awareness training for a software security company I worked for. I would print out the SANS OUCH! newsletters and put them above the coffee pot in the breakroom, on the mirror between the sinks in the bathroom, or above the copier. I put them wherever I knew people congregated or were a captive audience. Every other month, I would have a contest that would involve some of the information in the newsletter, and the reward could be a day off or some type of recognition. People started paying attention. When IT periodically phished our internal employees, they recognized the telltale signs and were able to send that phishing to the proper authorities at the company.

If you think you've been a victim of a social engineering campaign and have revealed sensitive information, report it to the right people—including network administrators. They have tools and can be on the alert for any suspicious behavior. If you believe you have financial accounts that have been compromised, contact that organization immediately. Close that account and watch for anything unexplainable. Watch your credit reports for any accounts that are opened that you did not authorize. I have my credit and my children's credit accounts locked down. Unfortunately, I was a victim a few years ago in the U.S. Office of Personnel Management hack, and in my clearance paperwork was all the personally identifiable information about my family.

Lastly, password hygiene is a fiercely debated topic in IT. If you think you're compromised, immediately change any passwords you might have revealed. If you use the same password on multiple sites for different accounts, change those as well, and don't ever use that password again. Some sites require the password to be a certain length with uppercase, lowercase, and special characters. Some people swear by using password managers like LastPass, Keeper, and Dashlane. A password manager is a tool that does the work of creating and remembering all the passwords for your accounts. For me, it sounds great but is a single point of failure.

To make accounts safer, you should make sure your passwords are

- Long and complicated. Ideally, your password should be totally randomized with uppercase and lowercase letters, making it very difficult to remember. Try to create a long password out of one of your favorite books—for example, Wh0i$J0hnG@1t!

- Do not write them down or use birthdays.

- Always use multifactor authentication, whenever possible.

- Don't be too terribly social on social media. Nearly 90 million Facebook accounts had their profile information shared by researchers using a third-party quiz app. If you aren't paying for it, you are the product. Nothing is ever truly private on social media.

Lastly, if you have chosen to create your passwords yourself, you do have another option. A friend of mine, Michael Hawkins of Wantegrity, has a site he built especially for his customers but has made it available to anyone who would like to play with it. If you visit www.wantegrity.com/passwords.php, you can use your regular-sized normal password as the master key and the account you are using it on as the site key. As you see in Figure 13.1, you enter your password and account and generate a unique complicated password for that credential pair. If you're concerned about password-harvesting, right-click and review the code. What's typed on the page stays on the page.

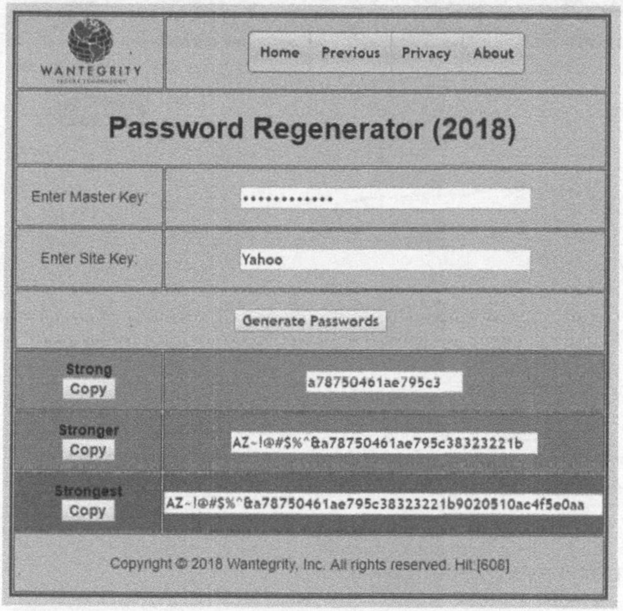

Figure 13.1: Creating unique credentials for web accounts

The Social Engineer Toolkit

According to the global statistics provided by gs.statcounter.com (see Figure 13.2), 70.22 percent of all global desktop users are using Windows—more than 50 percent of those users are on Windows 10, and interestingly enough, 2.22 percent are on Windows XP. According to this graph, there are more global users of Windows XP than Linux, statistically speaking. I have done my best to show you mainly tools of the Windows persuasion. However, we've gotten to a tool that only runs on Linux and macOS. But I may have a few tricks.

Windows 10 has an interesting tool called the Windows Subsystem for Linux (WSL). It is a compatibility layer for running a Linux-compatible kernel interface that can then run GNU on top of it. GNU is actually not an acronym—it is an antelope this project was named after. GNU is an operating system composed wholly of free software like Ubuntu, openSUSE, Debian, or Kali Linux. This type of user space will allow you to use a bash shell or programming languages like Ruby or Python.

Figure 13.2: 70.22 percent of the planet runs Microsoft Windows.

There are pros and cons for everything, and there are times and places for tools. WSL has its benefits as well as drawbacks. A lot of great tools have been developed for Linux that are free, and WSL supports a wide variety of Linux distributions. WSL is easy to install, and it takes about 5 minutes (not counting the reboot). While WSL is running, you can access your local machines filesystem from the subsystem. The flip side of this is that WSL is almost like a Linux lite. It was not engineered for heavy-duty production loads, and it might be more efficient and faster to run a full-fledged virtual machine. WSL is command line only. There is no GUI, so that can be a drawback for some. As a friend of mine, Josh Franz, a security consultant at Rapid7, told me, "It can just be buggy." He's right. The earlier iterations had limitations with what networking commands worked. Like any security tool we use, WSL will continue to evolve.

The Social Engineer Toolkit was written by David Kennedy and with a lot of help from the security community has evolved into a tool specifically used against people and their weaknesses. The attacks that are built into this toolkit are reminiscent of Metasploit; however, instead of focusing on network or application attacks, it assists penetration testers to target a person or organization.

Before you can install the Social Engineer Toolkit (SET), you have to turn on WSL in Windows 10 and reboot the machine. Go to your Control Panel, open

Programs And Features, and find the option to Turn Windows Features On Or Off. Scroll down toward the bottom until you find Windows Subsystem For Linux; then check that box and click OK, as you see in Figure 13.3. The system should prompt you to reboot the computer so this feature can be available.

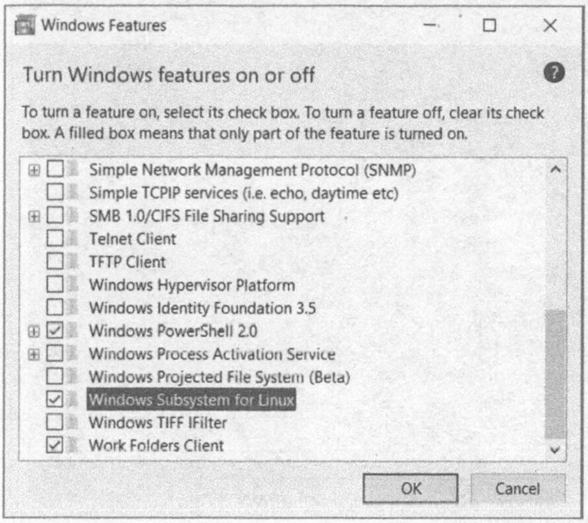

Figure 13.3: Turning on the Windows feature of the Windows subsystem for Linux

Once your machine has rebooted, go to your Start menu, and it is time to go shopping at the Microsoft Store. Open the Microsoft Store and look for the magnifying glass in the upper right. In the Search field in the upper right, look for Ubuntu. There are several flavors for you to choose from. Open Ubuntu 18.04 LTS. As you see in Figure 13.4, this version of Ubuntu 18.04 on Windows will let you run an Ubuntu Terminal and run the Ubuntu command-line utilities, including bash, ssh, apt, and many more.

If you click the More hyperlink above the word *Free*, you're reminded that this tool is used through a command prompt so you need to turn that feature on. As you see in Figure 13.5, it also contains a link to Windows help documents, but there are also help documents on www.ubuntu.com.

In Lab 13.1, you'll install Ubuntu 18.04 on a Windows machine.

We all have our heroes. Linus Torvalds is one of mine. His philosophy is "Intelligence is the ability to avoid doing work, yet getting the work done." At 10 years old, he was not happy with the MS-DOS and decided to create his own operating system based on UNIX. In 1991, he posted a message that he was ready to share what would become Linux. The original code and Linux kernel version 1.0 was released in 1994, and it has been the operating system of choice of geeks everywhere. In addition to being free, it rarely crashed and can be modified by anyone. Not only is Torvalds father of Linux, he also created Git.

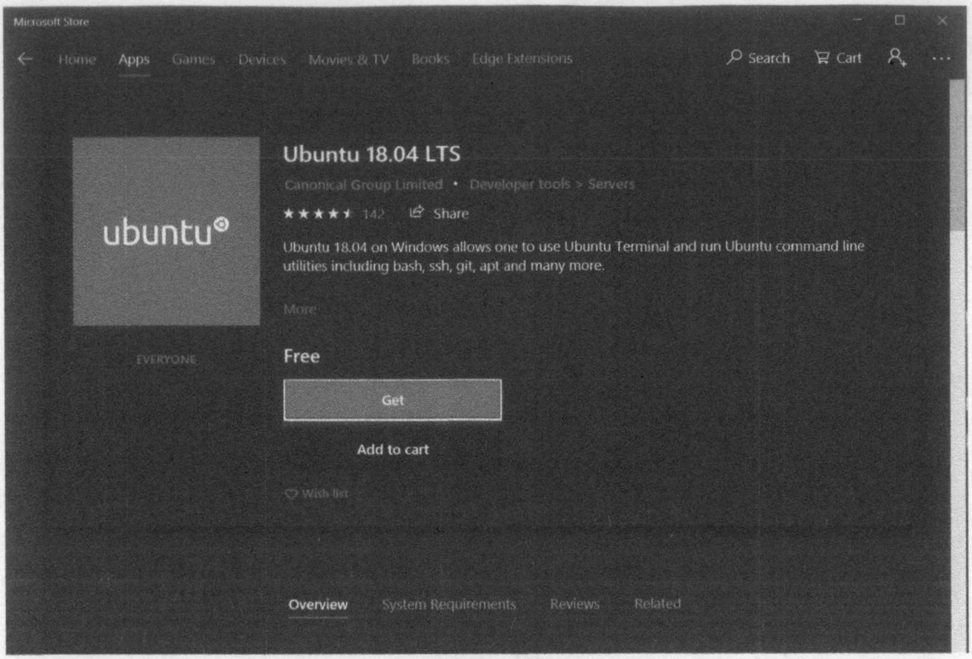

Figure 13.4: Finding Ubuntu 18.04 on Windows WSL

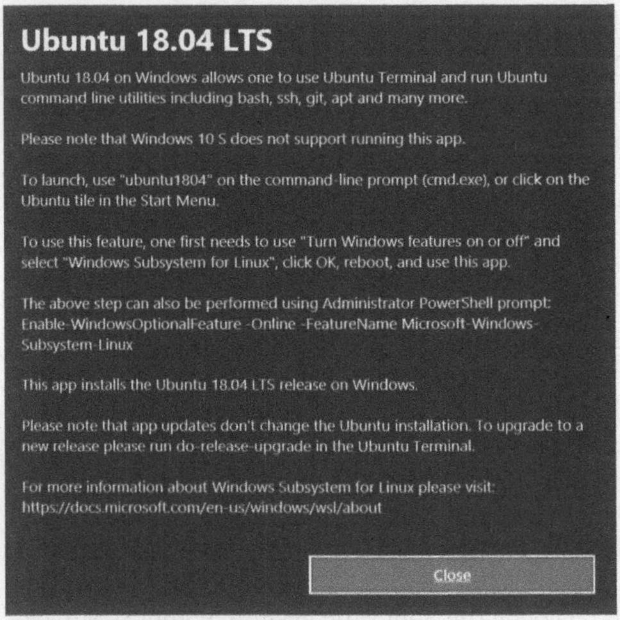

Figure 13.5: Details of Ubuntu 18.04 LTS

LAB 13.1: INSTALLING THE LINUX OS UBUNTU 18.04 ON A WINDOWS MACHINE

1. On a Windows machine, use the search tool for Windows Features. As you saw earlier in Figure 13.3, check the box for Windows Subsystem for Linux. Reboot the system. Now open the Start menu, pull up the Microsoft Store, and search for *Ubuntu*.

2. Open the dialog box for Ubuntu 18.04 LTS and click the Get button. This will download the file you need to complete this installation. The Install button will light up in the upper right. If you are asked to sign into your Microsoft account, click Not Now.

3. The install will take over, and then you will see the Launch button in the upper right of the window, as shown in Figure 13.6. Click Launch.

Figure 13.6: Ubuntu 18.04 successfully installed

4. The first time you launch your Ubuntu install, you have a little housekeeping to do. As you see in Figure 13.7, you will have to wait a few minutes for the install to complete, and then you will need to create a UNIX username and password. After you have completed the installation successfully, launch a new Ubuntu command prompt screen.

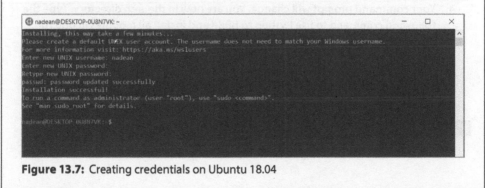

Figure 13.7: Creating credentials on Ubuntu 18.04

Git is what we call a distributed version-control system. What this means to developers is that if you clone a Git project, you have the entire project history. You can develop all you want on your local machine with no need of server interaction. GitHub also stores a copy of your project. You designate the project's central library or repository, and developers can push and pull all they want. Git is the system; GitHub is the service. I explained it because you're about to install it.

In Lab 13.2, you'll install the Social Engineer Toolkit in the WSL.

LAB 13.2: INSTALLING SET IN WSL

1. From the command prompt in the new Ubuntu 18.04 asset you just installed from the Microsoft Store, type in sudo apt-get install git.

2. Next, git SET and put it in the set folder by entering the following command:

   ```
   git clone https://github.com/trustedsec/social-engineer-toolkit/
   set/
   ```

   As you see in Figure 13.8, this will start cloning the toolkit to your machine. You want to make sure all objects, deltas, and files are at 100 percent.

Figure 13.8: Cloning SET to your set folder

3. When Git has completed installation and you are back at a command prompt, change the directory by typing in cd set.

4. Your command prompt will change. You are now in the set directory. Type the following command to use Python to build and install all modules in one run:

   ```
   python setup.py install
   ```

5. When the install completes, you can type in sudo setoolkit and see something similar to Figure 13.9. This is the welcome page to SET.

   NOTE   Like Metasploit Framework, HD and David have a quirky sense of humor, and the welcome page changes each time you log in.

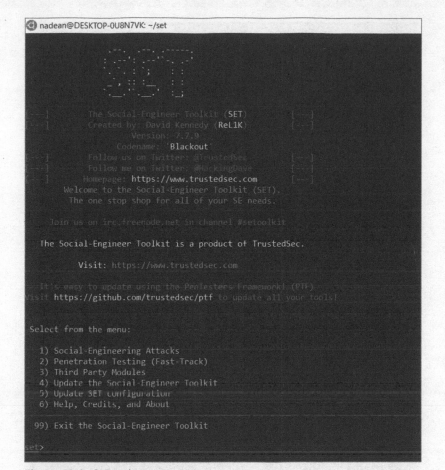

Figure 13.9: SET welcome screen

6. From the menu at the bottom, shown in Figure 13.10, choose 1) Social Engineering Attacks. Then press Enter. From the Social Engineering Attacks menu, choose 5) Mass Mailer Attack.

Continues

LAB 13.2 (CONTINUED)

```
xxxxxxxxxxxxxxxxxxxxxxxxxxxxxxxxxxxxxxxxxxxxxxxxxxxxxxxxxxxxxxxxxxxxxxxx
xxxxxxxxxxxxxxxxxxxxxxxxxxxxxxxxxxxxxxxxxxxxxxxxxxxxxxxxxxxxxxxxxxxxxxxx
   .o88o.                                      o8o                   .
   888 `"                                     `"'                   .o8
  o888oo  .oooo.o  .ooooo.   .ooooo.   oooo   .ooooo.   .o88oo oooo      ooo
   888   d88(  "8 d88' `88b d88' `"Y8 `888   d88' `88b    888   `88.   .8'
   888   `"Y88b.  888   888 888        888   888ooo888    888    `88. .8'
   888   o.  )88b 888   888 888   .o8  888   888   .o    888 .    `888'
  o888o  8""888P' `Y8bod8P' `Y8bod8P' o888o  `Y8bod8P'   "888"     d8'
                                                              .o...P'
                                                              `XER0'


  [---]        The Social-Engineer Toolkit (SET)         [---]
  [---]        Created by: David Kennedy (ReL1K)         [---]
                      Version: 7.7.9
                     Codename: 'Blackout'
  [---]        Follow us on Twitter: @TrustedSec         [---]
  [---]        Follow me on Twitter: @HackingDave         [---]
  [---]       Homepage: https://www.trustedsec.com        [---]
       Welcome to the Social-Engineer Toolkit (SET).
        The one stop shop for all of your SE needs.

      Join us on irc.freenode.net in channel #setoolkit

   The Social-Engineer Toolkit is a product of TrustedSec.

          Visit: https://www.trustedsec.com

   It's easy to update using the PenTesters Framework! (PTF)
Visit https://github.com/trustedsec/ptf to update all your tools!


Select from the menu:

   1) Spear-Phishing Attack Vectors
   2) Website Attack Vectors
   3) Infectious Media Generator
   4) Create a Payload and Listener
   5) Mass Mailer Attack
   6) Arduino-Based Attack Vector
   7) Wireless Access Point Attack Vector
   8) QRCode Generator Attack Vector
   9) Powershell Attack Vectors
  10) SMS Spoofing Attack Vector
  11) Third Party Modules

  99) Return back to the main menu.
```

Figure 13.10: Social engineering attacks

7. Once you have selected Mass Mailer Attack, you are ready to use all the quirks of human nature combined with the art of persuasion to develop the content of your phishing campaign. As you see in Figure 13.11, you have a choice of either spear phishing one person or casting a wider net by importing a list of email addresses in the Social Engineer Toolkit Mass E-Mailer. Choose option 1, E-mail Attack Single Email Address, and SET will guide you through the creation and delivery of a phishing campaign. Happy phishing!

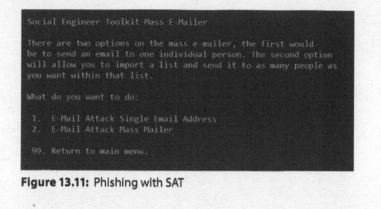

Figure 13.11: Phishing with SAT

Kali Linux

WHAT YOU WILL LEARN IN THIS CHAPTER:

➤ Virtualization

➤ Kali Linux

➤ Optimizing Kali Linux

➤ Using Kali Linux Tools

Most of what I teach is done virtually with customers over teleconferencing. The most difficult thing to do with virtual training is to engage the student. They don't see me, and I don't see them. I do not have the ability to read body language. I cannot see the crinkle between their eyes when they're confused. I also can't see when they have gotten up to get more coffee or are sidetracked by emails and phone calls, so student engagement is key. One of our conversations in the Nexpose Vulnerability Management class centers around the cybersecurity philosophy of viewing you and your ecosystem as an attacker would. I ask the question, "What do new pen testers or hackers download as their operating system of choice?" I'm surprised by how many blue-teamers have never heard of Kali Linux. I've been playing Kali since before it was Kali and was called Backtrack.

Kali Linux debuted in 2013 as a total rewrite of the free Linux distribution called BackTrack. BackTrack was based on the Knoppix Linux OS, whereas now Kali Linux is based on the Debian Linux OS and is funded and maintained by Offensive Security. Kali Linux still remains free and contains more than 600 penetration tools with a wide range of wireless device support. BackTrack was started as an answer to Mati Aharoni's need for a tool to take on an engagement where he could not bring any hardware except a laptop, which would be taken from him at the end of the engagement. Mati is the founder and core developer of the Kali Linux and is the CTO at Offensive Security. Interestingly enough, Kali is the Hindu goddess who brings the death of the ego. I think this software is aptly named.

We have examined many tools throughout this book, and now we've reached one of my favorites. Some of the tools in Kali Linux have entire chapters devoted to them in this book, such as Metasploit Framework, Nmap, Wireshark, and Burp. The best way to master any skill or tool is hands-on practice. One method you could take is to load these tools on your computer and use them to examine your personal systems. That is a great introduction, but it doesn't scale very well. Most of us don't have many systems in our own private network and may not be able to fully realize the usefulness of these tools. You could use these tools to examine Google or Yahoo! or some other production system out on the Web, but the major problem with doing that is that you don't have permission to do it. It could get you into a lot of legal trouble. Another alternative, and the one I use the most, is to use virtualization.

Virtualization

Virtualization is a technology that system administrators have been using in our datacenters for years, and it is at the heart of cloud computing infrastructure. It is a technology that allows the physical resources of a computer (CPU, RAM, hard disk, graphics card, etc.) to be shared by virtual machines (VMs). Consider the old days when a single physical hardware platform—the server—was dedicated to a single-server application like being a web server. It turns out that a typical web server application didn't utilize much of the underlying hardware resources available to it on the server. For purposes of this discussion, let's assume that a web application running on one of our physical servers utilized 30 percent of the hardware resources. That meant that 70 percent of the physical resources were going unused; thus, the server was being underutilized.

With virtualization, we could now install three web servers by using VMs each utilizing 30 percent of the physical hardware resources of the server. Now we are utilizing 90 percent of the physical hardware resources of the server, which is a much better return on our investment in the server. We will be using this technology to help us master the tools discussed in this chapter. By installing virtualization software on your computer, you can create VMs that can be used to work with the tools discussed. The rest of this chapter is concerned with doing just that.

Let's first define some of the proper vocabulary:

A *hypervisor* is the software that is installed on a computer that supports virtualization. It can be implemented as *firmware*, which is specialized hardware that has permanent software programmed into it. It could also be hardware with installed software. It is within the hypervisor that the VMs will be created. The hypervisor allocates the underlying hardware resources to the VMs. Examples of hypervisor software are VMware's Workstation and Oracle's VM VirtualBox. There are free versions of each of these hypervisors that you can download and use as we did in Lab 10.4 in Chapter 10, "Metasploit."

There are two types of hypervisors. Type 1 hypervisor runs directly on the bare metal of a system. Type 2 hypervisor runs on a host operating system that provides virtualization services. In our lab, you will be setting up a Type 2 hypervisor in the first lab of this chapter.

A *virtual machine* is a machine that is created on the hypervisor. It will have its own operating system and be allocated physical hardware resources such as CPU, RAM, hard disk, etc. Various network resources can also be allocated to each VM.

The *host operating system* is the operating system of the computer the hypervisor is being installed on.

The *guest operating system* is the operating system of the VM that resides within the hypervisor.

For example, I have a tower computer with an Intel i7 processor, 32 GB of RAM, and multiterabytes of hard disk space running Windows 10 Pro as the host operating system. I also have VMware Workstation Pro as my hypervisor with multiple VMs loaded in it, like Kali Linux and Metasploitable2. Linux is the guest operating system of both these instances.

Before you start this process, you need to make sure that the computer you plan to use for virtualization can support the VMs you intend to load on it as well as its host operating system. Table 14.1 lists the requirements for Windows 10, Ubuntu Linux, and Kali Linux.

Table 14.1: Resource requirements for Windows 10, Ubuntu, and Kali Linux

RESOURCE	WINDOWS 10	UBUNTU LINUX	KALI LINUX
Processor	1 GHz or faster	2 GHz dual-core processor	CPU supported by at least one of the AMD64, i386, armel, armhf, or arm64 architectures
RAM	1 GB for 32 bit 2 GB for 64 bit	2 GB	2 GB
Hard drive space	16 GB for 32 bit 32 GB for 64 bit	25 GB	20 GB
Graphics card	Direct 9 or later with WDDM 1.0 driver		
Display	800×600	1024×768	

```
https://www.microsoft.com/en-US/windows/windows-10-specifica-
tions
    https://help.ubuntu.com/community/Installation/SystemRequire-
ments
    https://kali.training/topic/minimum-installation-requirements/
```

Just like any environment, there will be pros and cons. Some of the pros of running Kali in a VM are that you can run more than one OS at a time; you can install, reinstall, or back up any time you want quite easily; and you can manage the allocation of resources. The cons would be that performance may not be as robust as if you were on bare metal, USB drives can cause issues, and some of us would rather roll back than actually troubleshoot the issue. I've been guilty of that because I was in a time crunch.

For demonstration purposes, in Lab 14.1, I walk you through installing VMware Workstation Player on my Windows computer and then importing a Kali Linux VM. Let's get started.

LAB 14.1: INSTALLING VM WORKSTATION

1. Download VMware Workstation Player for the Windows computer (if you did not already do so in Chapter 10 , "Metasploit"). As of the writing of this book, the link to Workstation Player is `https://my.vmware.com/en/web/vmware/ free#desktop _ end _ user _ computing/vmware _ workstation _ player/15 _ 0`, which you see in Figure 14.1.

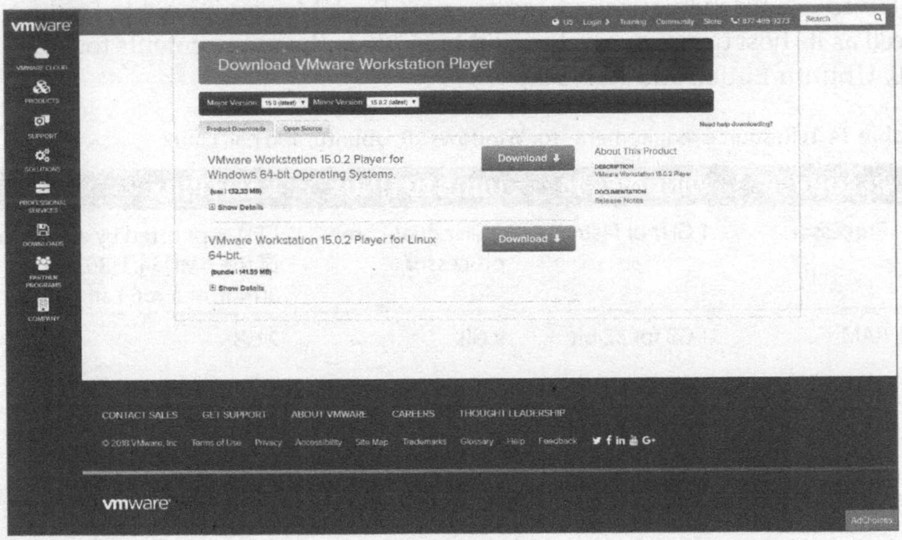

Figure 14.1: Download VM Workstation Player page

2. After you have VM Workstation downloaded, open the install file and double-click. A User Account Control (UAC) window will be displayed where you will need to click Yes to allow the program, as shown in Figure 14.2.

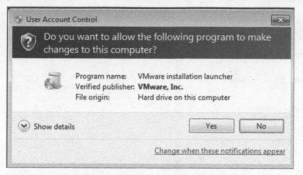

Figure 14.2: VMware UAC

3. Click Next to advance to the Setup Wizard. You can click Next five times to accept the EULA, install at the default location, accept the User Experience Settings, add shortcuts, and then finally click Install. The next window you see is the installation starting, as shown in Figure 14.3.

Figure 14.3: Installing VMware Workstation 15 Player page

4. The VMware Workstation player icon will be on your desktop. Double-click the icon to access the Welcome screen. You have two options at this point of installation. If this is for noncommercial use, as you see in Figure 14.4, leave the default and click Continue and on the next screen Finish.

Continues

LAB 14.1 (CONTINUED)

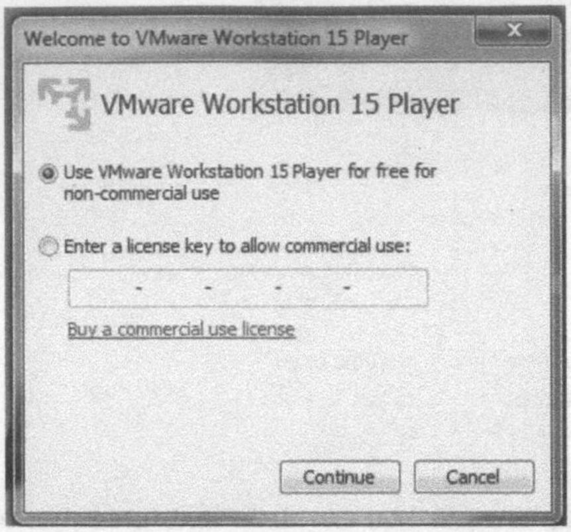

Figure 14.4: Accepting the free noncommercial license

5. **When you open the player, it will prompt you if you have any updates. As you see in Figure 14.5, you will make the educated decision to download the update, especially if you read Chapter 12, "Patch and Configuration Management." You are not too busy to make sure you have the latest updates and patches and bug improvements.**

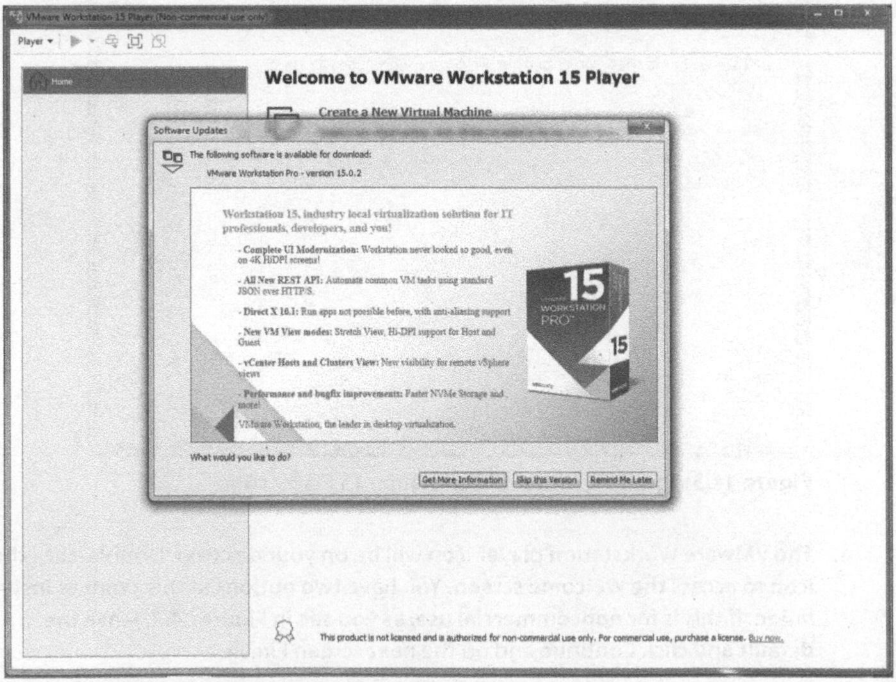

Figure 14.5: VMware Workstation Player software updates

6.   With VMware Workstation 15 Player, you have the ability to create a new VM from scratch or open one that already exists.

7.   The next level of this process will be to download the Kali Linux VMware image.

There are several Kali Linux distributions to choose from. You have the WSL version that can be pulled directly into a Windows OS. From www.kali .org, every few months there is a new Kali image you can download. From www .offensive-security.com, the VMs are already created for you. They are shared with the disclaimer that they are maintained on a "best-effort" basis, and all future updates will be listed here:

www.offensive-security.com/kali-linux-vm-vmware-virtualbox-image-download/19/

There are a few more important things I want to mention before we open Kali. Offensive Security does not supply technical support for Kali images, but support can be found on the Kali Linux Community page. Odds are if you have a question or problem, someone else has experienced the same thing. Scroll down the page until you see the Kali Linux VM for the architecture of your machine. As you see in Figure 14.6, there will be a version as well as a hash.

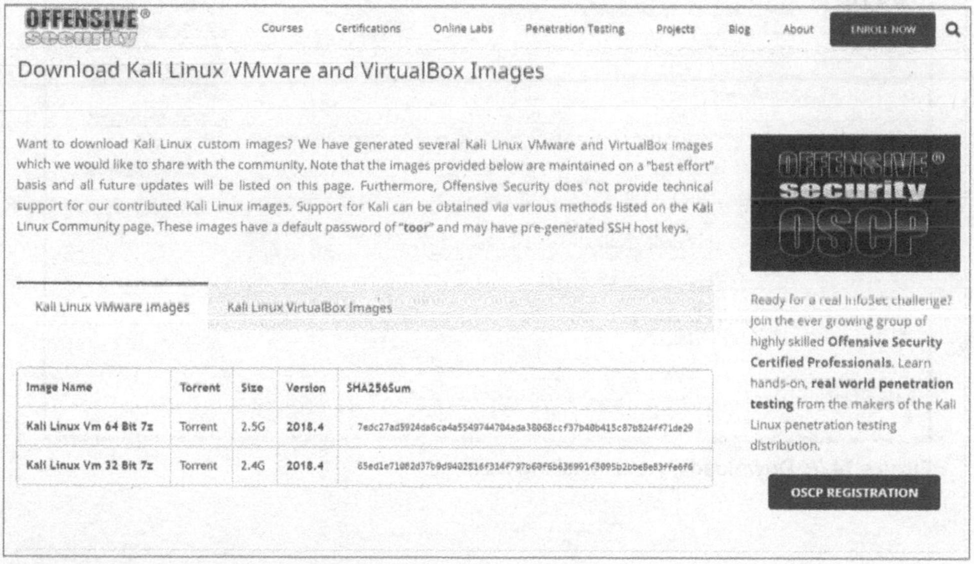

Figure 14.6: Downloading Kali Linux

NOTE   If you are interested in using an Android distribution for penetration testing, I have run Kali NetHunter on my tablet. It's a lot of fun on an airplane, but please remember to make ethical decisions. I had an interesting conversation on a flight from Denver to Los Angeles sitting next to a physician using the wireless service the airline offers. He was obviously reading confidential patient information that I could see because he had no privacy screen on his laptop. A peek at his taskbar told me a lot about the precautions he was taking. I pulled up NetHunter on my Android tablet and asked if he wanted to see something interesting. I'm not sure if I was supposed to be flattered that he said I looked like a librarian, not a hacker.

Download the appropriate VMware image, and in Lab 14.2, you'll unzip it and open it with the player.

LAB 14.2: INSTALLING 7-ZIP AND USING KALI LINUX IN VMware WORKSTATION

1. The file you just downloaded ends with the extension .7z. 7-zip is open source and free software that is a file archiver that utilizes a high compression ratio. To download the 7-Zip software for Windows, go to www.7-zip.org. Like you see in Figure 14.7, you have a choice between 32-bit and 64-bit architecture. It is a teeny tiny file, so it takes only a few seconds to download. Double-click the 7-zip icon and install the software.

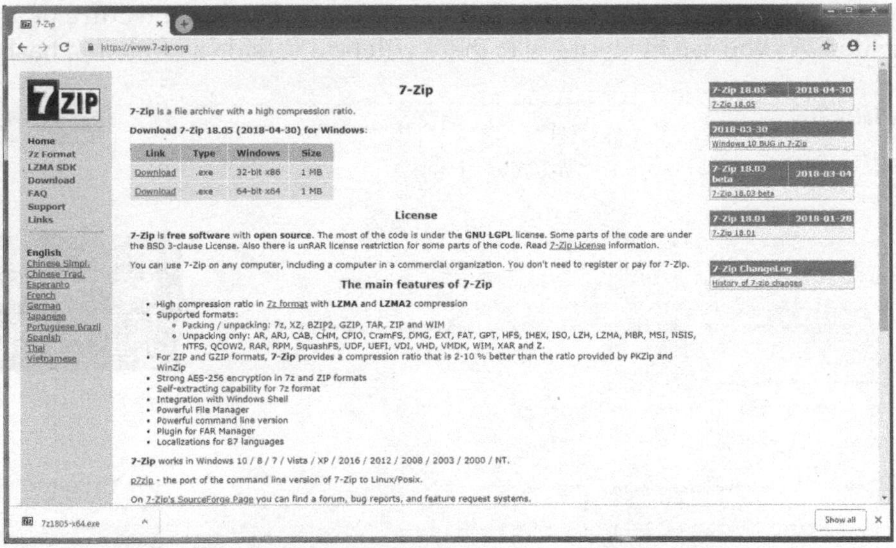

Figure 14.7: Downloading and installing 7-Zip

2. Now that you have 7-Zip installed, find your download of Kali Linux. Right-click the file and choose 7zip And Extract Here. This will unpack the zipped file create folder with the VM inside.

3. Open your VMware Workstation Player and choose the Open A VM option. When the Open dialog box opens, navigate to the proper folder and, like you see in Figure 14.8, the Kali Linux VM will be an option. Select the folder and then click Open.

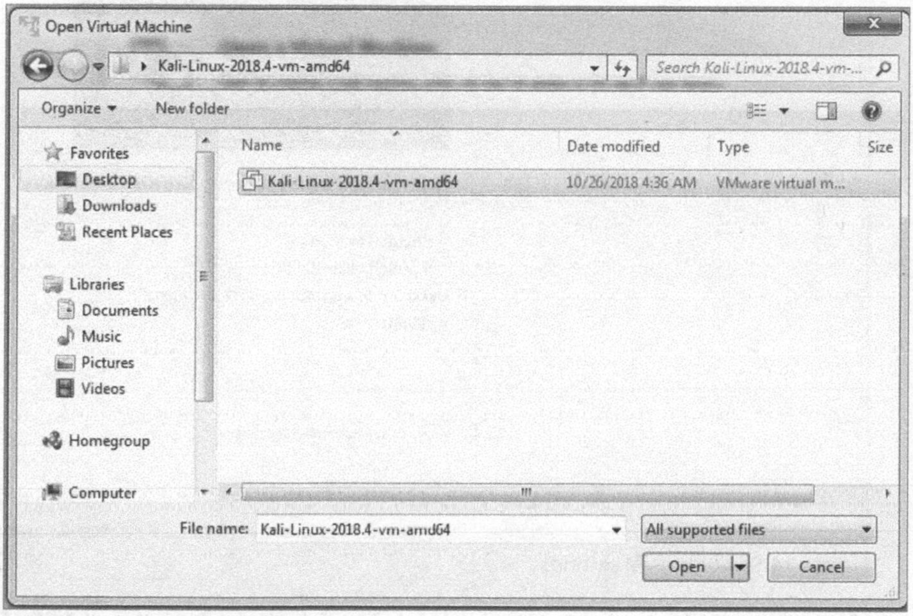

Figure 14.8: Opening Kali Linux VM

4. Once the Kali Linux VM is open, you will have several options. As you see in Figure 14.9, you have the ability to power on the VM or edit the settings. If you click the Edit VM Settings link, you will be able to allocate more resources to the virtual environment before you hit the Play button.

Continues

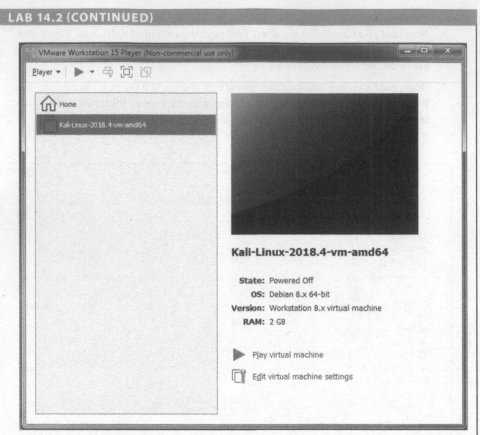

Figure 14.9: Editing VM settings

5. In Figure 14.10, you see the Hardware tab. The default configuration of 2 GB of memory, four processors, a 80 GB hard drive, a CD/DVD that will auto-detect if one is installed on your host and a NAT network adapter. For most workloads, CPU virtualization adds only a small amount of overhead, which means it will be very close to what you see on a bare-metal installation. The host operating system will not perform very well when it runs low on memory, so be careful about giving yourself too much memory. If the host OS doesn't have enough memory for itself, it can cause thrashing, constantly swapping data between memory and the paging file on disk. If you want this VM to connect to the Internet using the host's network, NAT is often the easiest way to go. The sound card and display will auto-detect unless you make a change. Take note of the defaults currently displayed for future performance tuning.

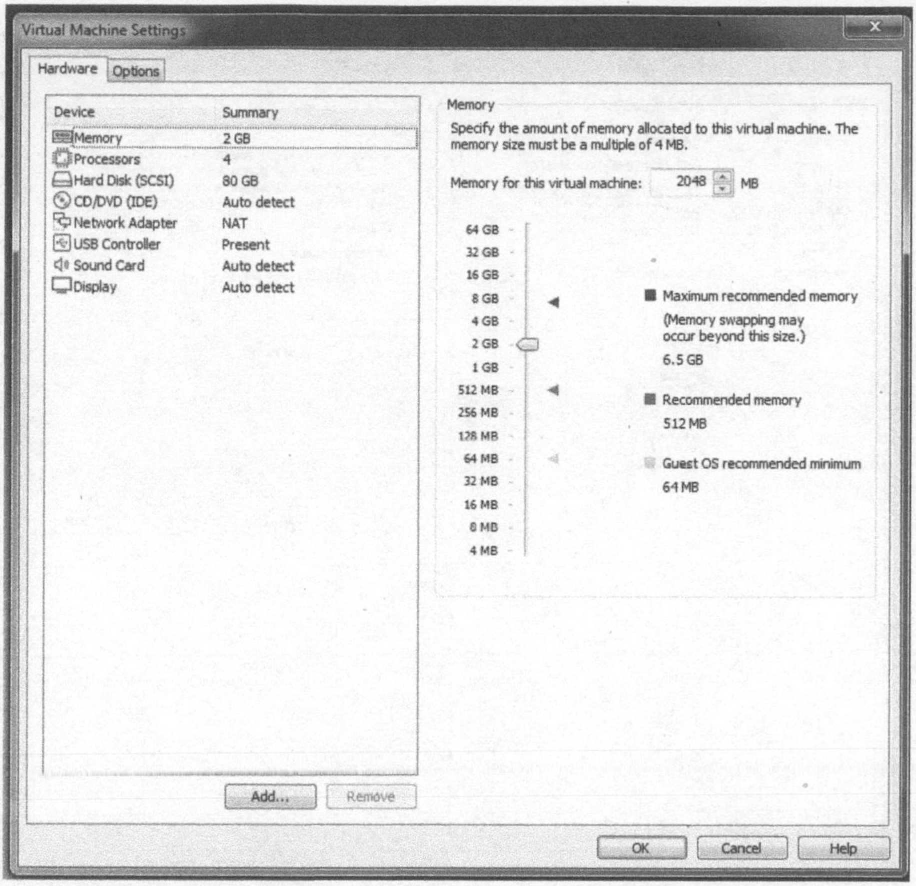

Figure 14.10: Default configuration for Kali Linux

6. The next tab to the right of Hardware is Options. The options for your Kali Linux VM include giving the VM a new name, using power options such as entering full-screen mode when the VM is ready to be powered on, and enabling or disabling folders. Considering this is Kali Linux and you will be compromising machines, I usually disable this. Shared folders will expose your host files to programs in the VM. In Figure 14.11, you see the option to disable shared folders or enable if you trust the VM with the data you have stored on the host. Edit your Power options to enter full-screen mode after powering on by selecting the box to the left and clicking OK.

Continues

LAB 14.2 (CONTINUED)

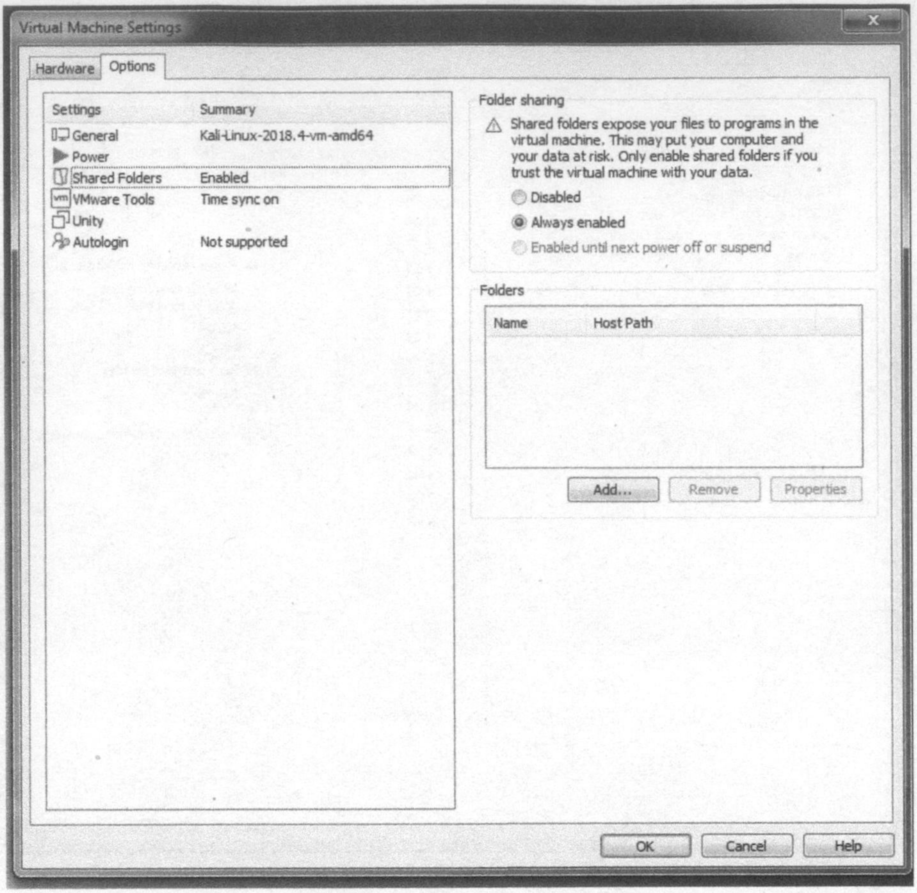

Figure 14.11: Disabling shared folders

7. The only other viable option to consider is Unity. Unity in VMware is the ability to display applications directly on the host desktop. The VM console is hidden, and you can minimize the Workstation window. If you're feeling really fancy, you can change the border color around the applications that run in Unity mode on the desktop, as shown in Figure 14.12.

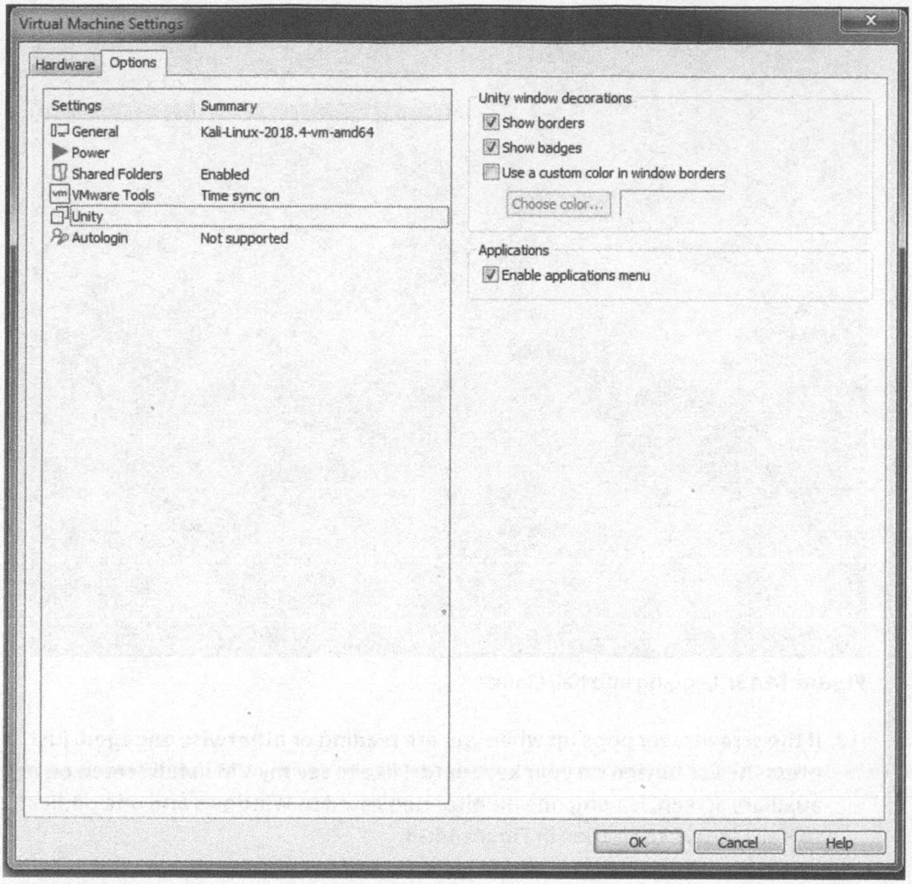

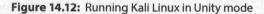

Figure 14.12: Running Kali Linux in Unity mode

8. Click the OK or Cancel button after you have made your VM modifications, and from the Home page, click the Play Virtual Machine green triangle. You will see the Kali Linux machine spin up. The first time you spin up this VM, it may ask if you moved it or copied it. Select the I Copied It option. "It" is the VM you have created or downloaded.

9. When the Kali Linux VM is ready, you will see the login screen that's shown in Figure 14.13. The default username is **root**, and the password is **toor**.

Continues

LAB 14.2 (CONTINUED)

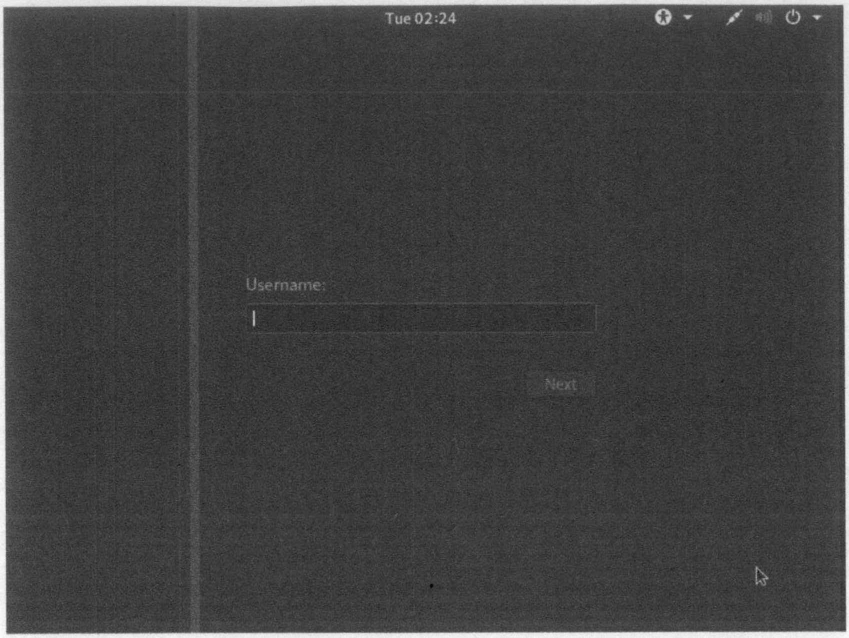

Figure 14.13: Logging into Kali Linux

10. If the screensaver pops up while you are reading or otherwise engaged, just press the Esc button on your keyboard. I like to see my VM in full screen on my auxiliary screen, leaving one monitor dedicated to Windows and one dedicated to Kali Linux, like you see in Figure 14.14.

Figure 14.14: Kali Linux desktop

Optimizing Kali Linux

One of the first things I do as a habit is update Kali Linux every single time I open it up. Offensive Security pulls updates from Debian four times a day. This ensures patches and updates are getting incorporated into Kali Linux on a daily basis. Keep your system up-to-date and make it part of your routine. As soon as the OS loads, open a terminal, and run `apt-get update`, as shown in Figure 14.15. When that process completes and you get your command prompt back, run `apt-get dist-upgrade` (also shown in Figure 14.15).

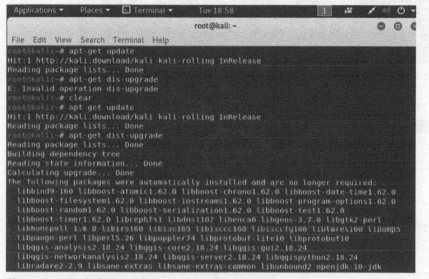

Figure 14.15: Updating Kali Linux through a terminal

Next, think about the credentials you used to log into this VM of Kali Linux. Those are root credentials. This book has cautioned you with a discussion on least privileges. Adding a nonroot user to Kali Linux is pretty easy. You can still use the root/toor credentials as needed. As you can see in Figure 14.16, the commands to add a user and password are simply `useradd -m nt -G -s /bin/bash` and `passwd nt`, respectively.

You will probably want to use your name or initials, not mine (even though mine are pretty awesome considering I'm in IT). Be cognizant of using any information or credentials that someone else could use nefariously.

You also might want to consider disabling the screen lock feature. The easiest and fastest way to disable the screen lock feature is to navigate the menu on the left to the very bottom. There is an icon of nine dots, which is your Show

Applications icon. At the top of the window is the Search field. Type **Settings**, navigate toward the bottom of the page, and choose Power. Like you see in Figure 14.17, choose Never as the Blank Screen option.

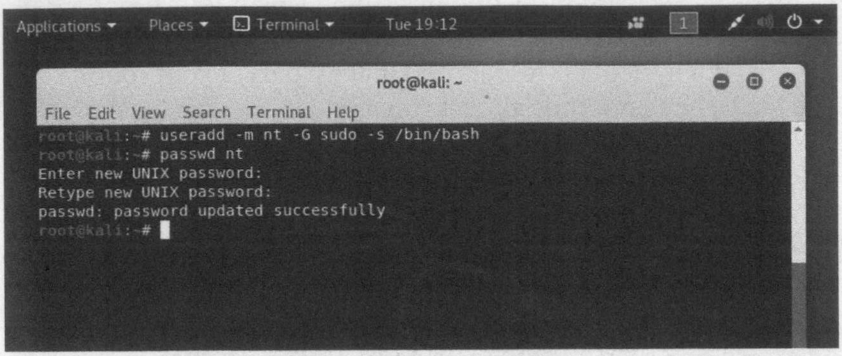

Figure 14.16: Adding a nonroot username and password

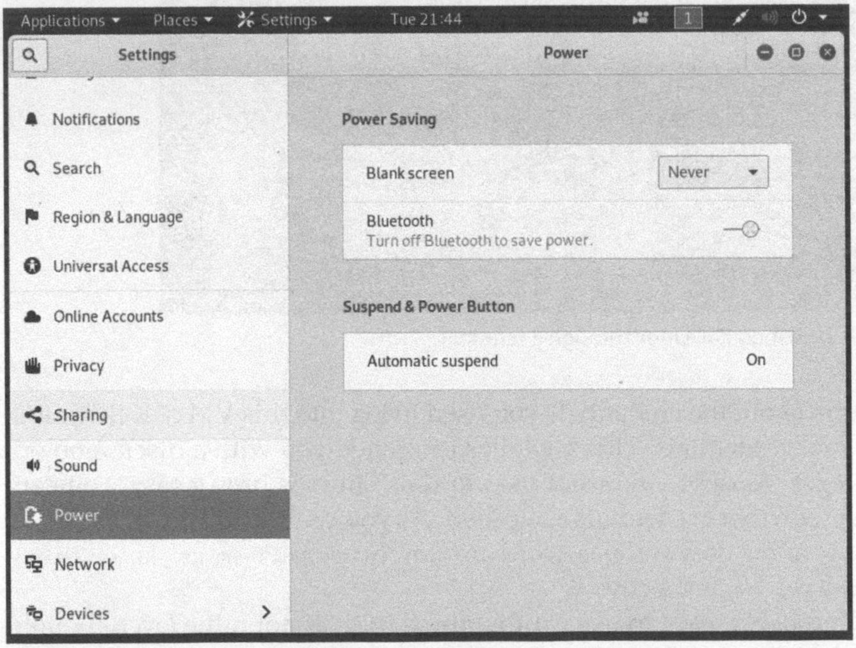

Figure 14.17: Turning off the Blank screen saver

The next feature you might want to disable is the Automatic Screen Lock. You will find this under Privacy in the Settings menu, as shown in Figure 14.18.

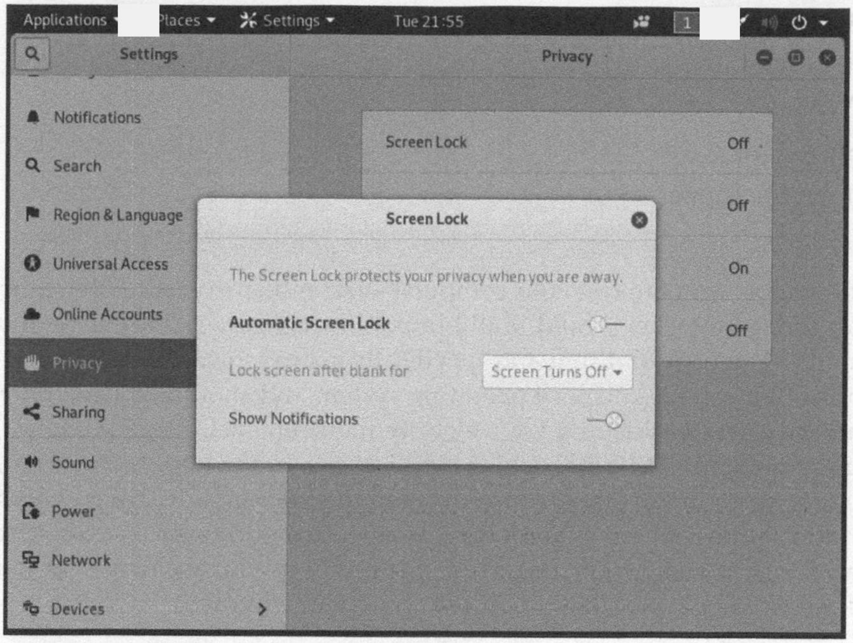

Figure 14.18: Configuring Automatic Screen Lock

Using Kali Linux Tools

Some of the tools in Kali Linux have been discussed in previous chapters of this book—including NMAP, Burp, Wireshark, Social Engineer Toolkit, and Metasploit Framework—but there are so many more. Here are some of my favorites out of hundreds that are extremely specialized but can be put in the following categories:

- Information gathering
  - Maltego
  - Recon-ng
  - Sparta
- Utilities
  - MacChanger
  - Nikto

- Wireless
  - Kismet
  - WiFite
- Brute forcing
  - John the Ripper
  - Hashcat

With these tools, you can test your computer system security using the same techniques that an attacker would. Kali Linux is specifically built to meet the requirements of security auditing and specifically geared toward security specialists. It is not a general-purpose operating system and should be used only while working toward achieving your security requirements.

As you see in Figure 14.19, by clicking Applications in the upper-left corner, the menu that drops down already breaks down the tools into different genres such as information gathering, password attacks, and forensics. Explore the menus in your own Kali Linux instance to get familiar with the names of the tools and recognize the placement of those you already know.

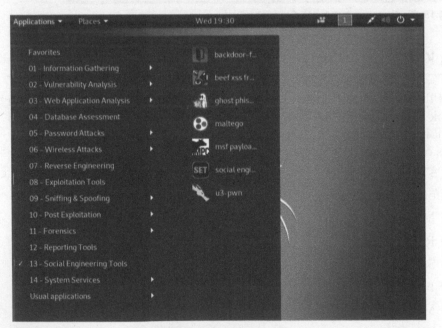

Figure 14.19: Kali Favorites menu

Maltego

In the beginning of any type of penetration test or campaign, you want to use your tools to gather as much information as you can. Maltego is one of the best. When you go to Applications ⇨ Information Gathering ⇨ Maltego, as shown in Figure 14.20, you have several choices that require a key. But there is a Community Edition, which you can access by clicking the Run button under Maltego CE (Free).

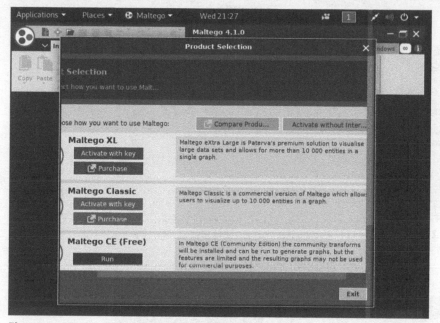

Figure 14.20: Starting Maltego CE in Kali Linux

After you have created a user login for Maltego, you will be able to fully utilize the features. As you see in Figure 14.21, after logging in, you will access Maltego and have a choice to build a new graphic interface or use an example to get familiar. This is the default example of what data mining looks like. Maltego renders graphs full of links based on relationships between pieces of data sprinkled across the Internet. Maltego uses the visual node representation to assist you in finding the information that is out in the wild that could possibly be used to compromise your environment. There is no graphical export in the community version, but the data is still there at your fingertips.

Recon-ng

While Maltego is one of my favorite ways to present the data, Recon-ng is a tool written by one of my favorite organizations: Black Hills InfoSec. Recon-ng is a Python web reconnaissance framework. It has modules, database interaction, and built-in functions to help you gather information. It looks like Metasploit and SET to reduce the learning curve, but even with the obvious simplicity, it is a rather complex tool. Type **help** at the default prompt for a list of all commands.

Next, type **show modules**. You will get a list of all the discovery, exploit, import, recon, and reporting modules. Next, type **user hackertarget** and then

show info, as you see in Figure 14.22. You can use this module to enumerate hostnames, among other things.

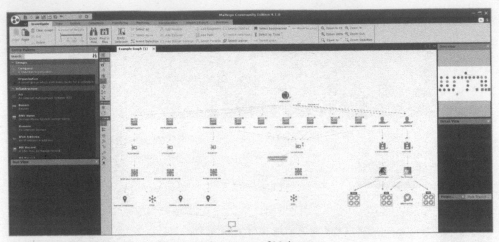

Figure 14.21: Data sources of Paterva, the owner of Maltego

```
                              /\
                            / \\ /\
      Sponsored by...     /\  /\/  \\V  \/\
                        / \\/ // \\\\\ \\ \/\
                        // // BLACK HILLS \/ \\
                        www.blackhillsinfosec.com

              [recon-ng v4.9.3, Tim Tomes (@LaNMaSteR53)]

 [75] Recon modules
 [8]  Reporting modules
 [2]  Import modules
 [2]  Exploitation modules
 [2]  Discovery modules

[recon-ng][default] > use hackertarget
[recon-ng][default][hackertarget] > show info

    Name: HackerTarget Lookup
    Path: modules/recon/domains-hosts/hackertarget.py
  Author: Michael Henriksen (@michenriksen)

Description:
  Uses the HackerTarget.com API to find host names. Updates the 'hosts' table wi
th the results.

Options:
  Name      Current Value  Required  Description
  ------    -------------  --------  -----------
  SOURCE    default        yes       source of input (see 'show info' for details)

Source Options:
  default           SELECT DISTINCT domain FROM domains WHERE domain IS NOT NULL
  <string>          string representing a single input
  <path>            path to a file containing a list of inputs
  query <sql>       database query returning one column of inputs

[recon-ng][default][hackertarget] >
```

Figure 14.22: Recon-ng welcome prompt

Sparta

Sparta is another Python tool that is a GUI application that assists in the scanning and enumeration phase. It feels like Zenmap in the beginning when you define the parameters of the network you would like to investigate, as shown in Figure 14.23.

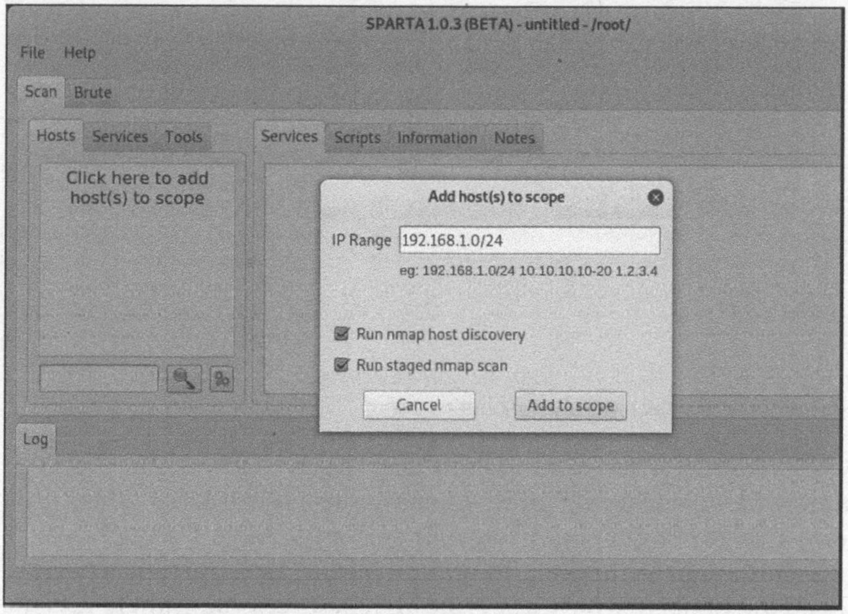

Figure 14.23: Defining parameters in Sparta

However, when you launch Sparta, after the initial Nmap scan and some data collection, it proceeds to run additional tools against the discovered services such as nikto, smbenum, snmpcheck, and more. Figure 14.24 shows an example of some of the data that can be extracted, such as the Sign In screen for the ASUS router on 192.168.1.117.

Services that need a login like telnet or SSH can be sent to the brute-force tool on the next tab to attempt to crack the password. Right-click any service that has been discovered and select Send To Brute. Sparta attempts to automate several tasks that you would normally manual execute separately.

MacChanger

After you have all the information from the three previous tools, you may want to change or fake your MAC address if you are attempting to disguise any of your exploit attempts. First, to find a list of all MAC vendors, type `macchanger -l` in your terminal window. You will get a list of all hardware vendors if there is a specific one you want to impersonate.

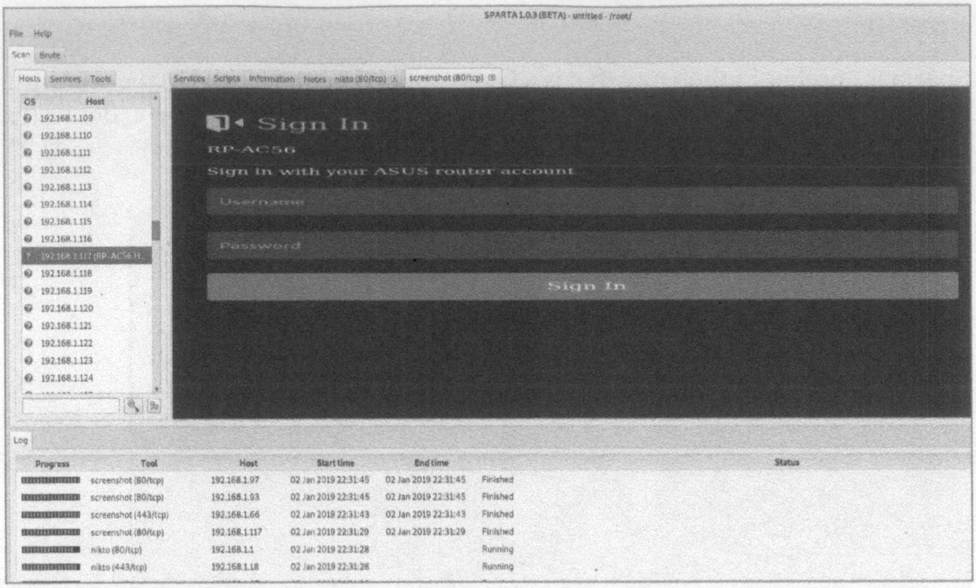

Figure 14.24: Sparta data collected while running a scan

Next, type `ifconfig eth0 down` in your terminal window so that you can reassign a new MAC address to eth0, as shown in Figure 14.25. Then type `macchanger -s eth0` to figure out what your current MAC is. Change `-s` to `-r` to reassign a random MAC to eth0. To bring the eth0 back up, type `ifconfig eth0 up`. If you did happen to have a specific MAC address you want to use, the command you would type is `macchanger -m 00:00:00:00:00:00 eth0`. A MAC address is hexadecimal, so instead of 0s, you could use any number from 0 to 9 and any letter from *A* to *F*.

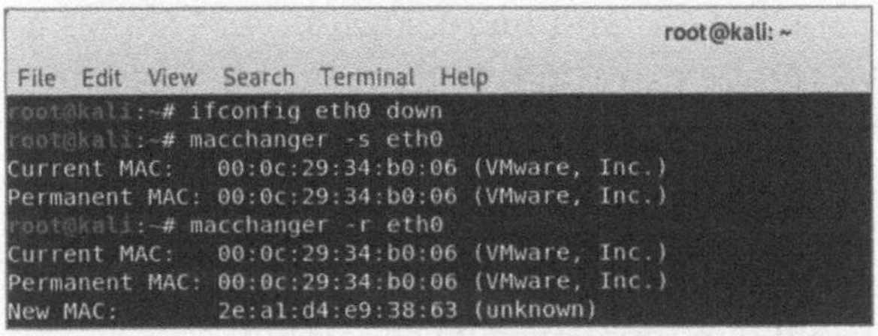

Figure 14.25: Spoofing your MAC address

Nikto

Now that you're flying incognito with a spoofed MAC address, you can use a tool like Perl-based Nikto to find vulnerabilities in web servers. One caveat: Nikto is not very stealthy. In fact, just about any IDS or security measure will detect it. We are using it to test for security—it was never designed to be stealthy. I do find it a little funny that the Nikto icon is the same as my Alienware Start button.

Go to the grid array of nine dots at the bottom of your Start menu to bring up the Show Applications window. At the top of the page, search for *nikto*. Do you still have your Metasploitable2 VM from Chapter 10, "Metasploit"? Spin it up, find its IP address, and once you have the terminal window open, type `nikto -host` and then add the IP address of the web server you would like to scan for vulnerabilities. The `-host` option is used to specify host(s) to target for a scan. It can be an IP address, hostname, or text file of hosts. Try the example in Figure 14.26; in your Kali Linux terminal, type `nikto -host http://web-scantest.com`.

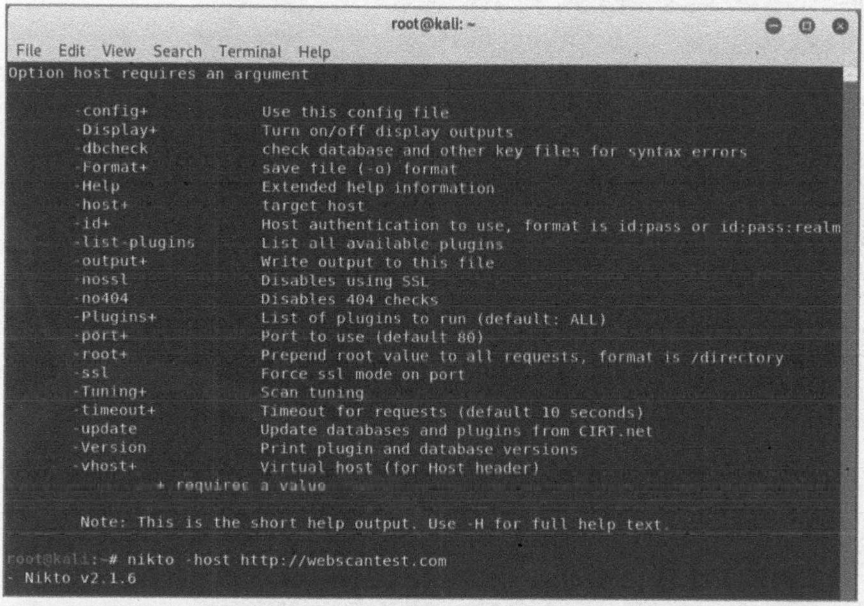

Figure 14.26: Nikto vulnerability scanning of `http://webscantest.com`

Kismet

For wireless, Kismet is a great way to view what is going on around you. Kismet uses a wireless network card in monitor mode to silently scan Wi-Fi channels. By capturing all this data, Kismet can visualize the wireless networks around you as well as the activity of any devices. How useful the data is depends on who you are and what you want to do. Kismet can detect wireless cameras, smartphones, and laptops. By using Kismet, you can easily war drive in your neighborhood looking for Wi-Fi signals and combine it with GPS data to build a map. In fact, you may not even have to get in your car. Visit `https://wigle .net` to see a global picture of Wi-Fi networks. Those purple dots are Wi-Fi networks geographically mapped for you. Guess what helped build this map. Yes, Kismet. Type in your address and zoom in. Do you recognize any of those networks? I recognize the names of networks that populate my Wi-Fi list. Now

I know where they live. Are any of those MAC addresses yours? If so, you may consider turning off your Wi-Fi when you're not using it.

Starting Kismet is easy. Simply type `kismet -c YourCardName`. As you see in Figure 14.27, you can make permanent changes to the configuration file and set up options for logging as well as the GPS location.

```
                              root@kali: ~                          ⊖ ⊡ ⊗
 File  Edit  View  Search  Terminal  Help
Usage: /usr/bin/kismet_server [OPTION]
Nearly all of these options are run-time overrides for values in the
kismet.conf configuration file.  Permanent changes should be made to
the configuration file.
*** Generic Options ***
 -v, --version                   Show version
 -f, --config-file <file>        Use alternate configuration file
     --no-line-wrap              Turn of linewrapping of output
                                 (for grep, speed, etc)
 -s, --silent                    Turn off stdout output after setup phase
     --daemonize                 Spawn detached in the background
     --no-plugins                Do not load plugins
     --no-root                             Do not start the kismet_capture binary

                          when not running as root.  For no-priv
                          remote capture ONLY.

*** Kismet Client/Server Options ***
 -l, --server-listen             Override Kismet server listen options

*** Kismet Remote Drone Options ***
     --drone-listen              Override Kismet drone listen options

*** Dump/Logging Options ***
 -T, --log-types <types>         Override activated log types
 -t, --log-title <title>         Override default log title
 -p, --log-prefix <prefix>       Directory to store log files
 -n, --no-logging                Disable logging entirely

*** Packet Capture Source Options ***
 -c, --capture-source            Specify a new packet capture source
                                 (Identical syntax to the config file)
 -C, --enable-capture-sources    Enable capture sources (comma-separated
                                 list of names or interfaces)

*** Kismet Net Tracking Options ***
     --filter-tracker            Tracker filtering

*** Kismet GPS Options ***
     --use-gpsd-gps (h:p)        Use GPSD-controlled GPS at host:port
                                 (default: localhost:2947)
     --use-nmea-gps (dev)        Use local NMEA serial GPS on device
                                 (default: /dev/ttyUSB0)
     --use-virtual-gps
              (lat,lon,alt)      Use a virtual fixed-position gps record
     --gps-modelock <t:f>        Force broken GPS units to act as if they
                                 have a valid signal (true/false)
     --gps-reconnect <t:f>       Reconnect if a GPS device fails
                                 (true/false)
root@kali:~# █
```

Figure 14.27: Kismet server options

WiFite

If Kismet is the tool to use for Wi-Fi network detection and sniffer and you need to take this a step further, then think about using Aircrack-ng or WiFite. These tools can be used for auditing or cracking to recover WEP/WPA/WPS keys once enough packets have been captured. WiFite is called the "set it and forget it" Wi-Fi cracking tool. As you see in Figure 14.28, there are many options for you to set with WiFite. However, you can simply automate the wireless capture of access points over 40 dB of power using the WPS attack with the command wifite -pow 40 -wps.

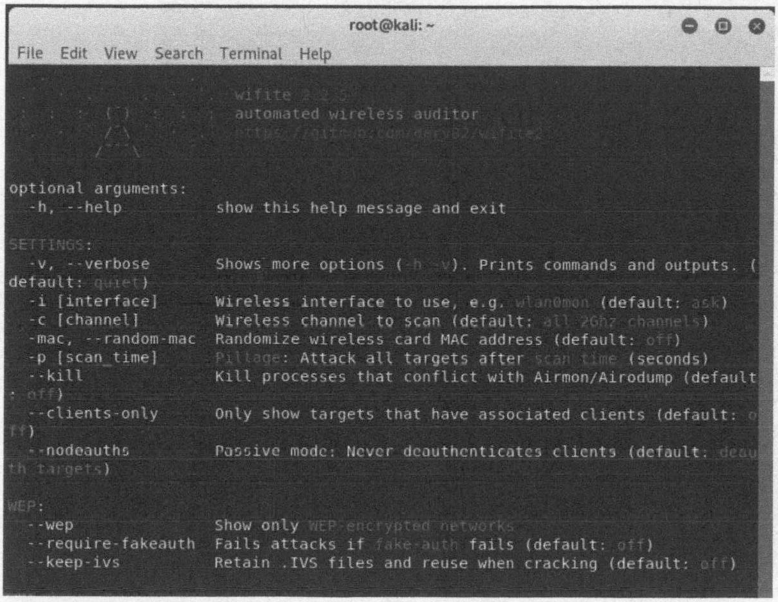

Figure 14.28: WiFite options

John the Ripper

Two community favorite password tools are Hashcat and John the Ripper. If you ask people which one is their favorite, chances are the answer will depend on the person. I like both. If I am not successful with one, I will try the other. I usually use John the Ripper first.

John the Ripper was originally designed to crack Unix passwords. Now it runs on pretty much everything and cracks almost any password. The original version is maintained by Openwall. The version that comes in Kali Linux is called the Jumbo version because it has more hash types and new attack modes. John the Ripper stores cracked passwords in the john.pot file, and its main configuration file is john.conf. There are lots of command-line options and more options in the configuration file, as you see in Figure 14.29.

At the simplest level, you can just point John the Ripper at a pwdump file, tell it what type of hashes you want it to crack (NTLM), and let it go. This is the tool that Metasploit Pro by Rapid7 uses to reverse engineer hashes. I've gotten to the point where I recognize the MD5 sum hash for a blank password as well as *password* for a password.

```
                                root@kali: ~

 File  Edit  View  Search  Terminal  Help
Created directory: /root/.john
John the Ripper password cracker, version 1.8.0.6-jumbo-1-bleeding [linux-x86-64-avx]
Copyright (c) 1996-2015 by Solar Designer and others
Homepage: http://www.openwall.com/john/

Usage: john [OPTIONS] [PASSWORD-FILES]
--single[=SECTION]        "single crack" mode
--wordlist[=FILE] --stdin wordlist mode, read words from FILE or stdin
                  --pipe  like --stdin, but bulk reads, and allows rules
--loopback[=FILE]         like --wordlist, but fetch words from a .pot file
--dupe-suppression        suppress all dupes in wordlist (and force preload)
--prince[=FILE]           PRINCE mode, read words from FILE
--encoding=NAME           input encoding (eg. UTF-8, ISO-8859-1). See also
                          doc/ENCODING and --list=hidden-options.
--rules[=SECTION]         enable word mangling rules for wordlist modes
--incremental[=MODE]      "incremental" mode [using section MODE]
--mask=MASK               mask mode using MASK
--markov[=OPTIONS]        "Markov" mode (see doc/MARKOV)
--external=MODE           external mode or word filter
--stdout[=LENGTH]         just output candidate passwords [cut at LENGTH]
--restore[=NAME]          restore an interrupted session [called NAME]
--session=NAME            give a new session the NAME
--status[=NAME]           print status of a session [called NAME]
--make-charset=FILE       make a charset file. It will be overwritten
--show[=LEFT]             show cracked passwords [if =LEFT, then uncracked]
--test[=TIME]             run tests and benchmarks for TIME seconds each
--users=[-]LOGIN|UID[,..] [do not] load this (these) user(s) only
--groups=[-]GID[,..]      load users [not] of this (these) group(s) only
--shells=[-]SHELL[,..]    load users with[out] this (these) shell(s) only
--salts=[-]COUNT[:MAX]    load salts with[out] COUNT [to MAX] hashes
--save-memory=LEVEL       enable memory saving, at LEVEL 1..3
--node=MIN[-MAX]/TOTAL    this node's number range out of TOTAL count
--fork=N                  fork N processes
--pot=NAME                pot file to use
--list=WHAT               list capabilities, see --list=help or doc/OPTIONS
--format=NAME             force hash of type NAME. The supported formats can
                          be seen with --list=formats and --list=subformats
root@kali:~#
```

Figure 14.29: John the Ripper password cracker

Hashcat

Hashcat provides much of the same functionality as John the Ripper. They are both open-source and share the same features. Hashcat is built around using the GPU rather than the CPU for cracking as John the Ripper does. A CPU is the central processing unit, often called the brains of a PC. A GPU is the graphics processing unit, which comprises the chips that render the display images to the monitors. If the CPU is the brain, some call the GPU the brawn. A GPU is better at focusing all the computing power on a specific task. If you're looking to do password-cracking on a system that has GPU, then use Hashcat. It will be better and faster for many complex passwords.

Remember, passwords should not be stored in clear text. They are stored in one-way encryption called *hashes*. There are a couple different ways of obtaining these hashes, but once you grab them, the next step is to reverse-engineer the hash, unless you want to Pass the Hash in Metasploit. There are gigs of wordlists available on the Internet, but Kali Linux already has some built in. A *wordlist* is a text file that contains a collection of words to be used in a dictionary attack.

The first thing you want to do is open a terminal window and type in `locate wordlist`. As you see in Figure 14.30, there are many wordlists available. (I just happen to know that the wordlist built for sqlmap has more than a million words in it.)

```
Applications ▾    Places ▾    ⬚ Terminal ▾         Thu 02:50
                          root@kali: ~
File  Edit  View  Search  Terminal  Help
* https://hashcat.net/wiki/#howtos_videos_papers_articles_etc_in_the_wild
* https://hashcat.net/faq/
root@kali:~# locate wordlist
/usr/sbin/remove-default-wordlist
/usr/sbin/select-default-wordlist
/usr/sbin/update-default-wordlist
/usr/share/wordlists
/usr/share/applications/kali-wordlists.desktop
/usr/share/dict/README.select-wordlist
/usr/share/dict/wordlist-top4800-probable.txt
/usr/share/dirb/wordlists
/usr/share/dirb/wordlists/big.txt
/usr/share/dirb/wordlists/catala.txt
/usr/share/dirb/wordlists/common.txt
/usr/share/dirb/wordlists/euskera.txt
/usr/share/dirb/wordlists/extensions_common.txt
/usr/share/dirb/wordlists/indexes.txt
/usr/share/dirb/wordlists/mutations_common.txt
/usr/share/dirb/wordlists/others
/usr/share/dirb/wordlists/small.txt
/usr/share/dirb/wordlists/spanish.txt
/usr/share/dirb/wordlists/stress
/usr/share/dirb/wordlists/vulns
/usr/share/dirb/wordlists/others/best1050.txt
/usr/share/dirb/wordlists/others/best110.txt
/usr/share/dirb/wordlists/others/best15.txt
/usr/share/dirb/wordlists/others/names.txt
```

Figure 14.30: Hashcat wordlists

After you choose a wordlist, it's time to grab your hashes. In Kali Linux, they are stored in the `/etc/shadow` file, so if you type in `tail /etc/shadow`, you should see something like what's shown in Figure 14.31. (I cut off my hashes on purpose—you never know if someone would take the time to reverse engineer my hashes.)

```
root@kali:~# tail /etc/shadow
saned:*:17820:0:99999:7:::
avahi:*:17820:0:99999:7:::
pulse:*:17820:0:99999:7:::
dradis:*:17820:0:99999:7:::
king-phisher:*:17820:0:99999:7:::
beef-xss:*:17820:0:99999:7:::
Debian-gdm:*:17820:0:99999:7:::
systemd-coredump:!!:17830:::::::
nadean:$6$rR35MVQD$D8ouZRf1RSsR5HceVtodJI6xc.Vk8mvtkXpyZjmcQiiMuL7iQWxV5VPsBmaYDDARF
nt:$6$u3VuhsyC$97mWrGIYhOxlj/MYcPxIGWOIIe.Db0T2mwU.85vEboMkMKq9HaUINWHwZ421gJh1MWDA
```

Figure 14.31: Hashes collected on Kali Linux

Now we need to figure out what hashing algorithm was used. To open that file, type `more /etc/login.defs`.

The more command allows you to page down line by line through this file. Once you're about 80 to 85 percent down the page, you should see what's shown in Figure 14.32.

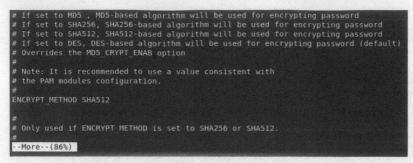

```
# If set to MD5 , MD5-based algorithm will be used for encrypting password
# If set to SHA256, SHA256-based algorithm will be used for encrypting password
# If set to SHA512, SHA512-based algorithm will be used for encrypting password
# If set to DES, DES-based algorithm will be used for encrypting password (default)
# Overrides the MD5_CRYPT_ENAB option
#
# Note: It is recommended to use a value consistent with
# the PAM modules configuration.
#
ENCRYPT_METHOD SHA512

#
# Only used if ENCRYPT_METHOD is set to SHA256 or SHA512.
#
--More--(86%)
```

Figure 14.32: Kali Linux using Encrypt_Method SHA512

Now you can put all the puzzle pieces together. Make a copy of your hashes in a separate file by using the following cp command:

```
cp /etc/shadow hash.1st
```

To make sure that it worked, type the following:

```
More hash.1st
```

To prepare this file for cracking, you need to remove everything but the hashes. Open the hash.1st file with gedit or vim and delete all the usernames and the colon. Remove the ending colons too. Now the file is only the raw hash itself. To crack these hashes, I used the following:

```
hashcat -m 1800 -a 0 -o success.txt -remove hash.1st
/usr/share/sqlmap/txt/wordlist.txt
```

where

- -m 1800 is the type of hash I'm cracking.
- -a 0 is a dictionary attack.
- -o success.txt is the output file.
- -remove says delete the hash after it was cracked.
- hash.1st is the input file.
- /usr/share/sqlmap/txt/wordlist.txt is the path to the wordlist.

Open your success.txt file. It took me a little over 10 minutes to get the cracked passwords. If you have issues, try running the command again with a --force at the end. If that doesn't work, you may have to give the Kali Linux box a few more than the default resources.

As I tell my classes, if at first you don't succeed, try again. You are attempting to force machines to behave in a way they were not originally intended to behave. We are trying to use these machines and vulnerabilities like attackers would. Using that mind-set is critical to securing our environments. Kali was designed to work even when used in a very hostile environment. The Kali motto is ``The quieter you become, the more you are able to hear''. Kali is designed to be as quiet as possible so that you can hide its presence on your network. This chapter was meant to be an introduction to penetration testing and what you have learned is a good foundation. You are now ready to learn more in order to fully exploit the power of Kali Linux, the best penetration testing framework.

CISv7 Controls and Best Practices

WHAT YOU WILL LEARN IN THIS CHAPTER:

➤ CIS Basic Controls—The Top Six

As an educator, I firmly believe that humans have to know the "why" to accept change. Most of us are curious creatures of habit and do not change unless sufficiently motivated. Most of us are motivated by either the love of something or the fear of it. In our cyber society, people need to know why certain controls are important, and they have to understand why they are important on a personal level. Knowing something and understanding it are very different. As a cybersecurity trainer, it is my personal mission to educate the public and bring understanding to cyber threats in a personal way. I believe we have to hope for the best but prepare for the worst.

When you are evaluating and auditing your environment for managing your processes and systems, you should determine whether the options you are following are the best practices of conducting inventories, adopting computer policy, and communicating to the people using those systems. You also have to evaluate whether people in the management roles have the practical and technical expertise to assess these options and can provide support and training for users.

The Center for Internet Security (CIS) is a self-described forward-thinking, nonprofit entity dedicated to protecting private domains and public society against cyber threats. The controls they publish are the global standard and are the recognized best practices for security. As our cyber worries evolve, so do these best practices. As a cybersecurity professional, I refer to these CIS top 20 controls fairly often as a reminder to secure the world to the best of my ability.

The CIS top 20 controls are broken into three sections. The first six controls are the basic ones. These six controls are essential in any organization for cyber defense. The rest of the controls are divided into foundational and organizational, which focus on technical best practices and processes.

CIS Basic Controls—The Top Six

I recommend that you go to the SANS website, www.sans.org, and look for conferences that are happening near you. In the evenings, they will have mini-sessions free to the public, usually about an hour long each, of interesting security topics taught by the certified SANS instructors. Sometimes, if you're lucky, they will have an assortment and up to three or four in one evening. In the dozens of sessions I've attended, the one that stands out the most is the one Eric Conrad did a couple years ago in Orlando, Florida. He talked about the top six CIS controls. He said that while he was consulting for a governmental organization on another continent, implementing the top six controls negated about 80 percent of the problems resulting in more security and less likelihood of a breach.

The top six CISv7 basic controls are as follows:

- Inventory and Control of Hardware Assets
- Inventory and Control of Software Assets
- Continuous Vulnerability Management
- Controlled Use of Administrative Privileges
- Secure Configuration for Hardware and Software on Mobile Devices, Laptops, Workstations, and Servers
- Maintenance, Monitoring, and Analysis of Audit Logs

If you read about the major breaches in the last five years, most of them could have been avoided if the organization had subscribed to and executed these six controls. The CISv7 controls have cross-compatibility or directly map to other cyber compliance and security standards like NIST 800-53, PCI DSS, and HIPAA. This translates to other organizations using these suggestions as regulations to aid in their respective compliance. The NIST Cybersecurity Framework is another tool that organizations use to organize and strengthen their security posture using the CIS top controls as their baseline for several of their best practices. Let's look at these in more detail.

Inventory and Control of Hardware Assets

One of my favorite sayings in class is that "you cannot protect what you don't know you have." This control specifically addresses the need to know what is connected to your network. You must develop policy and procedures around maintaining an accurate inventory. It can be rather tedious, but it is critical. If you do it right, it reduces loss risks. You must know what is on your network and who the system belongs to and use that data to prevent anyone unauthorized from accessing the network.

Creating a system inventory is a common task for system and network administrators. An open source security audit tool Nmap or Zenmap has all the necessary features needed to run an ad hoc or automated inventory process. By simply scanning a network using the operating system identification (-o) command switch and possibly verbose output (-v) command switch, you can get a list of systems and their protocols. The inventory created provides information that is critical to system, application, and protocol management. The inventory will not include information such as how much memory the system has or how many processors there are. This type of hardware inventory requires either an SNMP agent on the system or a script running on the system to determine the hardware in the system.

What do all network-connected devices have in common? They speak to each other using a logical address called *IP addresses*. Who manages IP addresses? Dynamic Host Configuration Protocol (DHCP) manages IP addresses. DHCP also generates logs. For DHCP-enabled networks, deploying a mechanism to focus on combining system inventory with configuration management and network access control is a win-win. The inventory management portion is usually based on some type of endpoint management software like System Center Configuration Manager (SCCM). SCCM is a Microsoft systems management software product for managing large groups of computers from servers to workstations to mobile devices. Do not forget IoT when you are coming up with a management policy of your hardware inventory.

If you are a Microsoft customer with an existing Microsoft enterprise agreement, you may already have an SCCM license. SCCM provides software distribution, operating system deployment, and network access as well as the CIS control hardware inventory. There are a couple of options when implementing at SCCM. There is a datacenter edition as well as a standard edition. Both editions include the following tools:

- Configuration Manager—for managing the deployment of applications and devices in an enterprise network
- Data Protection Manager—for performing backup and recovery for business continuance and disaster recovery
- Endpoint Protection—for managing anti-malware and firewall security
- Operations Manager—for monitoring the health and performance of operating systems and hypervisors
- Orchestrator—for standardizing and automating processes for operational efficiency

- Service Manager—for change control and asset lifecycle management
- Virtual Machine Manager—for provisioning and managing resources used to create virtual machines

Inventory and Control of Software Assets

Taking an inventory and control of software installed on your assets is taking the first control to the next level. You should be able to see what software is on your systems, who installed it, and what its function is. You need this information to prevent software that is not authorized from being installed on endpoints. Some organizations see this as a very complicated, highly managed process, but there are several ways to do this efficiently and automatically.

Many of the methods used to implement the inventory of authorized and unauthorized software will also improve the implementation of other controls relating to network access, asset configuration, and system management. Administrator access and installation rights should not be granted for every user. I have worked for organizations where all employees, including the warehouse personnel and receptionist, had administrative rights on their computer and could download any application they wanted with no processes in place to protect the network. Limiting who can install software also limits who can install seemingly innocent applications or games that include malware, adware, and other unwanted code.

Once installation rights have been limited, the next stage is creating a list of unauthorized and authorized applications. This is called *blacklisting* and *whitelisting*. Blacklisted software should never be allowed on the network, and whitelisting is the software the organization needs to get the job done. This can be rolled out as an authorized software policy first and followed up with scanning, removal, and, then, central inventory control. The inventory management portion is usually based on a software inventory tool or endpoint management services such as SCCM or based on GPO and local policy controls on Windows.

AppLocker, natively in Windows 10 and Server, can help you control which apps and files users can run on their systems. AppLocker can define rules based on file attributes, assign a rule to a group or user, and create exceptions to rules. It also helps reduce what is seemingly complicated, like standardizing approved software configuration to disallowing unlicensed software or certain apps from running.

Aside from AppLocker, Microsoft allows Group Policy–based whitelisting for supported versions of Windows. These can be edited locally using secpol .msc unless you have the Home version of Windows. If your organization has a domain controller or Group Policy Objects, you can use the same process by accessing Software Restriction Policies (SRP). For more general-purpose workstations, a number of client-based solutions exist, including antivirus and endpoint protection suites that limit software from a central console, like Carbon Blacks Consolidated Endpoint Security.

You can use software inventory to collect information about files on client devices that already exist. It can be a specific file, files with a specific extension, or all files on the computer. Software inventory can also collect files from client devices and store them on the site server. SCCM is an option for this kind of mature process, especially if you have it in place for hardware management as well. All the machines in an SCCM environment will have an SCCM client agent installed on them. This helps a machine to be able to communicate with the SCCM servers to receive their respective packages. Packages contain the executable files and the command lines for an application to be installed. These packages are then replicated on distribution points. Distribution points are servers used to store the content of the packages for a particular region. Machines that are remotely located can locally download the application from a distribution point, rather than connecting all the way to the SCCM primary server.

A deployment of approved software is created by the SCCM administrator. With the help of the SCCM client agent installed on the end user's machine, it keeps checking for new policies or deployments. After software inventory is enabled, clients run a software inventory cycle. The client sends the information to a management point in the client's site. The management point then forwards the inventory information to the SCCM site server. This information is stored in the site database. When software inventory runs on a client device, the first report is a full inventory. In the next cycle, the reports contain only updated inventory information, giving you the most current information of what is on that system.

Continuous Vulnerability Management

Organizations today operate in a constant dynamic stream of new security information: software updates, patches, and security advisories. It is easy to become overwhelmed with the amount of cybersecurity threat advisories that bombard our inboxes daily. Being able to understand and manage vulnerabilities is a continuous activity and requires a significant amount of time and attention to do it well.

A big part of your assessment and remediation has to do with scanning and finding the vulnerabilities in the hardware and software you have the inventory of from CIS controls 1 and 2. By not proactively scanning for vulnerabilities and addressing discovered flaws, the likelihood of an organization's computer systems becoming compromised is high. Identifying and remediating vulnerabilities on a regular basis is also essential to a strong overall information security program. Depending on your organization's maturity, you may scan monthly or weekly. Some three-letter-agencies I have worked with scan for vulnerabilities every single night and patch every day. You have to create a process around remediation and ensure that the most mission-critical assets with the most dangerous vulnerabilities get fixed first.

One of my favorite sites that I recommend you add to your RSS feed is www.us-cert.gov/ncas/current-activity. This web page by the United States Computer Emergency Readiness Team is regularly updated with the most frequent and high-impact security incidents. Another site is https://nvd.nist.gov/vuln/search. Here you can search the vulnerability database for a product, vendor, or specific CVE. Finally, https://cve.mitre.org/ is an extremely valuable resource for a list of entries with each containing an identification number, a description, and a reference for every publicly known cybersecurity vulnerability. I normally check in with these sites once a week to see what is out there.

Controlled Use of Administrative Privileges

Have you noticed that the critical controls are following a logical progression? As you gradually improve your security posture, they layer on top of each other. Now that you know what you have and what's on those machines, including vulnerabilities, you need to control who has access to those machines.

One of my favorite penetration tester's story is of a targeted phishing campaign launched against a specific department where six people clicked the link in the email, and two of the six were logged into their administrators account when they clicked and were compromised in 22 seconds. Within hours, the entire network belonged to the pen tester. You have to control who has administrative privileges and even how those administrators use their credentials. When you are logged in as an admin, you should not be opening your email under any circumstances. That is what your user account is for.

Two very common attacks rely on privilege to execute. That is one reason CVSS actually measures if privilege is necessary for exploitability. The first type of an attack is like the one I described previously where a user with elevated credentials opens a malicious attachment. The other is the elevation of privilege when cracking a password for an administrator. If the password policy is weak or not enforced, the danger increases exponentially.

Educate your leadership and help create a robust security posture where you restrict admin privilege. Have your IT admins make a list of the tasks that they do on an average day. Check the tasks that require administrative credentials. Create an account for normal tasks that all users can do and use the admin account for only those tasks where it's necessary. If you have executives insisting that they need admin privileges, remind them that they are the ones that hackers are targeting.

Microsoft has guidance on implementing least privilege. For Linux, each sysadmin should have a separate account and enforce the use of sudo by disabling su. You should also change all default passwords on all assets in your environment as well as making sure that each password is as robust as possible. Use multifactor authentication and configure systems to issue an alert if an admin mistypes his or her password.

The most secure admin credentials I've personally used were on a military network. My password was at least 16 characters, uppercase, lowercase, special characters, and could not spell anything in Meriam Webster's dictionary. I also had a lockout policy of one mistyped password. I was logging into upwards of 40 to 80 machines multiple times a day. If I locked myself out, I was basically in limbo for the rest of the day because I had to call the help desk to have them reset my password, which could take hours. That might be a bit extreme for the average organization, but the fundamentals are the same. By using robust passwords, limited privilege accounts, and a lockout policy, you are making it more difficult for the attacker to compromise your account or steal important data.

Secure Configuration for Hardware and Software on Mobile Devices, Laptops, Workstations, and Servers

If you have ever opened a new laptop freshly imaged with an operating system, you have to know that the default configuration you're working on setting up is extremely vulnerable. There are open ports open and services running and default accounts preinstalled for ease of use and deployment, which are all exploitable. In Windows, for example, there are a couple things you should do immediately after taking it out of the box.

In Lab 15.1, you'll be securing a Windows workstation.

LAB 15.1: SECURING AND CONFIGURING A WINDOWS WORKSTATION

1. **Enable system protection and create a restore point. If you accidently install a bad piece of software, you need a system restore point when everything was shiny and clean. (Strange, I know, but system protection comes disabled.) Search for restore, as shown in Figure 15.1.**

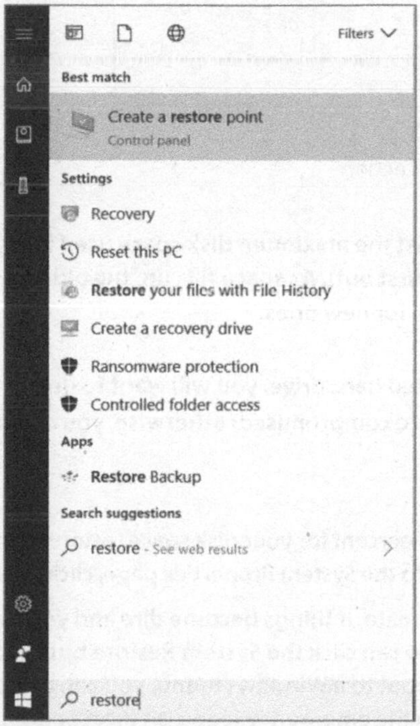

Figure 15.1: Creating a restore point in Windows

Continues

2. Open the Create A Restore point menu item. A System Properties dialog box opens, showing you all the options for System Protection, as shown in Figure 15.2. Click the Configure button in the lower-right corner.

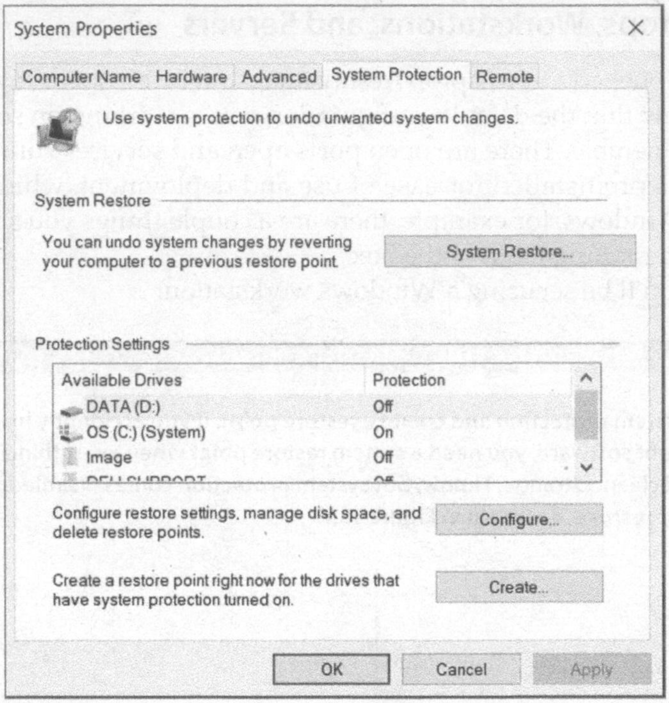

System Properties   ✕

Computer Name   Hardware   Advanced   System Protection   Remote

    Use system protection to undo unwanted system changes.

System Restore

You can undo system changes by reverting your computer to a previous restore point.   [System Restore...]

Protection Settings

Available Drives	Protection
DATA (D:)	Off
OS (C:) (System)	On
Image	Off
DELL SUPPORT	Off

Configure restore settings, manage disk space, and delete restore points.   [Configure...]

Create a restore point right now for the drives that have system protection turned on.   [Create...]

[OK]   [Cancel]   [Apply]

Figure 15.2: Configuring system protection

3. Turn on System Protection and adjust the maximum disk space used for system protection. This file is FIFO (first in, first out). As space fills up, the older restore points will be deleted to make room for new ones.

    TIP If you ever have an infected hard drive, you will want to delete the restore points you may believe are compromised; otherwise, you could end up reinfecting your systems.

4. After you set a drive space of about 3 percent for your disk space restore point allocation, click Apply. When you return to the System Properties page, click Create.

5. Name your restore point and click Create. If things become dire and you need to restore from one of these points, you can click the System Restore button on the System Protection tab. If you can't boot to a Windows menu, you can press F1, F8, or Shift+F8 during boot to get to the emergency menu on most computers. If F8 doesn't work, Google your make and model of laptop for boot menu options.

6. By default, Windows now hides most file extensions, so when you're browsing through your files, you can't easily see what type of file they are. Your résumé, for example, will appear as `myresume` instead of `myresume.docx`. Microsoft has been disabling extensions by default for the past several versions of its OS in a misguided effort to simplify the file system for users.

   In an effort to protect you from yourself, Microsoft also hides certain operating system files from you by default. But what if you need to find these files or edit them to troubleshoot? Navigate to the Control Panel.

7. With the Control Panel open, in the upper-right corner next to View By, choose Large Icons. Open File Explorer Options like you see in Figure 15.3.

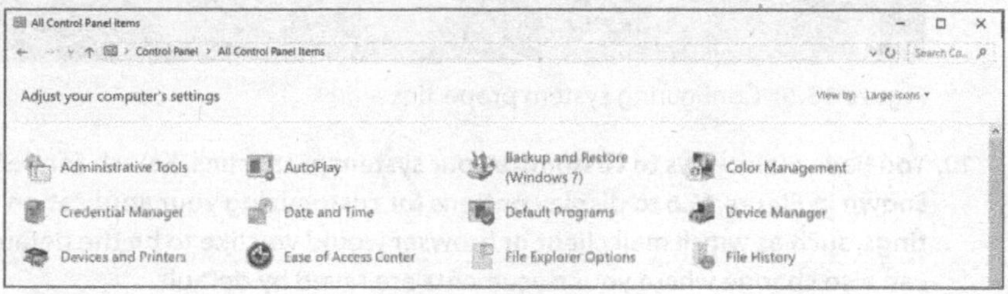

Figure 15.3: Configuring File Explorer Options

8. Make changes on the General tab to suit your workflow. Open the View tab and review the settings. If you look at Figure 15.4, you'll notice I've made some changes to my machine. I like to see the full path of my file structure, showing hidden files and folders and unhiding empty drives as well as extensions. You should make an educated decision about unhiding protected operating system files. It is recommended to keep them hidden.

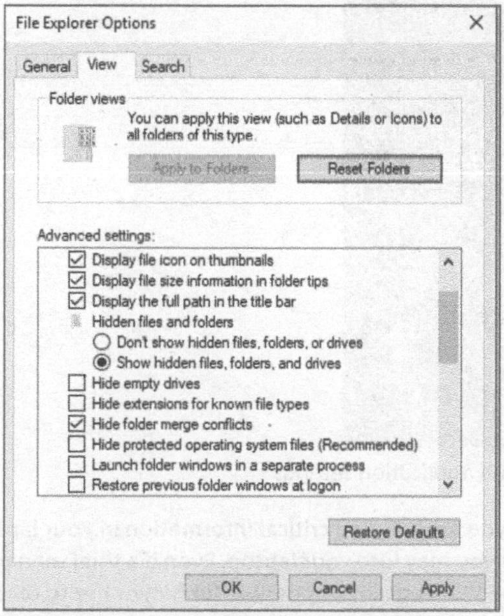

Figure 15.4: Configuring file properties

Continues

9. Once you have your files the way you want them displaying, open your settings. From the Start menu, type in **settings**. Open your System settings, as shown in Figure 15.5.

Figure 15.5: Configuring system properties

10. You have many ways to customize your system properties. Search for **default** as shown in Figure 15.6 to display options for customizing your application settings, such as which mail client or browser would you like to be the default. You can also change where your documents are saved by default.

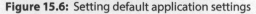

Figure 15.6: Setting default application settings

11. Encryption is essential if you are keeping critical information in your laptop. There could be situations you may lose your laptop. Even if a thief manages to steal your laptop, it will be theoretically impossible for him or her to read your data. Most Windows users can use easy tools like BitLocker to encrypt your data. From your search menu, look for BitLocker and turn it on.

12. Look for Windows Defender in your search menu. Review the settings for your machine. As you see in Figure 15.7, you may need to turn on protection for your system.

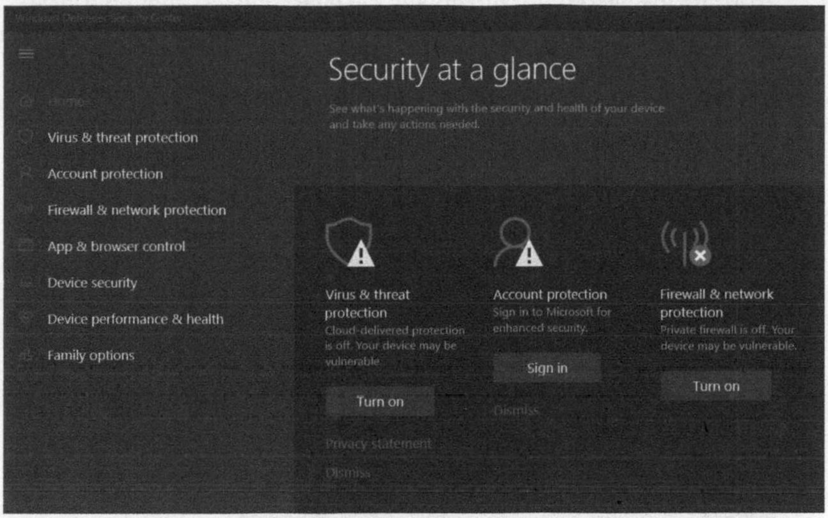

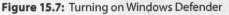

Figure 15.7: Turning on Windows Defender

13. Now that you have antivirus and firewall settings, if you are using the Chrome browser, there are features that will check for malware. Open the Chrome browser. Type in the URL **chrome://settings/**, as shown in Figure 15.8. Scroll to the bottom of the page and click the Advanced button in the middle. This will open the advanced features available in your browser. Again, scroll to the bottom of the page where you will see Clean Up Computer. Click the button Check For Harmful Software. This will take a few minutes to run.

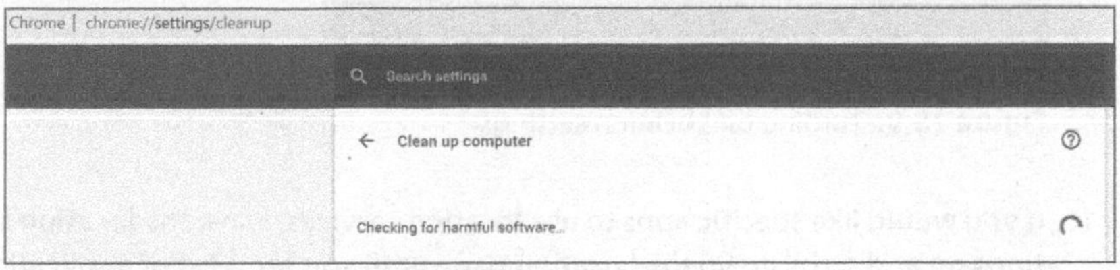

Figure 15.8: Removing unwanted programs

14. People may track your online behavior as you browse the Web, allowing marketers to create a profile based on your interest and provide you with relevant advertising messages. It's not a good thing to allow people to observe what you do online. To disable advertising ID, search for **privacy** and go to Privacy Settings under System Settings. Go to General ⇨ Change Privacy Options and turn off the first option to disable interest-based advertising.

    After you disable interest-based ads, marketers won't be able to track your online behavior. You will still get ads, but they are generic ones.

Continues

15. Windows can track your location, which is helpful for many people. It helps you to locate the nearest restaurants and get latest updates about the local weather. But if security is your top priority, it is a good idea to prevent Windows from tracking your location, like you see in Figure 15.9. Go to the Location section in privacy settings and disable the location service option.

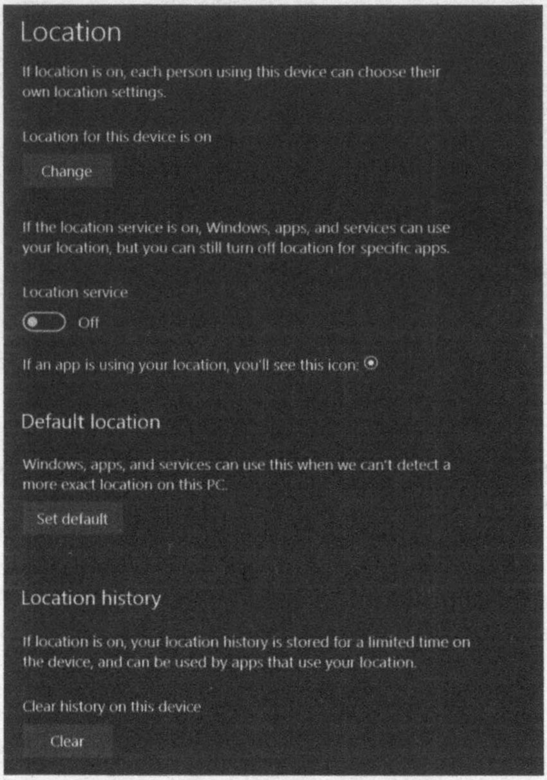

Location

If location is on, each person using this device can choose their own location settings.

Location for this device is on

Change

If the location service is on, Windows, apps, and services can use your location, but you can still turn off location for specific apps.

Location service

◯ Off

If an app is using your location, you'll see this icon: ◉

Default location

Windows, apps, and services can use this when we can't detect a more exact location on this PC.

Set default

Location history

If location is on, your location history is stored for a limited time on the device, and can be used by apps that use your location.

Clear history on this device

Clear

Figure 15.9: Turning off Location settings

16. If you would like specific apps to use location services, leave the location settings on and scroll down the Location page until you see a list of applications that would like to use location services. These applications can be individually turned on or off. When you disable this feature, Windows will keep the past location history until you delete it. To delete your past location history, click the Clear button for Location History to remove all saved locations.

Maintenance, Monitoring, and Analysis of Audit Logs

Without appropriate logging, an attacker's activity could go unnoticed, and evidence can be inconclusive. Regular log collection is vital to understanding a security incident during an investigation. Logs are useful for baselines, trends, and support. At a minimum, log events should include the following:

- Operating system events
  - Startup/shutdown of the system
  - Startup/shutdown of a service
  - Network connection changes or failures
  - Changes to, or attempts to change, system security settings and controls
- OS audit records
  - Logon attempts (successful or unsuccessful)
  - Functions performed
  - Account changes, including creation and deletion
  - Successful/failed use of privileged accounts
- Application account information
  - Successful/failed application authentication attempts
  - Use of application privileges
- Application operations
  - Application startup/shutdown
  - Application failures
  - Major application configuration changes

One of my favorite resources for logging is on a site called Malware Archaeology.

`https://www.malwarearchaeology.com/cheat-sheets/`

As you can see in Figure 15.10, it has a variety for everything logging.

Cheat Sheets to help you in configuring your systems:	
• The Windows Logging Cheat Sheet	Updated Mar 2018
• The Windows Advanced Logging Cheat Sheet	Updated Mar 2018
• The Windows HUMIO Logging Cheat Sheet	Released June 2018
• The Windows Splunk Logging Cheat Sheet	Updated Mar 2018
• The Windows File Auditing Logging Cheat Sheet	Updated Nov 2017
• The Windows Registry Auditing Logging Cheat Sheet	Updated Oct 2018
• The Windows PowerShell Logging Cheat Sheet	Updated Sept 2018
The Windows Sysmon Logging Cheat Sheet	Coming soon
MITRE ATT&CK Cheat Sheets	
• The Windows ATT&CK Logging Cheat Sheet	Released Sept 2018
• The Windows LOG-MD ATT&CK Cheat Sheet	Released Sept 2018

Figure 15.10: Logging cheat sheets

After you have a strong foundation around the six basic CIS controls, it's time to add on the Foundational and Organizational controls. In Figure 15.11, you see a list of the next layers of defense in depth that cybersecurity professionals put in place to keep organizations and users secure.

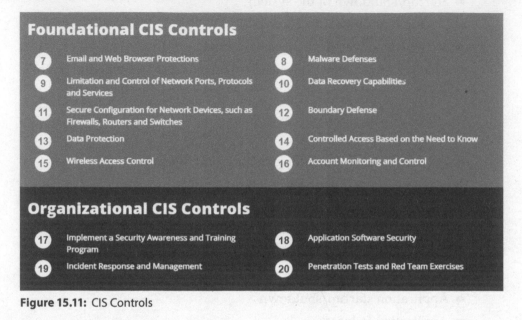

Figure 15.11: CIS Controls

In Conclusion

When my husband suggested that I write a book I wanted to read, I decided to write the book I wanted to read when I was starting in IT. My career has bounced between doing and then teaching, and I love my niche. Being in IT as a technical educator is not just my job, it is my passion. I try to give my students the tools and knowledge they need to be successful in what they have chosen to do.

The last six months' writing journey has pushed me to put down on paper what I know and how I've used it to make the world a safer place. As Ryan said in the Foreword, in the world of cybersecurity, we are constantly bombarded with new products, new tools, and new attack techniques. We are pulled daily in multiple directions on what to secure and how to secure it. I hope I've given you tools to make you successful.

What now? Keep going. Keep learning and growing your toolkit. Our industry will keep evolving, and you will have to keep up or, even better, become a leader. Share your knowledge. Remember, as you learn more, you realize there is so much more out there to know, and if you understand it well enough, you will be able to explain it simply.

Index